Hypnosis in Therapy

HYPNOSIS IN THERAPY

H.B. GIBSON
The Hatfield Polytechnic, U.K.

M. HEAP
University of Sheffield, U.K.

LAWRENCE ERLBAUM ASSOCIATES, PUBLISHERS
Hove and London (UK) Hillsdale (USA)

Lawrence Erlbaum Associates Ltd., Publishers
27 Palmeira Mansions
Church Road
Hove
East Sussex, BN3 2FA
U.K.

British Library Cataloguing in Publication Data

Gibson, H.B.
Hypnosis in therapy
I. Man. Mental disorders. Hypnotherapy
I. Title II. Heap, Michael
616.89162

ISBN 0-86377-155-6 (HBK)
0-86377-170-X (PBK)

Typeset by Key Origination, Eastbourne
Printed and bound by BPCC Wheatons, Exeter

Contents

Acknowledgements

We gratefully acknowledge help from a number of people. We have made some substantial quotes from *Hypnotherapy of pain in children with cancer* by Josephine Hilgard and Samuel LeBaron, copyright William Kaufmann Inc., and the authors and publishers have kindly given their permission for the use of this material. We have also used short quotes from the works of a number of authors, and received substantial advice from others, notably from the late Anthony Basker of Burnham-on-Crouch, Kenneth Bowers of the University of Waterloo, Canada, Harold B. Crasilneck of Dallas, Texas, Catherine Dunnet of the Royal Infirmary, Glasgow, Ilana Eli and Moris Kleinhauz of Tel Aviv University, Ernest Hilgard and the late Josephine Hilgard of Stanford University, Samuel LeBaron of the University of Texas, Ronald Melzack of McGill University, Bernard Oliver, late Editor of the BSMDH *Proceedings*, David Rowley of Leicester Polytechnic, Patrick Wall of London University, André Weitzenhoffer of the V.A. Hospital, Oklahoma. We are very grateful for the help and inspiration that these people, and many others, have given us in the writing of this book. We should also like to express our appreciation of the assistance given by Carol Graham in reading and advising on the readability of the manuscript, and by Valerie Heap in typing much of the manuscript and references.

Dr H.B. Gibson
President of the British Society of Experimental and Clinical Hypnosis
Honorary Senior Research Fellow, The Hatfield Polytechnic

Dr M. Heap
Principal Clinical Psychologist, Sheffield Health Authority,
Lecturer in Psychology, University of Sheffield
Honorary Secretary of the British Society of Experimental and Clinical Hypnosis

Acknowledgements

1 What is Hypnosis?

It is difficult to define very precisely what is meant by hypnosis, but this need be no bar to discussion. A similar difficulty arises when we try to define other concepts such as pain, and no one would deny the reality of the latter (except perhaps Christian Scientists) , but authorities on the subject are agreed that pain can only be defined ostensively. Ostensive definition of a word indicates that we make its meaning clear by giving various examples which illustrate the correct usage of the term. So it is with hypnosis, and perhaps we can illustrate its nature best by describing the various procedures that are used to induce a state of hypnosis, assuming that hypnosis can correctly be designated as a "state". We shall discuss some controversy relating to this matter later. If hypnosis is conceived of as a psychological state, then by hypnotism we mean the processes adopted to enable a subject to achieve that state.

In our state of normal waking consciousness we are constantly receiving impressions from the environment, examining them critically and relating them to the stored impressions in our memory, and thus making sense of the world. We do not, of course, pay attention to all the stimuli that impinge upon us; this would be unnecessary and really impossible under normal circumstances for we are constantly being bombarded with such a wealth of stimuli. Rather, we pay attention to what is meaningful to us, and waking consciousness involves a constant activity of processing and evaluating information. When we relax that activity we may drift off into sleep. While falling asleep in front of the TV screen (or during a lecture) we still "hear" what is being said in so far as the mechanisms of hearing are concerned, but as we have given up processing the information it means nothing to us. Keeping closely in mind this model of information-processing determining what we perceive, we can discuss the process of hypnotism.

INDUCING HYPNOSIS

The general techniques of hypnotism will be described in order to illustrate the principles involved. When a subject is being hypnotised two things are being accomplished. First, the subject agrees to relinquish the activity of critically processing all the information impinging from without and leaves this task to the hypnotist. No part of the subject's autonomy is relinquished, nor is "compliance" increased (a point that will be discussed later). It is merely a matter of altering the manner of perception, just as when we witness an enthralling play we are content to leave to the actors the structuring of present reality. Second, only the limited range of stimuli and ideas that the hypnotist suggests are attended to, the hypnotist's voice becoming more and more the sole channel of information. Put like this, a psychologist familiar with the mechanisms of information-processing can understand what is going on, but how, it may be asked, do we explain to the naïve subject just what is required in order to achieve hypnosis? The problem is to choose language that is meaningful to the subject, and this may require the use of metaphors describing behaviour and feelings in everyday terms. It is, of course, necessary initially to discuss what the subject understands by the word "hypnosis", and to dispel any common misapprehensions such as that it involves the domination of one mind over another.

There are numerous techniques of hypnotising. According to Hilgard and LeBaron (1984) there are three main components of the process of inducing hypnosis, *relaxation, imagination*, and *enactment*, and these will now be discussed in relation to three types of induction technique.

Induction by Relaxation

Getting a subject to relax all the musculature is commonly used as the basis of one type of technique, a technique that often employs the metaphor of sleep. William Edmonston (1981, p.13) presents a case for relaxation being the *essential* component of hypnotism, and throughout his book he argues against the over-simple dismissal by many modern writers of the traditional sleep-hypnosis connection. He writes:

> Bramwell (1903) argued against the analogy of hypnosis with sleep , but like others before and after him, his argument seemed based on absolutism—that hypnosis and natural sleep are not *identical*. There is no argument here; they are not identical, but there are points of similarity. And these points did not begin with Pavlov ... but have been the common thread in the history of hypnosis.

One type of technique involves repeated suggestions of muscular relaxation, and then going on to encourage the subject to go to sleep, while at the same time preventing them from actually going to sleep not only by continuing to talk to them but insisting that they pay close attention to all that is said. In practice this works pretty well, as by "going to sleep" people understand ceasing to attend to all the multitude of stimuli impinging from the environment and critically evaluating and processing them. We do this every night of our lives when we go to bed, so it is a well-practised skill. Here we may usefully quote an actual induction process, that of the modern Stanford Scale (Weitzenhoffer & Hilgard, 1959, pp. 15–16) which begins with repeated suggestions for muscular relaxation and then continues with the sleep metaphor:

> You feel drowsy and sleepy. Just keep listening to my voice. Pay close attention to it. Keep your thoughts on what I am saying—just listen. You are going to get much more drowsy and sleepy. Soon you will be deep asleep but you will continue to hear me. You will not awaken until I tell you to do so ... you will feel yourself going down, down into a deep, comfortable, a deep restful sleep. A sleep in which you will be able to do all sorts of things I ask you to do ... Pay attention only to my voice and only to such things as I may call to your attention.

There are many other wordings for this type of induction process employing relaxation and the metaphor of sleep that have been used by other hypnotists, but they all have in common encouraging the subjects to go to sleep while at the same time preventing them from really going to sleep by insisting that they continue to pay attention to what the hypnotist is saying. The subjects are thus caught in a "double-bind" situation, a situation which they can resolve only by accepting the suggestions of the hypnotist as interpreting and structuring reality.

The sentence "A sleep in which you will be able to do all sorts of things I ask you to do", defines a very special sort of "sleep", in fact a condition of sleepwalking or somnambulism. This was apparent to the early experimenters as long ago as the eighteenth century, and to this day deeply hypnotised subjects who are carrying out purposeful acts are known as "somnambules".

Induction by Imagination

Sleep and drowsiness need not be mentioned in the induction process, nor indeed need subjects be physically relaxed. By the use of guided imagery the hypnotist can encourage the development of a fantasy, and by concentration of attention on that fantasy to the exclusion of every other idea hypnosis may be achieved. For instance, the hypnotist may suggest the vivid experience of lying in the warm sunshine on the sea shore, listening to the sound of the waves, smelling the sea, and feeling a beautiful calm and peace.Thus a word-picture of the scene is gradually built up so that subjects get "carried away", just as they can enter into the experience of a scene cleverly presented on stage, on film or in a vividly written book. The device of capturing the subjects' whole attention by describing a very vivid scene is intended to effect the desired change in the whole mode of perception. Hypnotised subjects come to rely on the hypnotist's words as the sole channel of experience of the world. Thereafter, whatever the hypnotist suggests, providing that it is reasonably acceptable, becomes actual reality for the subject.

It should be pointed out right away that although hypnotised subjects are experiencing an unreal world,they *know* that they are hypnotised, and can attribute the strangeness of the phenomena they experience to their being in this state. It is understood that this unreal world has been built up by the hypnotist's words and at one level of thinking it is acknowledged that it is unreal. This need not occasion us surprise, for when we have the experience of witnessing a very moving play performed by great actors, we may, at the time, feel all the emotions appropriate to the play even to the point of weeping, while knowing that the scenery is made of cardboard and that the characters before us are paid actors.

Induction by guided imagery is used by many clinicians. Kroger and Fezler (1976, p.38) write:

> Vivid images are accomplished by focusing on a subject's sensory recall. Every image should be experienced in all five senses if possible and just as if it were really happening. A sensation once experienced is never forgotten. It is recorded for ever. We have the ability to recall a sensation in its entirety but we seldom utilize this potential. A sensation is imaginarily going back in time to a point where that particular sensation was received and re-experiencing it. For example, if the relaxing image is seeing yourself on the *beach*, you smell the salt not by saying over and over, "I smell salt" but by recalling a particular point in time when you experienced that smell and reliving it.

Thus although the scene is created by the hypnotist's words, the vivid detail comes from the storehouse of the subject's own memories. The hypnotist must therefore choose words with great care so that it is pretty certain that all the details mentioned will have been within a particular subject's personal experience. This necessitates some preliminary discussion before deciding on the exact nature of the guided imagery to be used. It is useless to expect just anyone to build up pleasant fantasies about lying in the hot sun on a sandy beach by the sea, for a few people just do not like this form of relaxation. However, they might be very willing and capable of remembering and re-creating pleasant scenes of walking in the mountains.

Here it may be appropriate to use the analogy of lucid dreaming when discussing hypnotism by means of guided imagery. Lucid dreaming refers to a phenomenon that has come into prominence in recent years, and has been intensively studied by some investigators such as Stephen LaBerge (1985). In ordinary dreaming the dreamer accepts as reality the bizarre events of dreams and may be genuinely distressed, pleased or excited by the dream content. In a lucid dream, however, the dreamer knows very well that it is only a dream and does not accept it as reality.

Although the dreamer is creating the lucid dream, it involves the curious experience of being a passive spectator of what is happening, or an actor fulfilling a predetermined part, as though it were being produced by an agency other than ourselves. If the lucid dream becomes unpleasant it is generally possible to wrench ourselves out of it and wake up. This is very like what takes place in hypnosis. The outside agency is the voice of the hypnotist unlocking memories and building fantasies out of their raw material, and if the hypnotised subject does not like what is suggested, hypnosis can be easily terminated.

Induction by Enactment

Induction by enactment involves affecting the motor control of the subject. One classic form of induction is to get the subject to stare at a fixed point rather above the level of the eyes, and to give verbal suggestions that the eyes are getting tireder and tireder and that they will soon begin to close of their own accord. As will be discussed in the next chapter, the pioneer James Braid (1843), who first coined the word "hypnotism", initially believed that the phenomenon was explicable in terms of the fatigue of the muscles of the eyes and the cortical centres concerned with vision. He abandoned this simplistic theory of hypnotism later and advanced to a more sophisticated theory (Braid, 1846, 1855). Again we may quote the induction procedure of the modern Stanford Scale (Weitzenhoffer and Hilgard, 1959, p.14).

> Just relax. Don't be tense. Keep your eyes on the target. Look at it as steadily as you can. Should your eyes wander away from it that will be all right ... just bring your eyes back to it. After a while you may find that the target gets blurry, or perhaps moves about, or again, changes colour. That is all right. Should you get sleepy, that will be fine too. Whatever happens, let it happen and keep staring at the target for a while. There will come a time, however, when your eyes will be so tired, will feel so heavy, that you will be unable to keep them open any longer and they will close, perhaps quite involuntarily. When this happens, just let it take place.

Concentrating on the involuntary closure of the eyelids is related to the companion technique of using the metaphor of going to sleep.

The muscles of the eyes are not the only target for the hypnotist's suggestions in this type of induction technique. To quote Bernheim (1973, pp. 138–139):

> The mechanism of suggestion in general, may then be summed up in the following formula: *increase of the reflex ideo-motor, ideo-sensitive, and ideo-sensorial excitability*.... In the same way in hypnotism, the ideo-reflex excitability is increased in the brain, so that any idea received is immediately transformed into an act, without the controlling portion of the brain, the higher centres, being able to prevent the transformation.

A variety of suggested movements have formed the basis of techniques of hypnotism by enactment. The postural sway test of Hull (1933) forms the first item in the Stanford Scale which has been referred to already. Here it is a pre-induction item designed to give the subject experience and to demonstrate that standing up with the eyes closed, listening to suggestions of postural sway will actually affect the postural equilibrium without there being any conscious intention to move. Many people are very surprised when they find themselves swaying on this test. There is also the hand levitation technique that has an ancient lineage and has been popularised by Erickson (1961). This technique is administered as follows: the subject is asked to look steadily at one hand resting in the lap, and it is suggested that in a little while some movement will develop in that hand, such as the twitching of a finger. The hypnotist goes on making references to this potential movement, and if and when it occurs (it may not occur in some insuggestible subjects) additional suggestions are given to the effect that the hand will experience sensations of tingling and lightness, and that it will begin to float up in the air of its own accord. Some hypnotists (see Barber, Spanos, & Chaves, 1974, p.131) believe in providing the subject with a cognitive strategy for a "goal-directed" imagining, that is, to suggest a specific situation which, if it were the actual state of affairs, would tend to produce the behaviour and experience that is being suggested. "For instance, a suggestion for arm levitation might ask the subject to imagine a large helium-filled balloon tied to the wrist which is raising the arm."

Once the hand and arm float upwards, the hypnotist's suggestions are directed towards getting the hand to approach the forehead, with the assurance that when the forehead is reached the eyes will close and a state of hypnosis will be achieved.

As well as techniques of suggestion that involve the enactment of muscular movements, there are others that concentrate on the *inhibition* of movement, and inviting the subject to test how the usual voluntary movements will not take place. Again, to quote the Stanford Scale (Weitzenhoffer & Hilgard, 1959, p.21)

> Please extend your left arm straight out and make a fist... Arm straight out, a tight fist. I want you to pay attention to this arm and imagine that it is becoming stiff ... stiffer and stiffer very stiff. ... and now you notice that something is happening to your arm ... you notice a feeling of stiffness coming into it ... It is becoming stiff ... more and more stiff ... rigid ... like a bar of iron ... and you know how difficult ... how impossible it is to bend a bar of iron like your arm ... See how much your arm is like a bar of iron ... test how stiff and rigid it is ... *try* to bend it ... *try*.

Such challenge techniques may be adapted for inducing hypnosis, but more commonly they are used to test the degree of responsiveness of a subject, and also to "deepen" the state of hypnosis. They give subjects the opportunity of experiencing the fact that they are indeed in an altered state of consciousness in which unusual phenomena occur

THE CHARACTERISTICS OF HYPNOSIS

Having outlined in general terms the methods that are commonly employed to induce a state of hypnosis (assuming that hypnosis can properly be designated as a state — see later), we may list the main characteristics, most, although not all, logically follow from the methods of hypnotism employed:

1. The subjects are less likely to initiate action. They depend passively on the hypnotist to direct the course of their interaction (see Hilgard, 1965).
2. Subjects attend selectively to the range of ideas and the happenings around them that the hypnotist calls to their attention, and they tend to ignore things outside this range (see Bowers, 1983, pp. 138–139).
3. Reality testing is reduced. Subjects tend to accept ideas and even distorted perceptions that are presented to them without much concern for logical consistency (see Sheehan & Perry, 1976, pp. 201–202).
4. Suggestibility is increased (see Hilgard & Tart, 1966). An enhanced imaginative capacity is displayed but subjects are no more compliant than in their ordinary waking state, in that they may not accept suggestions that are displeasing to them (see Orne, 1980a).
5. There is an enhanced capacity for enacting roles. Thus if it is suggested that hypnotised subjects return to a much younger age they will play the childhood role more convincingly than is normally characteristic of them (see Sarbin, 1950; 1965).
6. Some amnesia for events in hypnosis may be present after hypnosis. There is some controversy about this, some writers maintaining that post-hypnotic amnesia has to be suggested directly or indirectly for it to occur (see Nace, Orne & Hammer, 1974).
7. Behaviour and experience after hypnosis has ended may be affected by what has been suggested during hypnosis. Thus if it is suggested that the subject will perform a certain action when a relevant cue is given post-hypnotically, this post-hypnotic suggestion may be performed without conscious awareness on the part of the subject. Alternatively, the subject may perform the act but be well aware of where the idea originated. Similarly, post-hypnotic amnesia for a certain event may be suggested, and the subject may be unable to remember it until a pre-arranged releasing cue is given (see Orne, Sheehan, & Evans, 1968).

CRITICISMS AND RESERVATIONS

Rowley (1986) lists seven different theories of hypnosis. Because there is considerable divergence of opinion about the topic it is natural that all the characteristics that have been listed above are subject to questioning and different interpretations by people who have their own theoretical positions to defend. It would be tedious to discuss each of the seven different viewpoints, but instead we will consider two main differences of approach taken respectively by those who consider it useful to refer to a "state" of hypnosis, and those who take a "non-state" position and question this approach (see Coe, 1973). This controversy has generated a great deal of discussion, perhaps more than it warrants, and is regarded by some as no more than a verbal quibble. When we refer to the "state" of hypnosis we are referring to a psychological state, just as when we refer to a state of expectation, a state of anger, a state of anxiety, a state of disappointment, and so on. All these are *psychological* and not *physiological* states, although at the extreme there may be physiological concomitants. A person who is extremely angry or extremely anxious may have a raised blood pressure, etc. But we do not define psychological states in terms of the possible physical indices, for these are by no means unique to a particular psychological state. It is the lack of any unique physiological criteria of hypnosis that is one of the main objections of the "non-state" theorists. Barber (1969, p.10) writes: "The topic needs to be approached from a new perspective *which does not assume that the behaviours to be explained are a function of a unique state*". As a matter of fact, those theorists who find it useful to talk about a "state" of hypnosis are not bothered whether or not such a state is unique. Indeed, if we examine many other areas of study where we find the use of the "state" concept—a state of sleep or a state of pain for instance—we find that there is no uniqueness, and we get on very well in scientific discourse without such an assumption. Turning to criticisms of the view that relaxation is the essential component of hypnosis, as maintained by Edmonston (1981) we can refer to an interesting study by Banyai and Hilgard (1976) who demonstrated that subjects vigorously pedalling an exercise bicycle could be hypnotised, the suggestions emphasising alertness, freshness, and wakefulness. The hypnotic state they entered was in every way similar to that achieved by a relaxing and sleepy-type induction. If muscular relaxation is not really necessary to induce hypnosis, we may ask why is it so commonly used both by experimentalists and by clinicians when they hypnotise? Apart from tradition, the answer probably refers to the immense facility which the hypnotist enjoys when influencing the subject by suggestions for relaxation. When we suggest muscular relaxation we can be pretty sure that practically all subjects will respond appropriately. The subject then has the experience of responding physically to spoken suggestions, and becomes more and more passive, leaving direction of the situation to the hypnotist, confident that whatever the hypnotist says will be followed by further appropriate reactions. Very soon a change coming over the whole body is experienced, and this is the first step towards hypnosis.

Edmonston's thesis may be saved from rejection, however, if we consider further just what is meant by "relaxation". Ordinarily we think of muscular relaxation, but is it the sheer loss of muscular tonus that is important? Wolpe (1958) in his original therapeutic method of desensitising patients with phobic and similar complaints, proceeded with psychological work only after he had induced complete muscular relaxation. He reasoned that a patient could not be anxious and psychologically tense if at the same time the musculature was completely relaxed. As discussed by Rachman (1968), subsequent workers did indeed find that the therapeutic success of psychological desensitisation was greater if the preliminaries of inducing muscular relaxation were observed. However, other clinicians found that there was little correspondence between the degree of muscular relaxation (as shown on physiological monitoring apparatus) and subjects' own report of how mentally calm they felt. In accordance with these findings Rachman argues that what is important for therapy is not the *physical* relaxation but the degree of *mental* relaxation, i.e. how calm the patient feels. Presumably in the study by Banyai and Hilgard where the subjects were on exercise bicycles, the hypnotic suggestions engendered a feeling of relaxed calmness even though they were pedalling energetically.

The extreme of mental relaxation is, of course, sleep, and one can drop off to sleep while performing some simple physical task that does not require any mental effort or planning. Edmonston has already been quoted on the points of similarity between hypnosis and sleep. Here we come across some very sharp controversy. Insistence that "hypnosis is not sleep", which characterises a number of modern books on hypnosis, is probably an over-reaction against the many nineteenth-century hypnotists who, since the time of José de Faria in the early part of the century, invariably used the sleep metaphor in hypnotising. As noted above, the induction process of the modern Stanford Scale continues to do just this, but some writers, particularly social psychologists, are strongly opposed to the classical sleep-hypnosis connection emphasised by Edmonston. One social psychologist (Wagstaff, 1981, p.214) goes so far as to write:

> I feel that no amount of claims that the terms "trance", "somnambulism" and "waking" are only metaphorical can really justify their continued usage unless it is made abundantly clear to all subjects receiving suggestions that they *are* only metaphors, i.e. "hypnosis" is *nothing like* sleep or sleep-walking.

In fact, many modern hypnotists would not agree with this at all, and in the explanation of hypnosis given to subjects prior to induction in the Stanford Scale (Weitzenhoffer & Hilgard, 1959, pp.14–15), which is still the most frequently used modern scale in its various forms, it is specifically stated that:

> Many people report that becoming hypnotised feels at first like falling asleep, but with the difference that somehow or other they keep hearing my voice as a sort of background to whatever other experience they may have. In some ways hypnosis is like sleepwalking; however, hypnosis is also an individual experience and is not just alike for everyone. In a sense the hypnotised person is like a sleepwalker, for he can carry out various and complex activities while remaining hypnotised.

Books on hypnosis frequently mention the fact that the electroencephalograph (EEG) of the hypnotised person does not resemble the record of a sleeping person, and hence it is argued that the two states cannot be considered as similar. When the EEG first came into widespread use, various investigators studied the records of hypnotised subjects to see if the "brain waves" were sleep-like, and the general consensus of opinion was that they were not (see Evans, 1979). This finding weakened the traditional sleep-hypnosis connection, but on reviewing the evidence, Edmonston (1981, pp. 37–38) writes:

> Unanimity with respect to EEG evaluations of the relationship between hypnosis and natural sleep is certainly not apparent as yet, and my earlier admonition (Edmonston, 1967) to suspend judgement seems as reasonable now as it did then. At this juncture it is more important to recognize that, despite the methodological difficulties Evans (1979) noted, some EEG data have suggested that while hypnosis is not total sleep, it may reside on an EEG continuum between wakefulness and total sleep.

It is relevant to consider here just what we mean by that ambiguous term "sleep". Traditionally it has been assumed that we all know just what we mean by the term, but it was the investigation of sleeping subjects by means of the EEG in the 1950s that first alerted researchers to the fact that "sleep" is by no means a simple and easily defined state of consciousness — just like "hypnosis" in fact. Sleep research over 30 years has now made it clear that "sleep" has to be defined by three different criteria; psychological, physiological, and behavioural. In some states of consciousness the three criteria do not coincide. For instance, in lucid dreaming the dreamer is psychologically "awake" in that there is complete awareness of what is going on, but physiologically the dreamer is "asleep" in terms of the EEG record. We must accept the fact that "sleep" is a rather vague, rag-bag category of different states of consciousness, and while the hypnotised subject is not what we would ordinarily call "asleep", the nineteenth-century researchers who referred to hypnosis as "lucid sleep" were not far wrong.

MYTHS ABOUT HYPNOSIS

While there is a lot of room for argument about the different interpretations of the known facts, some of the folk-lore about hypnosis can definitely be dismissed in the light of modern knowledge. We shall deal with the more common myths about hypnosis.

Alleged Connections with "The Occult"

Because the history of hypnosis is connected with that of mesmerism, as is outlined in the next chapter, the topic has inherited many of the strange beliefs that were current in the mesmeric movement. Mesmerism has been a frequent subject for writers of fiction such as Edgar Allen Poe (1871) and many other nineteenth-century novelists as discussed by Ludwig (1963). One of the beliefs of the mesmerists was that the mesmerised subject could exhibit occult powers such as reading without the use of eyesight, and the ability to communicate thought at a distance. Early in his career Pierre Janet investigated some of these beliefs with respect to hypnosis rather than mesmerism, and eventually came to the conclusion that such beliefs were without factual basis (see Ellenberger, 1970, p. 338). Bernheim (1973, p.406) also investigated such beliefs and concluded, "I have found nothing definite, and here also I remain in doubt". Whereas adherents to occult beliefs will always claim for hypnosis supernormal mental powers, at the level of rational science one can safely say that such beliefs are without any supporting evidence.

Hypnosis Itself Abolishes Pain

The idea that the hypnotised subject feels pain very much less than in a state of normal waking consciousness again relates to the old association between hypnotism and mesmerism. As is discussed in the next chapter, some subjects could be put into a curious, trance-like state by the techniques of the mesmerists, even to the degree that severe surgical operations could be performed painlessly. This has given rise to the mistaken belief that hypnosis *per se* confers analgesia. This is quite untrue, and the facts of the case will be explained in Chapter 8 of this book.

Although hypnosis itself makes no difference to the perception of pain, it can be attenuated in some people, sometimes to a surprising degree, by deliberate hypnotic suggestions that are carefully designed to build up this effect. These suggestions work in two ways, first, by allaying the anxiety of the patient (and this applies to a clinical situation in which a patient is anxious) less pain is likely to be felt because pain is partly a function of anxiety; second, a negative hallucination for pain may be induced by hypnotic suggestion, just as other sensory experiences can be wholly or partially ablated by suggestion. This effect is not easily achieved, and the phenomenon should not blind us to the fact that hypnosis does not automatically confer analgesia.

Hypnosis and Super-normal Strength and Endurance

It is widely believed that when hypnotised, subjects can exhibit physical strength greater than their normal capacity. This belief is often capitalised on by stage hypnotists who, by a number of conjuring tricks, often purport to demonstrate this alleged phenomenon. A typical example of this is the so-called "human plank feat". A subject is hypnotised and it is suggested that the body will be rendered very strong and rigid.

When a sufficient degree of stiffness is obtained, the subject is supported horizontally with the head on one chair and the feet on another. This sounds as though it were an extraordinary feat and it looks it, but in reality it is not so difficult to perform *without* hypnosis. According to Barber (1969, pp. 68–69) it has been shown that when men and women are suitably instructed they can perform this apparently difficult feat for over two minutes without being hypnotised. In the experiment to which Barber refers, subjects were amazed at their own ability;

comparing people in the waking and hypnotised state, hypnosis did not appear to make a great deal of difference.

The older literature contains accounts of a number of badly conducted experiments that have bolstered the myth of the super-normal ability of hypnotised subjects. Hypnosis cannot give people supernormal strength. What hypnosis does do is enable them to concentrate rather better on a particular task, provided it is simple, and perhaps increase their performance by this means (see Gibson, 1977, pp. 95–97).

Hypnosis and Memory

Many people believe that hypnosis can be used greatly to improve the memory, so that many events that have been forgotten can be remembered within hypnosis. This is not entirely a myth since it is founded on some rather complex facts about the nature of memory. The belief has come up for special scrutiny in recent years because of the vogue in the United States for hypnotising witnesses in the course of police investigations in order to help them remember details of what they have observed at the scene of crimes. An enormous amount has been published on this subject, and a general tendency in all recent forensic studies and laboratory experiments on memory and hypnosis has been a growing scepticism as to the usefulness of hypnosis in this matter. The British Home Office, benefitting from the American experience, and having taken the opinion of various learned societies, has finally come round to a very sceptical view of the matter that contrasts with the earlier enthusiastic advocacy from such writers as Reiser (1980). This advocacy has been criticised by authors such as Perry and Laurence (1982). The British Home Office, while not absolutely forbidding the use of hypnosis, has proposed very stringent safeguards in their guidelines to the police (see Fellows, 1988a).

There are two main drawbacks to the use of hypnosis in attempting to get a subject to recover memory. First, if the hypnotised subject believes that forgotten material *ought* to be recoverable, then there is a tendency for memories of similar events, and creative fantasy material, to take the place of true memory, the subject innocently believing that what he appears to recall is true. The subject having thus concocted a "false memory" out of the material available, this distorted version becomes believed in henceforward as though it had actually occurred. The police may then be given totally false leads in their investigation, and a witness may even give false evidence in court quite innocently.

After various legal debates in the United States, the practice of hypnotising witnesses in the course of investigations has been subject to more and more stringent restrictions in various states. The matter has been the subject of several investigative studies (see Perry & Laurence, 1983), and in 1984 the American Medical Association made an official statement (published 1985) on the matter concluding that "recollections obtained during hypnosis can involve confabulations and pseudomemories and not only fail to be more accurate, but actually appear to be less reliable than nonhypnotic recall".

Apart from the forensic field, hypnosis has long been in use in therapy in attempts to enable patients to recover memories from the past that may be relevant to their condition. Here it may not matter if the events they "remember" actually took place the way they recall, for what may be more important is their perception of these events in relation to the problems they now experience. This will be discussed further in Chapter 6. Experimental work on revivifying memory in hypnosis shows that hypnotised subjects tend to produce *more* material than in their normal waking state, but because some of it is inaccurate and subject to all kinds of distortion, hypnosis is not a suitable technique if it is desired to obtain veridical accounts of past events.

The Question of Compliance

It is widely believed that people who are easily hypnotised are of an especially "compliant" nature; that is, they are very prone to do as they are told. Associated with this belief is the idea that, when hypnotised, people will become more submissive and obedient than they are in the normal waking state. Both these ideas are mistaken yet they are rather fundamental to the image of hypnosis that is very common—the idea of the phenomenon involving the dominance of one person's will over another's.

This myth of hypnosis being a matter of compliance on the part of the subject is, of course, one of the major stereotypes that have been created by writers of fiction. Both Ludwig (1963) and Schneck (1978) identify George Du Maurier's best-selling novel *Trilby* as the major source of the public image of hypnosis involving compliance and a dominance-submission interpersonal relationship. Ludwig gives many other examples of writers of fiction supporting this idea of hypnosis. It is difficult to produce evidence that counteracts this myth.

For hypnosis to take place subjects must in the first place be willing to co-operate; they agree to suspend their normal activity of critical judgement and reality testing, just as we do this when settling down to enjoy a dramatic performance. When watching a play, with one part of our minds we may actually criticise the acting and production, but our empathy and enjoyment depends upon our reacting as though these were real events and real human emotions taking place before our eyes. This involves the *willing* suspension of disbelief; there is no compliance with authority involved. So with subjects in hypnosis; they are entirely autonomous and in no way dominated by the hypnotist, although they are "going along with" the situation and responding to the suggestions like a rapt member of an audience who has been "carried away".

It is easy to understand how an onlooker may get a quite mistaken idea of the situation when watching hypnosis, and construe it in terms of dominance–submission. Earlier, when discussing the phenomenon of *enactment*, the arm rigidity test of the

Stanford Scale was described. Here it is suggested to subjects that they imagine that their arms are stiff like bars of iron, and then they are invited to test how stiff and rigid their arms are by trying to bend them. Frequently they try — and fail! Subjects sometimes say afterwards that they were genuinely surprised to find that their arms would not bend, but this is the sort of "surprise" one encounters in dreams where the products of one's own fantasy go counter to mental processes in another part of the mind. This is the phenomenon known as "dissociation" which has a long history in psychology, and is discussed at length by Hilgard (1986).

Although it is difficult to demonstrate that people who have a high capacity for hypnosis are *not* especially compliant individuals, this is indicated by such evidence as we have. London and Fuhrer (1961) demonstrated that unhypnotisable individuals tended to be rather more compliant than hypnotisable individuals in that they were more willing to exert themselves to please an experimenter both *before* and *after* an attempted induction procedure than were hypnotisable individuals. Wagstaff (1981) attempts to explain away such evidence by suggesting that individuals low in hypnotic performance feel guilt towards the experimenter and hence seek to propitiate by being extra-compliant in other contexts. This fails to account for why the subjects were extra-compliant *before* the fact of their hypnotic insusceptibility had been established.

In general, although lay people will no doubt continue to believe in the myth of hypnosis being a form of extra obedience and compliance, and see the hypnotist as a sort of Svengali figure, researchers have discovered that this is not the case, even against their previous expectations, as in the case of Orne (1980a, p.32) who writes:

> there is no evidence that hypnotised individuals are more willing to carry out simple requests from the hypnotist because they are hypnotised. This has been documented in experimental contexts with some care when some time ago I summarised the evidence (Orne, 1966) that, contrary to my own early views (Orne, 1959), the hypnotised individual is not necessarily more motivated than the unhypnotised individual to comply with the requests of the hypnotist.

The folk-lore about the compliant hypnotic subject and power-hungry hypnotists compelling their victims to perform all sorts of immoral and criminal acts is the topic of a whole issue of the *International Journal of Clinical and Experimental Hypnosis* to which six authors contributed papers discussing the issue (IJCEH, 1972).

Myths about Hypnosis in Therapy

Some of the most common myths about hypnosis concern its use in therapy. This matter will be dealt with in detail in Chapter 4 where the general therapeutic uses of hypnosis are examined, and again in Chapter 13 where the use of hypnosis by various professions is considered.

SUMMARY

As properly conducted research in hypnosis has proceeded, mainly in university-based laboratories, over the last 44 years, much of the aura of magic that has surrounded hypnosis for so long has been dispelled. The topic is still the subject of lively debate and controversy among psychologists and other professionals who investigate hypnosis, but all reputable scientists and clinicians are now agreed that it is simply an interesting psychological phenomenon with some physiological correlates, and that there is no need to invoke occult and mystical concepts to explain it. That it has important implications for the work of health professionals is undeniable, and this book will examine its various practical applications in therapy.

2 Historical Background

In the previous chapter it was indicated that hypnosis is not easy to define, there being several different theories advanced by people from rather differing standpoints, although all are agreed that we are discussing a very real psychological phenomenon. In delineating the history of hypnotism in Western society, say over the past 200 years, this latitude of definition causes some imprecision in just what social, intellectual, and scientific movements we are prepared to consider relevant to the topic of "hypnosis".

Many books dealing with the history of hypnotism trace its origins to the work of Franz Anton Mesmer, the physician who began his work in Vienna in the 1770s, and who caused a furore when he established a flourishing practice in Paris in 1778. This furore led to the establishment of a Royal Commission of inquiry under the chairmanship of Benjamin Franklin in 1784. This matter has been much written about by historians of hypnotism such as Bernheim (1886), Binet and Féré (1888), Bramwell (1903), Buranelli (1975), Darnton (1968), Ellenberger (1970), Hull (1933), Janet (1925), Sheehan and Perry (1976), Thornton (1976), and Tinterow (1970). It is not proposed to deal with this interesting period in French and European history in any detail in this book.

Shor (1972) divides the history of hypnotism into four stages: (1) presomnambulistic mesmerism; (2) somnambulistic mesmerism; (3) the early psychological period; (4) the later psychological or modern period. This chapter will be arranged approximately according to Shor's headings, although the matter will not necessarily coincide with what Shor presents.

PRESOMNAMBULISTIC MESMERISM

Hypnotism arose out of mesmerism but it should be noted that if we use the strict definition of the former term, then we cannot say that Mesmer himself ever used hypnotism. Hypnotism implies the deliberate induction of an altered psychological state by means of verbally conveyed ideas. The technique of mesmerism is not quite the same. It consists essentially of inducing in the subject something like a state of shock which is followed by a degree of torpor and perhaps insensibility. Mesmerists who adhered to Mesmer's original practice tried to initiate what was called a "crisis", something like an epileptic fit, and indeed Thornton (1976) has suggested that many of the patients with whom Mesmer was successful were people disposed to epilepsy. The mesmerists did this, not by verbal suggestions as in hypnotism, but by working up their subjects to a high degree of emotionality by various procedures including physical manipulations, the theory being that they were imbuing their patients with "animal magnetism", an invisible fluid that was supposed to flow from the mesmerist to the subject. Indeed, mesmerists claimed to be able to "magnetise" inanimate objects such as trees, so that people could receive the "animal magnetism" by touching the object, much as we receive a flow of static electricity from a charged body.

This first period is referred to as "presomnambulistic mesmerism" as originally there was no intention of producing any sort of "somnambulism". This matter will be discussed later when we refer to the work of Puységur and his inheritors. While mesmerism and hypnotism are basically distinct processes producing rather different states, it should be noted that these two states probably co-existed to a greater or lesser degree in many cases.

Mesmer's Sources, Practices, and Theory

It is of interest to consider the main sources from which Mesmer derived his theory and practices. Priests had long been treating various types of emotional and physical disorders by the ceremony of exorcism that was designed to cast out the demon allegedly responsible. In the eighteenth century there was a very popular exorcist, Father Gassner who operated in Austria, Switzerland, and Germany, and treated many people with nervous diseases by the ceremony of exorcism. This ceremony, when successful, threw the patient into a sort of fit or convulsion when the demon was supposed to depart from the body and leave the sufferer cured. In many cases of psychosomatic and hysterical disorders when the patient strongly believed in demonic possession, such an experience would alleviate the disorder. But Mesmer, a child of the Scientific Enlightenment, did not believe in the supernatural causation of disease. However, he was influenced to some extent by Father Gassner's methods. He held that such disorders were caused by a derangement of the sufferer's "animal magnetism". He held that this fluid permeated the whole universe and that some individuals, such as himself, were specially richly endowed with it. Mesmer's theories were not particularly original; in his dissertation *The influence of the planets on the human body* we can trace his ideas back to Paracelsus who wrote in the sixteenth century and, as detailed by Pattie (1956), to the English doctor Richard Mead who had published similar speculations much earlier. The reason why he chose to call this postulated fluid "animal magnetism" is to be found in the elementary scientific thought of the time that was fascinated by the mysteries of electricity and the power of the lodestone and iron magnets. Since ancient times it had been believed that magnets had a curative power when applied to sick persons, and for a time Mesmer worked with Father Hell, a Jesuit professor of astronomy in Vienna who attempted to use magnets therapeutically . To quote Sheehan and Perry (1976, p.6):

> Mesmer proceeded to demonstrate in meticulous detail that the magnets had no effect in themselves. He kept in touch with Father Hell and conducted many tests in his presence. To show that the magnets were not the crucial factor in the cure, he demonstrated that almost anything—other metals, paper, wool, silk, stone, glass, and water could conduct the magnetic forces.

The "magnetic force" referred to here was not that of ordinary electromagnetism, of course, but Mesmer's own "animal magnetism". It is to Mesmer's credit that he was shrewd enough to discover the uselessness of magnets in therapy; it is less creditable that he continued to trade upon the public belief that magnets were therapeutically effective. In the *baquet* of his Paris salon he had iron filings and bottles of water, all supposedly "magnetised", with iron conducting rods projecting out that sufferers could hold, all a piece of flummery designed to play upon the emotions of his patients. When patients were treated in groups they crowded round the *baquet* holding the iron rods and getting emotionally aroused by the music, the mirrors, and the general atmosphere of a magician's den that was cultivated in the salon. Individual treatment consisted of, among other things, the mesmerist making "passes", stroking movements up and down the body either in contact with the clothes or a few inches away. This was supposed to "magnetise" the patient, just as a piece of iron may be magnetised by repeated stroking with a steel magnet. Ideally, according to Mesmer's theory, when sufficiently "magnetised", the patients would experience a "crisis" in which they were physically prostrated and recovered only slowly, as after a fit. Some patients did indeed have quite severe fits and were carried out to a room with a quilted floor where they could recover. Whatever disorder the patient suffered from would then be alleviated by the experience. In many cases all this did happen, and patients responded favourably just as the believers had responded to Father Gassner. However, in some cases the subjects of mesmerism did not respond at all, and we may presume that in the course of time Mesmer and his followers discovered empirically the sort of people and the varieties of conditions that would respond favourably to this treatment. Describing Mesmer's practice, Thornton writes (1976, p.6):

> He only treated diseases of the nervous system and these were the only ones he undertook to cure; sufferers from other diseases he referred back to their own doctors, the magnetic fluid having less influence over these disorders.

In this, of course, his practice was similar to that of Father Gassner who claimed to treat only the disorders that were of "preternatural" origin.

Thornton attributes the crises and ensuing comatose condition to the epileptic propensity of many of the patients with nervous disorders. However, as pointed out by Parsons and Hart (1984), epilepsy is a symptom and not a disease *per se*. It refers to seizures of greater or lesser severity due to a strong nervous discharge from the brain; some authorities such as Clemenow, King, and Brantley (1984) identify as many as eight types of epileptic seizure. Most "true" epilepsy is due to injury of the brain, but there are borderline cases of "hysterical" epilepsy in which there is no evidence of brain injury, and the symptom is generally triggered off by emotional excitement.

Nowadays doctors are somewhat chary of using the old label of "hysteric" for people, but even such staunch opponents of the over-use of the term as Elliot Slater (1965) concede that "It would be legitimate, I believe, in a given instance to say that a particular symptom was 'hysterical'".

In addition to epileptic and hysterical disorders there are other conditions that produce fits of one kind and another, and are followed by partial insensibility. One of these conditions which has come into prominence in recent years is narcolepsy, a condition quite distinct from epilepsy and surprisingly common in the population at large; about 3 sufferers in every 1000 of the population according to Williams and Karacan (1973). Apart from a general tendency to be very sleepy at all times, people afflicted with narcolepsy suffer from a variety of other symptoms. About half of them are subject to attacks of cataplexy if they are strongly aroused emotionally; that is, they lose all control of their muscles and appear to swoon, sometimes experiencing hallucinations. Descriptions of the behaviour of some of Mesmer's patients resemble descriptions of narcoleptic attacks given by modern authors such as Mendelson, Gillin, and Wyatt (1977), and it seems very likely that sufferers from this disorder became patients of the mesmerists and exhibited behaviour that was attributed to their "magnetic" state.

Mesmerism and Pain

As well as seizures brought on by epileptic, hysterical, and narcoleptic conditions, we must consider a very curious phenomenon known as "tonic immobility" to which most animal species are subject, and is undoubtedly relevant to the conditions induced in their patients by the mesmerists. Tonic immobility, as discussed by

Gallup (1974) , which is otherwise known as "animal hypnosis", is easily produced in small mammals such as guinea pigs simply by turning them on their backs and gently immobilising them for a time. The animal remains immobile and apparently partially paralysed for a while, but strangest of all it does not react when pricked or otherwise injured. This has led to the term "death feigning" which was used by Charles Darwin. Darwin suggested that feigning death would protect a species from predators to some extent, in that if an entrapped animal remains absolutely motionless it is less likely to be killed as prey, for some predators will only attack a wriggling, moving prey. In the state of tonic immobility the animal appears to be immune to pain. New light was thrown on this phenomenon in the 1970s when the nature of endorphins was discovered. Endorphins are chemical substances similar to morphine that are secreted in the brain in certain circumstances and militate against the experience of pain. (Carli 1978), in a series of experiments with rabbits, has evidence that endorphins are produced in the condition of tonic immobility, and this would account for the apparent state of analgesia. The relevance of this to the mesmeric trance is that it was found possible in the nineteenth century to perform severe surgical operations upon patients who had been mesmerised without their experiencing pain. There is little doubt about the authenticity of this fact as details of such painless operations are given not only in the writings of mesmeric enthusiasts such as Elliotson (1843) and Esdaile (1845), but in the objective report of the Bengal Governor's Committee (*Zoist*, 1847–48) appointed to investigate Esdaile's mesmeric surgery. Also, cautious sceptics such as Forbes (1845), while dismissing many of the claims of the mesmerists as nonsense, were forced to acknowledge the reality of their painless surgery. Whether or not endorphins were involved in the analgesia conferred by the mesmeric trance, it is impossible to say. Mesmerism was essentially a physical procedure, based on an erroneous theory of "animal magnetism", which probably acted only on people suffering from somewhat unusual disturbances of the nervous system either permanently, or in the rather special circumstances of awaiting a grisly surgical operation. There was little evidence that mesmerism had much effect on normally healthy people, and this was admitted by the mesmerists themselves.

Once we have understood the essential nature of mesmerism it will be apparent that it had little in common with the techniques that were later to be known as hypnotism. As explained in the previous chapter, hypnotism is essentially a technique of altering the psychological state of subjects by strongly appealing to their imaginative capacities but not to disorganise their nervous system in any way.

SOMNAMBULISTIC MESMERISM

One of the best known accounts of a mesmeric subject becoming hypnotised and showing all the classic signs of what we now regard as the hypnotic state, concerns a young peasant called Victor Race. He was the patient of one of Mesmer's followers, the Marquis Chastenet de Puységur. Race was suffering from a respiratory illness and was also perturbed by some family troubles, and when Puységur tried to mesmerise him the usual sort of crisis did not take place. Instead, at first he appeared to go off to sleep and then began to converse quite rationally but in a manner quite unlike his usual peasant self. According to Puységur (quoted in Buranelli, 1976, p.118):

> He spoke frankly about his private affairs. When I saw his thoughts were having a bad effect on him I stopped them and tried to make him think of more pleasant things. It did not cost me much effort to achieve this. He imagined himself winning a prize, dancing at a fête, and so forth. I encouraged these images... When he enters the magnetic state he is no longer an ignorant peasant who can scarcely speak a word in response to a question. He is a different being whom I do not know how to identify.

When awakening from this trance state Victor Race apparently had no memory of what had been going on, and this and other features of the trance led Puységur to identify it with "somnambulism", the state of a natural sleepwalker who acts fairly rationally without full knowledge of what he is doing, and has no memory for the episode after awakening. To this day, subjects who act in deep hypnosis are known as "somnambules".

Mesmer was not pleased when Puységur related the results of his experiments with Victor Race and other subjects with whom he had begun to try this new technique designed to produce somnambulism. It did not accord well with the general theory of animal magnetism. The mesmeric movement began to be divided between those who held to the original doctrine, and continued the physical rituals designed to produce crises and subsequent insensibility, and the followers of Puységur. The latter were interested in producing lucid somnambulism in which the imagination of the subjects could be directed by talking to them, and during which the various phenomena that we now associate with hypnosis could be produced.

Mesmerism and Humbug

Both mesmerism and what we now call hypnotism became confused in a great morass of occult theories involving belief in spiritualism, foretelling the future, clairvoyance, telepathy, and all sorts of allegedly supernormal powers. In a masterly review of the subject an eminent Scottish doctor, John Forbes (1845), describes how the mesmerists were their own worst enemies in preventing the orthodox medical establishment from taking their more authentic claims seriously. Forbes carefully examined the evidence for the cases of painless surgery that were carried out in the mesmeric trance, and found that a lot of it was indeed genuine. But he pointed out that the mesmerists were unlikely to have their claims taken seriously because in addition they also alleged that they produced all sorts of parapsychological wonders. With commendable care Forbes examined evidence the mesmerists produced for their grandiose parapsychological claims and found that it just did not stand up to careful scrutiny. All the famous mesmerists of the early nineteenth century, Deleuze, Dupotet, Elliotson, Esdaile, Teste, and others, many of them men of considerable achievement and ability, lent their names to this superstructure of occult nonsense. Forbes pointed out with considerable acumen that whereas one mesmerist would claim that a particular marvel like "seeing" without the use of the eyes was "common" among magnetised subjects, another would admit that he personally had never witnessed the phenomenon. They all referred to one another as the authority for their preposterous claims and thus maintained an overblown mythology without any direct fraud or lying on the part of any of the more respectable mesmerists. In England, moreover, mesmerism was mixed up with the passing craze of phrenology, the alleged science of attributing character and ability to the contours of the skull. John Elliotson, sometime professor of medicine at University College, London, edited the quarterly the *Zoist* which was devoted to mesmerism and phrenology, and was published from 1843 to 1845.

Thus the one really valuable contribution that mesmerism made to medical science in the early nineteenth century, the demonstration that major surgery could be carried out painlessly with entranced patients, was largely ignored and disbelieved. All patients could not, of course, be mesmerised, and it was never investigated systematically just what factors were associated with susceptibility to mesmerism. The medical establishment chose to ignore mesmeric surgery, first because most doctors were so contemptuous of the occultism and humbug that characterised the general mesmeric movement, and second, because doctors had grown up in a tradition that took pain for granted as a necessary evil and were not seriously concerned to prevent it, as related by Haggard (1932). When a well authenticated case of the amputation of a leg performed painlessly under mesmeric anaesthesia was presented at a meeting of the Royal Medical and Chirurgical Society of London (Topham and Squire Ward, 1842) not only was frank disbelief expressed, but a Dr Copland expressed the view (quoted in Bramwell, 1903, p.10) that "...if the history of the man experiencing no agony during operation were true, the fact was unworthy of their consideration, because pain was a wise provision of nature, and patients ought to suffer from pain while their surgeons were operating; they were all the better for it and recovered better".

The history of mesmerism has adversely affected the rational acceptance of hypnotism and has caused endless confusions that are not yet eradicated. Many of the myths about the extraordinary powers that mesmerism was supposed to confer are now attributed to hypnotism by less educated people.

The Different Reactions to Mesmerism

Before leaving the subject of mesmerism we should comment on what must strike the modern reader as very strange—the great variety of reactions on the part of patients to the process of being "magnetised". At least three very different conditions ensued. For Mesmer and his orthodox followers the patient went into a "crisis", a fit followed by a sort of swoon from which it took some time to recover.

For Puységur and his followers, magnetising produced the appearance of quiet sleep and then somnambulism in which the patient could be quite active and lively, sometimes exhibiting a new personality. For Esdaile and other mesmeric surgeons, the patient gradually went into a state of profound insensibility with accompanying anaesthesia resembling the tonic immobility of animals. How can we explain these extraordinary differences in reaction to what was supposed to be the same process?

First we must consider differences in method, and then in types of patient. Mesmer did all he could to work up his patients to a pitch of emotional excitement: the strange salon with dim light, mirrors, music, the *baquet*, all the trappings of magic and Mesmer's own charismatic person played their part in overawing the patients. Puységur's approach was quite different; he dispensed with all such trappings and his manner was simple and kindly. We read that Victor Pace was "quietly sleeping in my arms". Although he used the mesmeric ritual of passes, he spoke to the patients and encouraged their fantasies. His methods were closest to what we now understand as hypnotism. The methods of Esdaile and his assistants, and presumably of all mesmeric surgeons, were direct and to the point according to mesmeric theory. The patients underwent a long process, sometimes lasting for hours, in which they were prone and immobile while the operator made passes up and down their bodies.

Second, we must consider the type of people who presented themselves for treatment. We have already described the sorts of disturbed people who probably made up the bulk of the clientele at the clinics of Mesmer and his pupil Deslon in Paris. Their crises would be a natural effect of over-excitement on their nervous disorders, and those whose disorders were purely hysterical would imitate what they saw others do. With Puységur the clientele were mostly poor peasants who suffered from various forms of poor physical health and who benefited from suggestive therapy and the placebo effect of being treated at all. With Esdaile and the other mesmerist surgeons, the patients would generally be in a state of acute apprehension and real terror at the prospect of having to undergo surgery, as in those days it generally entailed extreme pain and sometimes death. It has been found (see Gallup, Nash, Potter, & Donnegan, 1970) that factors that induce fear in animals potentiate the reaction of tonic immobility.

THE EARLY PSYCHOLOGICAL PERIOD

The Abbé de Faria

One of the first pioneers of hypnotism, although he did not call it by that name, was the Abbé de Faria. Little is known about this man, who was Portugese and came from Goa, but he is undoubtedly the real father of what we now know as hypnotism. He referred to the hypnotic state as "lucid sleep", and he rejected the whole theory of "animal magnetism" with scorn in the series of lectures he began in Paris in 1813.

Faria was amazingly energetic and collected data on over 5000 people in both clinical and experimental work. His principal method of inducing "lucid sleep" was to get the subject to sit comfortably with closed eyes and to concentrate thoughts solely on the subject of sleep. Faria would then give verbal suggestions of going to sleep. When successful, this method induced a condition of "lucid sleep" which was not, of course, real sleep, for Faria continued to talk to the subject directing thought processes by suggestions and inducing all the classic phenomena of hypnosis, such as positive and negative hallucinations, unwilled movements and inhibition of movements, and post-hypnotic actions that would occur without knowledge of the subject some time after awakening.

It is of interest that some of Faria's methods and the logic of his thinking are still employed today. In the modern Stanford Hypnotic Susceptibility Scale (Weitzenhoffer & Hilgard, 1959), which has been referred to in the previous chapter, suggestions for sleep are given, but it is insisted that the subject will continue to attend to all that is said by the hypnotist.

Faria's book *De la cause de sommeil lucide,* which was first published in the year of his death, 1819 (Faria, 1906), contains the substance of his theory. Nearly 70 years later Bernheim (1973, p.118), the leading figure in the Nancy school of hypnotism, followed directly in the line of Faria and explained the concept of "lucid sleep" in relation to natural sleep very well. He wrote:

> the *ordinary sleeper is in relation with himself only*, as soon as his consciousness is lost. The impressions conducted to his brain by the nerves of sensibility or of organic life, may awaken diverse memory-sensations or images, which constitute dreams. These dreams are spontaneous, that is to say, suggested by himself. The *hypnotized subject* falls asleep, with his thought fixed, *in relationship with the hypnotizer*; hence the possibility of the suggestion of dreams, ideas and acts, by this foreign will.

One of the great contributions of Faria stems from his scientific honesty and modesty. He frankly admitted that only a minority of people were capable of lucid sleep, "a ratio of one in five or six of the population". Perry (1976) points out that this is indeed the ratio that is found everywhere in modern research, if we consider only those people who are capable of experiencing deep hypnosis to the extent that we class them as somnambules. This frank admission of the limitations of hypnotism was possible because Faria realised that hypnotic susceptibility does not depend upon any special power of the hypnotist, but depends almost wholly upon the innate ability of the subject. The mesmerists had deluded themselves into believing that they were people gifted with a specially rich endowment of magnetic fluid which they could convey to their subjects, hence success reflected on their personal prowess. Faria recognised that success, or lack of it, was not a function of the ability or power of the operator.

Alexandre Bertrand

Much of Faria's theory was quite erroneous because he tried to base it on the incomplete and mistaken ideas about physiology current in the medicine of his day, but his understanding of the psychological realities of hypnosis was shrewd. His work was taken up and advanced by Alexandre Bertrand (1826) who had previously been an orthodox mesmerist until his views were changed by General Noiset, an enthusiastic supporter of the teaching of the now deceased Faria. In Bertrand's later work he studied the Reports of the Royal Commissioners of 1784 who had investigated the whole question of mesmerism in studying the work of Deslon. Bertrand commented on an interesting point that had been rather overlooked at the time. The Commissioners had reported that there was no evidence for the existence of the alleged magnetic fluid and that therefore, having no existence, it could not be of any use They attributed many of the curious phenomena they witnessed to the *imagination* of the patients and overlooked the fact that their investigations had established what a very powerful and important factor imagination was. Bertrand fastened on this fact; Faria had been working on the *imagination* of his subjects, a force so powerful that in the 16 per cent of the population who possessed unusually high imaginative capacity, a "lucid sleep" could be induced, a state in which all sorts of psychological phenomena could be manifest.

James Braid

We owe the word "hypnotism" to James Braid, a Manchester surgeon working in the 1840s, although, as Gravitz and Gerton (1984) have pointed out, the prefix *hypn-* had been in use in France for some decades before Braid's adoption of it to indicate the sleep-like states that could be induced by some forms of mesmerism. The work of Faria and Bertrand undoubtedly influenced him, although he tended to underplay the extent of their influence. At first he regarded all the work and claims of the "magnetic" movement with extreme scepticism. It should be mentioned that by the 1840s operators in the "magnetic" movement were not using mesmerism in its pure and original form, but were employing a mish-mash of mesmeric rituals, suggestive hypnotism, and the tricks of the stage magician. Mesmerists even demonstrated tonic immobility with animals at public performances, and showed how in a trance state animals such squirrels, lizards, and even young lions could be pricked without their reacting.

Although, like most serious medical men, Braid started off as a complete sceptic, he was impressed at a public demonstration by the French mesmerist Lafontaine, although he did not believe the mesmerist's explanation for the phenomena he produced. Braid tried some experiments of his own and at first sought an entirely physiological explanation for the phenomena of hypnosis and theorised about the results of exhaustion of the "cerebro-spinal centres" occasioned by fixed staring at a bright object, a method of induction that had sometimes been used by Faria. All that Braid wrote about the proposed physiological mechanisms involved in hypnotism appeared to be very scientific in terms of the knowledge of the time, but in fact it meant very little. In his own experiments Braid found that he could induce hypnosis in some suitably disposed subjects by getting them to stare steadily at a bright object, but he neglected to take into account that his subjects *knew what was supposed to happen to them*, if only by overhearing the conversation between Braid and his colleagues. Later on, Braid (1843, p.36) was more aware of the role of suggestibility and imagination in hypnotism even while he was still trying to build a scientific theory in terms of physiology, for he acknowledged that: "The oftener patients are hypnotized, from association of ideas or habits, the more susceptible they become, and in this way they are liable to be affected entirely through the imagination".

Reading Braid's earlier work we are conscious that he was trying to express himself in *physiological* rather than psychological terms, because the former were acknowledged to be within the domain of "science" whereas the latter were regarded as being within the muddled and mystic domain of the occult world that the mesmerists wrote about. Thus Braid tried to deny that he was influenced by Faria and Bertrand whose theories were primarily psychological in character, although sharply divided from those of the mesmerists.

To emphasise the "scientific" character of his theorising, Braid called the condition he produced "nervous sleep" and rendered it into Greek as "neurohypnology", shortened to "neurypnology", and finally to *hypnotism.* Thus Braid gave rise to the term that is known all over the world today and is part of our everyday language, just as the name of Mesmer gave rise to the word *mesmerism* which is also part of our language. Because of the historical events that have been related, the two terms are unfortunately misused and confused. More recent writers such as Gauld (1988), Gibson (1982, 1988a), McGarry (1987), and Pulos (1980), have begun to clarify and explore the essential differences between hypnotism and mesmerism.

In his later writings Braid (1846, 1855) abandoned much of his earlier physiological theorising and dealt more and more with the psychological realities of hypnotism, demonstrating that the observed phenomena are the product of the imagination of the subject powerfully influenced by the suggestions of the operator, given either deliberately or accidentally. He died in 1851, and surprisingly made very little impact on the world of medicine and science in his lifetime, all his careful theorising and exciting demonstrations being dismissed as mere "mesmerism", which of course they were not.

Charcot and Bernheim

For nearly 20 years after the death of Braid very little attention was paid to hypnotism; then there came a period of great interest and enthusiastic acceptance of it by many well-known and respected men in medicine and science. According to Ellenberger (1970, p.171): "After 1882 the medical world became infatuated with hypnotism; publications on it reached the hundreds until a point of saturation with it was reached and the trend abandoned. This may be true; but there must also have been factors inherent to hypnotism that caused the rapid decline". The period of the 1880s has been known as "the golden age" of hypnotism. The two outstanding theorists and practitioners were Charcot at the Salpêtrière Hospital in Paris and Bernheim at the University of Nancy. Charcot was the outstanding neurologist of his day, and his acceptance of hypnosis set the seal of respectability on the topic. He had at the Salpêtrière a number of patients showing the various manifestations of epilepsy which, as we have noted, is not a disease but a symptom. Some of these patients were "true" epileptics, in that their disabilities were the result of organic brain damage. In other patients their fits and odd behaviour were of a hysteric character in that their disabilities were entirely functional. In fact, the hysterics were probably copying the behaviour of the "true" epileptics.

Charcot's study of hypnotism led him to somewhat erroneous conclusions in various respects. He regarded all the phenomena that men such as Braid had investigated as being the result of psychopathology. He believed that these phenomena could be brought on by physical manipulations such as rubbing the top of the head. Since he experimented only with patients it was understandable that he viewed hypnotism entirely in terms of abnormal psychology and physiology. It is true that many of the classic phenomena that can be produced in hypnosis are very similar to those that occur spontaneously in hysteric disorders, but this does not imply an identity between hypnosis and hysteria.

Bernheim originally took his views from Liébault, a country doctor who had an enormous practice among poor people and who treated a lot of them by suggestion in hypnosis, using much the same methods as Faria and Braid. Although Braid's hypnotism had had very little impact in Britain after his death, it had become known in France, and Professor Velpeau read a paper on *Braidisme* at a public session of the French Academy of Sciences in 1860. It was this lecture that started Liébault on his researches which he carried out more or less in isolation for nearly 20 years. His book (Liébault, 1866) attracted very little attention until Bernheim took up his work.

Bernheim's views on the relation between the hypnotic state and natural sleep have been quoted earlier, but his great contribution was the emphasis he put on *suggestion* both within hypnosis and in the waking state. In this he was indebted to the later theories of Braid who, contrary to what is stated in some books, had a very good understanding of the role of suggestibility (see Bramwell, 1903, p.207). This was where Bernheim differed from Charcot, the latter appearing to neglect the fact that many of the phenomena demonstrated in patients with hysteric disorders, had been suggested to them indirectly by himself. With hindsight we can now see that the principal difference between Bernheim and Charcot and the basis of their great controversy, was that whereas Bernheim was concerned with phenomena we now regard as being within the domain of *hypnotism*, Charcot's researches and demonstrations were really within the domain of early *mesmerism*. However, Charcot had no truck with that rather disreputable movement that expressed belief in occult forces and paranormal powers. He was strictly a scientist trying to explain phenomena in what was known of the neurology of the time. From their side the mesmerists were sharply critical of Charcot. The 1889 International Congress on Mesmerism made it clear that mesmerism should not be confused with hypnotism and sought to maintain the truth of the original doctrines of Mesmer.

Although Bernheim continued the work of Braid, he introduced an important difference that was materially to affect the future course of practice and theory in hypnotism. As pointed out by Weitzenhoffer (1985), according to Braid a subject either was or was not hypnotised; it was an all or none affair just as it had been for Faria. However, Bernheim (1886/1973, pp.11–15) introduced the concept of there being *degrees* of hypnosis: a subject could be lightly, moderately or deeply hypnotised, and he gave a scale of nine degrees of hypnosis. This scale is of great historical importance, in that it is the ancestor of many scales of hypnosis that have been developed by experimental psychologists in the twentieth century and has conditioned our thinking about the phenomenon.

The long controversy between the two schools represented by the Salpêtrière Hospital and the University of Nancy was more or less decided by the time of the International Congress of Experimental Psychology, Second Session (1892), sufficient work had been done in hypnosis for Charcot's theories to be regarded as quite discredited and the future of hypnotism to be clearly founded on the Nancy school.

THE LATER PSYCHOLOGICAL OR MODERN PERIOD

When we have traced the history of hypnotism up to Bernheim, through Faria, Noiset, Bertrand, and Braid, we have really covered most of the important developments. When Pierre Janet, in the 1880s, then a rising young psychologist, began to study this "new" topic of hypnotism, he found to his surprise that all the important facts about it had been discovered many years ago in the earlier part of the century and that now doctors were apparently re-discovering facts that were already well known. Clark Hull (1933, p.18), some 40 years later, wrote:

> Practically all of the actual phenomena were discovered and described during the first fifty years, from 1775 to 1825. But the century since 1825 has shown a remarkable sterility. Almost nothing of significance has been accomplished during this period except the very gradual correction of errors which originally flowed directly from bad experimental procedures... The tardy development of the science of hypnotism, moreover, is especially striking when it is recalled that practically from the beginning hypnosis has been definitely an experimental phenomenon.... We have already seen the dominant motive throughout the history of hypnotism has been clinical, that of curing human ills. A worse method for the establishment of scientific principles among highly elusive phenomena can hardly be devised.

When Hull wrote of the "science" of hypnotism he was, of course, trying to divorce it from the huge superstructure of myth and magic that was the legacy of mesmerism. Very recently Weitzenhoffer (1985, pp. 73–74), basically in agreement with Hull on the confusing role of the clinicians, has commented on the twentieth-century developments in hypnotism in the following terms:

> research since Bernheim's time has done little to clarify the picture. By 1900, and really earlier, all the essential phenomenology of hypnotism had been described. Nothing new has been added, and much of the research since 1900 (and especially since 1920) has been characterized by re-discovery rather than discovery. In fact, modern and especially contemporary research have only further abetted the situation created by the clinicians. Today, some 200 years after the discovery of artificial somnambulism, researchers are divided on even such basic issues as the verdicality of hypnotic phenomena and whether or not hypnosis exists as a state.

These critical strictures by Hull and Weitzenhoffer are perhaps a little over-severe, and indeed it is Hull's work on hypnosis and suggestibility that is generally regarded as a milestone starting a new era in which the topic began to be examined with fresh enthusiasm by modern scientific methods using appropriate statistical techniques. More and more hypnosis began to be scrutinised by experimental psychologists in the setting of university laboratories, rather than by doctors observing the behaviour of sick people in their consulting rooms and clinics.

The Question of Suggestibility

Braid and Bernheim had written about "suggestibility" as though everyone were clear about what they meant by the term. The early history of suggestibility was reviewed by Janet (1925) but in spite of his erudition he never succeeded in elucidating just what was meant by the term. Confusion was made worse by the term being taken up by sociologists such as Tarde (1907) and in social psychology by McDougall (1908), who implied that all ordinary imitative and compliant behaviour lay on a simple continuum with hypnotic behaviour. This ancient fallacy found expression in the earlier work of Barber (1969) who went to elaborate lengths in designing experiments to try to demonstrate the validity of this belief.

According to Duke (1964), 40 tests of so-called suggestibility had been devised by psychologists in the late nineteenth and twentieth centuries. These tests had little in common, and only some of them predicted susceptibility to hypnosis. As will be discussed later, subsequent experimental work showed that only one sort of suggestibility, which was called "primary suggestibility" (Eysenck, 1943, Eysenck & Furneaux, 1945) is relevant to hypnotic susceptibility.

Other Modern Developments

A great expansion in research into hypnotism occurred after the Second World War in the American universities. Although it is true that nothing essentially "new" about hypnotism was discovered, a number of old questions were investigated more thoroughly and it became possible to give more definite answers. In the previous chapter various myths about hypnosis have been referred to, and it is possible nowadays to say with some confidence that they are myths because properly conducted scientific inquiries have been carried out in the spirit of the modern age.

One of the features of modern scientific inquiry is the use of control measures and control groups. It is true that the Royal Commissioners of 1784 used some sensible control measures when investigating the claims of the mesmerists, but in the long history of mesmerism and hypnotism the use of scientific controls has been largely rejected by the enthusiasts, particularly in the clinical field, hence the persistence of a huge folk-lore which dies hard. The modern period is characterised by a necessary scepticism and the testing of old beliefs which entails a de-mystification of the subject. This is often done in the teeth of opposition from some clinicians who see themselves as having a vested interest in preserving the mystique of hypnotism.

It has been noted that interest in hypnotism seems to wax and wane over periods of some decades. The 1880s were the "golden age" of hypnotism, but a decline came with the turn of the century. This decline has been attributed by some people to the growth of the psychoanalytic movement after Freud had abandoned the use of hypnotism, but this is certainly an over-simplification. The monumental work of Ellenberger (1970) discusses the many cultural, social, political, and scientific changes that led to the decline of what he calls "the first dynamic psychiatry" that centred around hypnotism in the nineteenth century.

In the United Kingdom the British Medical Association appointed two committees to report on the use of hypnotism in 1892 and again in 1953 (see BMA, 1955). Both these committees reported favourably and with guarded optimism. After the 1892 report interest in hypnotism actually waned, and the 1955 report was not followed by any noticeable change in interest by the medical profession for quite a long time. Between 1900 and 1965 there were no international congresses on hypnosis, but since 1967 the International Society of Hypnosis has run international congresses every three years. This society, which began as the International Society of Clinical and Experimental Hypnosis, was originally founded in the United States in 1959, and it now represents 36 countries. It appears then that we are now in a period of revival of interest in hypnotism.

In the United Kingdom the British Society of Medical and Dental Hypnosis was founded in 1968, exclusively for medical doctors and dentists, and in 1977 it was followed by the British Society of Experimental and Clinical Hypnosis (BSECH), mainly for psychologists but admitting doctors, dentists, and suitably qualified members of other professions who have a legitimate use for hypnosis (see Chapter 13). More recently we have seen the formation of the British Society for the Practice of Hypnosis in Speech Therapy, which confines its membership to speech therapists, and which became affiliated to the BSECH in 1987.

It has been suggested that what lessens interest in the practice of hypnotism in the long run as a serious professional skill is a tendency on the part of some clinicians to practise some mystification as though it were indeed an occult art to be reserved for the *illuminati*, and at the same time to over-sell its potentialities. Weitzenhoffer (1985, p.70) identified this tendency in the modern age thus:

> Around 1955, a small group of professionals banded together in the United States to teach and promote the use of hypnotism by physicians, dentists and psychologists. At their head was Milton Erickson. They set out with a certain evangelical zeal to sell hypnotism to as many professionals as they could. And sell it they did, frequently in an atmosphere reminiscent of religious revivals and seances.

Similar alarm has been expressed by Fromm (1987), Hammond (1984, 1988), and Heap (1988a) and by Kirmayer (Note 12) who speaks of the burgeoning of "fast-food therapies" arising from the proliferation of training courses in Ericksonian therapy.

Weitzenhoffer (1986) also relates how the Ericksonian cult has further developed into what he calls "the latest American potential fad", Neuro-linguistic Programming (NLP) which arrives at its ultimate definition by its popularisers Bandler and Grinder (1979), "all communication is hypnosis". NLP presents an elaborate framework of ideas on cognitive processing which along with the therapeutic procedures based upon them, have been influential amongst many practitioners of hypnosis, and in some cases quite extraordinary allegations have been made concerning their therapeutic efficacy (see Heap, 1988a,b). However, the protagonists of NLP appear to have been more zealous in selling their commodity than in critically examining its contents, and experiments reviewed by Sharpley (1985, 1987) and Heap (1988c; 1989) have failed to yield convincing evidence for the NLP model, likewise the few investigations of its therapeutic effectiveness (see Chapter 5). Nevertheless, some of the techniques may be usefully incorporated into a behavioural approach as we will describe in later chapters.

It must not be thought that all clinical use of hypnotism is committed to this approach. We have traced the history of hypnotism for 200 years up to the present day and indicated how one tendency has apparently taken us back to the salon of Mesmer. However, there are plenty of clinicians in different professions who are using hypnotism guided by common sense, and by the useful information about it that modern science has teased out from the mass of conflicting data and folk-lore that we have inherited. Recently there has been a growing sophistication in clinical research and many excellent journals and books are being published. It is the endeavour of this book to present an exposition of how hypnotic techniques can be a very useful adjunct to other procedures in therapy in various professional applications.

3 Differential Susceptibility to Hypnosis

One of the puzzles about hypnosis is that everyone is not able to experience the phenomenon to the same degree. As has already been made clear, the full co-operation of a subject or patient is a prerequisite for the induction of hypnosis. However, there are people who co-operate fully and are anxious to be hypnotised and yet are able to experience very little. By contrast a few people are very susceptible indeed and can go into a state of hypnosis "at the drop of a hat". This sometimes surprises a neophyte hypnotist who has only just begun to practise the technique. Most of us, however, are moderately susceptible to hypnosis and can experience some if not all of the phenomena, when the session is conducted by a properly trained hypnotist. This problem is one of great interest to clinicians. If hypnosis is to be used it is hoped that it will "work". It is naturally disappointing if when the clinician attempts to hypnotise the patient, the latter, after a genuine attempt to co-operate, complains that nothing at all has been felt, no particular imagery has been engendered, and there has not even been the experience of the relaxation suggested by the therapist. The patient remains tense and disappointed, and the therapist can be made to feel inadequate. Naturally, the therapist will take all possible measures to maximise the hypnotic responsiveness of the patient, but as we will see later, it is not easy to modify a person's natural degree of susceptibility to hypnosis.

In the previous chapter Weitzenhoffer has been quoted with reference to one line of development in clinical hypnosis in the United States. He refers to the fact that a self-proclaimed "hypnotherapist" can be defeated by a patient's resistance or simple lack of hypnotic talent, and explains the subterfuge that is sometimes adopted (Weitzenhoffer, 1985, p.71):

> The success rate was very much increased by the simple subterfuge of accepting indiscriminately any evidence of suggestibility as a sign of hypnosis. In the course of time any response, any spontaneous act (whether relevant or not to such suggestions as might have been given) was turned, at appropriate moments, into evidence of hypnosis.

Such a subterfuge is entirely unnecessary, and indeed it is likely to appear transparent to the intelligent patient. Later we will explore just what a competent clinician may do about the problem of the relatively unsusceptible patient, but first we must consider the whole question of susceptibility.

THE PROBLEM OF DEFINITION

In the first chapter we inquired into the question of "what is hypnosis?", and it was apparent that not everyone is agreed on how we should define it. We have seen that historically there have been different views about what percentage of the population are susceptible to hypnosis. For the Abbé de Faria, after he had applied his technique, subjects were either considered to be in a condition of "lucid sleep" or they were not. He reckoned that the proportion of the population who could achieve this state was only about 16 per cent, and all the others he would dismiss as being "insusceptible". For James Braid the position was much the same. He varied during his career as to what conditions he would call "hypnosis", as he did in his theory of hypnotism, but the state that Braid would describe as hypnosis in his later work (Braid, 1855) was achieved by about only one tenth of his subjects.

From the 1880s onwards—that is, following the great explosion of interest in hypnotism arising from the work of Bernheim and his contemporaries—a change of view occurred and it became usual to accept that hypnosis was a state experienced to a greater or lesser degree, and measurable on standard scales. Weitzenhoffer (1985, p.69), who started work on hypnosis research in 1947, expresses the matter thus:

> the hypnotism of Braid lost its unique identity to become a part or aspect of a wider condition now given the name of "hypnosis". Hypnotism had thus been redefined. Put another way (using Braid's criteria for hypnotism) the hypnosis of 1947 included behaviour he would not have agreed to call hypnotic.

This wider definition is generally accepted nowadays and so it is agreed that relatively few people can be classed as being "non-susceptible" to hypnosis.

THE STABILITY OF HYPNOTIC SUSCEPTIBILITY

First it must be established how stable is the trait of hypnotic susceptibility. Do people tend to be highly susceptible on one day and little susceptible on another? Are they easily susceptible with one hypnotist yet little influenced by another? There has been a good deal of research into this matter and the general findings are that hypnotic susceptibility is a very stable trait, varying little between different occasions and with different hypnotists. It makes no significant difference whether the hypnotist is male or female, old or young, prestigious or non-prestigious, the result is much the same. This matter was the subject of a great deal of research by Ernest Hilgard and his colleagues in the 1960s (1965, p.386), and he found that "Provided that the setting for hypnosis is one that evokes confidence, the initial responsiveness to attempted hypnotic induction depends very little on the personal characteristics of the hypnotist". This is understandable if we realise that hypnosis is very much a phenomenon that depends upon the subject's own capacity for imagination, and for letting go of the reality testing normal to ordinary waking life.

In experimental research into hypnosis various scales of hypnotic susceptibility have been developed, one of the earliest being that of Bernheim (1886; 1973). The Stanford Hypnotic Susceptibility Scale (Weitzenhoffer & Hilgard, 1959) has already been mentioned, but there are a number of similar modern scales. Some are mainly for experimental work, such as the Barber Suggestibility Scale (Barber, 1969); some are for the preliminary screening of groups of people, such as the Harvard Group Scale (Shor & Orne, 1962). There are also scales for use in clinical work, such as the Stanford Hypnotic Clinical Scale for Adults (Morgan & Hilgard, 1978a), which also has a children's version (Morgan and Hilgard, 1978b). A general description and discussion of these scales is given by Fellows (1988b).

All these scales consist of a number of items of typically hypnotic behaviour, some items characteristically being "passed" by most people. An example of an easy item is reacting to suggestions to imagine that a weight is pulling an outstretched arm downwards. A difficult item that is passed by relatively few people involves reacting to an imaginary mosquito attacking the back of one's hand. Considering the reaction of subjects to all the items on such a scale, subjects can each be awarded an individual score of susceptibility. The degree of susceptibility manifest on any occasion can be compared with that shown on future occasions, perhaps months or years ahead. It has been found that people change very little even when tested in different places by different people and under different conditions.

A minor difference that is observed in the testing concerns the very first occasion of a series of tests. Initially, scores are likely to be artificially low because the novelty of the first occasion makes some people hold back a little. When people are less apprehensive on future occasions, having found that hypnosis is perfectly harmless and quite enjoyable, the test scores are likely to be a little higher and reflect the true level of ability more accurately.

There have been attempts to increase hypnotic susceptibility by various measures such as sensory deprivation (Sanders & Reyher, 1969), muscle tone feedback (Wickramasekera, 1973), and operant conditioning (Delprato & Holmes, 1978). Where successes have been achieved they have been of a very modest extent, and other experimenters have not always succeeded in replicating them. This is hardly surprising for, as we shall see later, susceptibility reflects some very basic aspects of an individual's make-up, the product of his or her whole developmental history possibly interacting with factors of genetic endowment as implied by Morgan (1973). According to Bowers (1983, p.128): "It is becoming increasingly clear that hypnotic susceptibility and its correlates are deeply embedded in a person's biological organization. This is undoubtedly one reason for the relative stability of hypnotic susceptibility in mature people".

Such attempts to increase hypnotic susceptibility should not be confused with research in social psychology where the main object of the experimenters is to enhance the subjects' report about their experience and their overt behaviour after undergoing special courses of instruction. A recent example of such social psychological research is that of Spanos and his colleagues in which a special test was developed in order to achieve the stated aims. There are already about 15 tests of hypnotic susceptibility in existence, but this newly created test, the Carleton University Responsiveness to Suggestion Scale (CURSS) of Spanos, Radke, Hodgkins, Stam, and Bertrand (1983) has a special feature. According to Kihlstrom (1985, p.387): "While the CURSS clearly taps the domain of hypnosis to some degree, it also tends to define hypnosis in terms of the subject's willingness to cooperate with the procedures rather than in terms of subjective experience, as is characteristic of the Stanford Scales".

This follows Spanos's (1986, p.97) stated view that: "Highly susceptible subjects… respond to suggestions as tacit requests to enact the behaviours called for while interpreting their actions as involuntary occurrences". This is a rather unusual theory of hypnosis. No one would doubt that large increases in scores on the CURSS can be obtained by training programmes instucting subjects how to respond. But the exercise seems rather like drilling subjects in the correct answers to an I.Q. test, and if this were done, we might wonder whether the increased score truly reflected an increase in intelligence.

THE IMPLICATIONS FOR THERAPY

The work of Spanos that has been referred to may be meaningful and valuable in terms of social psychology, but it has little relevance to the problems of the clinician, who aims to maximise patients' capacity for hypnosis. The face-saving technique of the frustrated "hypnotherapist" described by Weitzenhoffer is relevant here, as its aim is to re-define hypnosis and to persuade the patient to accept that redefinition. An alternative approach is to accept patients as they are with regard to susceptibility, to explore what capacities they have, and then to utilise and build upon them. It is pointless to pretend that patients are more susceptible than they are and to raise expectations of performance too difficult for them to fulfil. Therapy may involve a good deal of self-hypnosis, sometimes with the aid of a tape specially recorded for the individual by the therapist. Between sessions it is useful for the patient to practise exercises that involve such self-hypnosis, the wording on the tape soon being over-learned (see Chapter 5). Only if the therapist is well aware of the level of the capacity of the patient and the nature of the responses available can such exercises be tailored appropriately. According to Hilgard (1982, p.394):

> To adapt hypnotic psychotherapy to the individual patient some kind of assessment of the patient's hypnotisability is essential. The choice lies between clinical judgement of responsiveness and measurement. Although measurement is desirable, care has to be exercised in selecting the appropriate measurement instrument, because an efficient scale must be based on sound psychometric considerations and avoid the illusions inherent in clinical intuition.

Some therapists such as Sacerdote (1982a) suggest that, if standardised rating scales such as the Stanford Hypnotic Clinical Scale are used, only some aspects of the hypnotic response are tested and there is no adequate measure of qualitative differences of the experience of hypnosis. Sacerdote is concerned that some patients' poor rating on a standard scale might preclude them from receiving the benefits of hypnotic treatment. But a competent therapist who is made aware of the level of susceptibility of a patient, even if it is rather low, will adapt a programme of therapy to the individual case.

Frankel (1962) has replied to Sacerdote's criticisms and advocated the use of scales of measurement in clinical interviews, arguing that for various reasons they provide both the therapist and the patient with a valuable experience relating to what phenomena the latter is capable of, and in enabling the patient to study how suggestions may be responded to. Sacerdote (1982b, p.393) has accepted the force of Frankel's arguments and stated in a later paper that: "As a result of this friendly controversy, I have decided to start comparing my clinical assessment of my patients' talent with their response to the Stanford Scales, to be administered after therapeutic trial".

It seems likely that clinical and educational psychologists will feel rather more at home with using scales of measurement in a clinical context because their past training has involved the measurement of human behaviour. Psychiatrists in general, on the other hand, are more likely to have training in a different tradition, and will be less willing to adopt this approach. Whereas psychiatrists such as Frankel stress the necessity for careful assessment of the patient's degree of susceptibility by means of standard tests as discussed above, some other psychiatrists such as Waxman (1981, p.73), are of the opinion that:

> It is worth repeating that these tests are neither necessary nor desirable, and rarely if ever would an experienced clinician use them…
>
> The best test of hypnotisability is *the assessment and instinct and experience of the doctor, his positive decision to use hypnosis and the co-operation and motivation of the patient.*

All therapists must form their own opinions on this matter. Christopher Clarke, a clinical psychologist, and Arthur Jackson, a psychiatrist (1983, pp.44–45), write: "the reader might wonder about hypnosis assessment. Is it necessary? Does it serve any purposes? The answers, without hesitation, are 'yes' to both questions. For a start ... there is no in-principle distinction to be drawn between scientific and clinical endeavours".

They then go on to discuss the extent to which research into therapeutic techniques involving hypnosis has revealed that in many treatments for disorders such as asthma (Collison, 1978) and pain conditions (Gottfredson, 1973), the patient's degree of hypnotisability is highly relevant to therapeutic success (see Chapters 4 and 7). Only if careful assessment of patients' varying degrees of talent for hypnosis has been made can such facts be determined.

Some clinicians may object that they have a record of quite a number of cases of patients who had very little manifest talent for hypnosis, but who were nevertheless cured or substantially improved in treatments that involved hypnosis. This is undoubtedly true, but, it may be asked, was the element of hypnosis in treatment of any particular significance? We should be well aware of the placebo component of *all* treatments, and it may be argued that for the relatively unhypnotisable patient the ritual of hypnotism may at least confer the benefit of a placebo. But if a clinician is using placebos , at least it should be a deliberate practice, and such a time-consuming procedure as hypnotism hardly commends itself for this purpose (see Gibson, 1987).

Whether formal scales of measurement are administered or not, all clinicians will gain a great advantage by familiarising themselves with the details of a number of scales and by acquiring some practice in their administration. As mentioned previously, Fellows (1988b) provides an excellent description and discussion of them. Those who rely entirely on the accounts of clinical hypnosis that are given in such textbooks as Hartland (1971) and Kroger and Fezler (1976) which do not advocate the measurement of susceptibility, miss a great deal in understanding the nature of individual differences in hypnotic susceptibility and becoming acquainted with the sort of suggestions that are easily responded to and those that are more difficult. The study of such individual differences has opened up a greatly increased understanding of the nature of hypnosis and an appreciation of the fact that it is not just one phenomenon but a whole group of phenomena relating to the individual's perception of and adjustment to the external world. An enormous amount of research effort in both the clinical and experimental fields has gone into the creation and standardisation of scales of measurement of hypnotic susceptibility, and they are indeed central to the impressive resurgence of interest in and respect for hypnosis in the clinical field that has occurred during the last 30 years in the English-speaking world.

THE CREATIVE IMAGINATION SCALE

It will be convenient to describe just one scale of measurement whereby individual differences that are relevant to hypnotic susceptibility may be measured, the Creative Imagination Scale (CIS) of Barber and Wilson (1978). This is not a specifically clinical scale nor does it involve actual hypnotic induction, but its great simplicity makes it easy to describe and to understand. For a beginner it is easy to administer, score, and interpret. The full text of the scale is given in the paper just cited.

The scale consists of 10 items that are read aloud to the patient, or subject, who sits relaxed in a chair with closed eyes. Each item is a simple description of a scene or situation, and patients are invited to imagine themselves in that situation as vividly as possible. There is no prior hypnotic induction; it is explained that the purpose of the test is merely to try to establish what sorts of things an individual finds most easy to imagine. When the test has been described and any questions about it answered, it is simply read out, or better still, presented from a tape recorder. The items of the test (Barber & Wilson, 1978, p.85) are as follows:

1. The left arm is held out horizontally with the palm upwards, and the patient is invited to imagine that one, two, and then three heavy dictionaries are being placed on the hand. Although the subsequent scoring is entirely in terms of subjective feeling of how 'real' the experience was, it may also be noted what movements, if any, are made, i.e. the degree to which any *enactment* of the situation occurs.
2. The right arm is held out horizontally with the palm facing downwards, and it is suggested that a strong stream of water from a garden hosepipe pressing upwards on the hand should be imagined. Again, any enactment may be noted.
3. The idea of an anaesthetic injected into the left hand is suggested, and imagining that the hand is becoming numb is encouraged by repeated suggestions.
4. The patient is invited to imagine being hot and thirsty while climbing in the mountains, and then to experience the sensations of drinking a cup of cold, refreshing water. Possible enactment may include swallowing movements.
5. This item consists of imagining peeling and eating an orange with suggestions concerning its smell, taste, and texture.
6. This involves imagining listening to powerful, thrilling music.
7. It is stated that by imagining the right hand being in hot sunshine an actual increase in warmth will be felt, and verbal suggestions to this end are made.
8. In this item it is stated that 'By controlling your thinking you can make time seem to slow down'. The suggestions largely depend upon slowing down the rate of

speaking, and repeating suggestions such as 'There is lots and lots of time between each second. Time is stretching out and there's lots of time ... etc'.

9. Here the patient is invited to imagine being back in primary school, and a fairly general but vivid description of being in a classroom is given; the senses of hearing, smell, and touch are invoked as well as perhaps 'seeing' the surroundings.

10. The suggestions conjure up a scene of lying on a beach on a warm summer's day, with all the pleasant and relaxing associations of that scene.

Items vary in length between 45 seconds and just over 2 minutes, and the whole test takes about 20 minutes. At the end of each item the scene is "cancelled" by an appropriate suggestion such as "Now tell yourself that it's all in your own mind and bring yourself back ... etc." After all 10 items have been read out, patients are asked to rate their experience for each item on the following scale printed on a rating form.

When you were asked to imagine (description of item) how similar was the experience to actually (reference to item)?
0 = Not at all the same.
1 = A little the same.
2 = Between a little and much the same.
3 = Much the same.
4 = Almost exactly the same.

Thus each item is scored by the patient 0–4 for the vividness of the experience, and as there are 10 items, by simple summation there is a range of possible total scores of 0–40. Although the total score is of interest in indicating an overall ability for imagination in response to suggestions, the information obtained by studying the pattern of responses to each item is also of importance in revealing the individual's response style in respect of different sorts of imagining in the various sense modalities. For instance, some people find it very easy to imagine muscular movements and sensations, such as the imaginary force of water pressing the arm upwards, but cannot easily imagine in the more subtle sensory modalities such as the item concerning eating an orange call for. Again, others may find it very easy to imagine listening to music, but difficult to imagine an "atmosphere" such as being back in the classroom of a primary school.

It is very helpful to find out just what sort of imaginings come most easily to the individual patient *before* deciding what techniques of hypnotism will be most appropriate. It should be explained to patients that everyone is different with respect to imagination, and it is their own personal talents that are of relevance and importance .

In interpreting the results of this test for an individual, it is of course necessary to refer the personal score and profile to the norms for the test. Normative data are given in the original paper of Barber and Wilson (1978) and later studies by Hilgard, Sheehan, Monteiro, and McDonald (1981), McConkey, Sheehan, and White (1979), Myers (1983), and Straus (1980). But perhaps the best data for British users of the test are those of Fellows (Note 8), who administered the test to 169 females and 121 males. From Fellows's data it may be seen that the responses to some items, e.g. arm heaviness, are much more easily imagined than others such as imagining the sun's warmth. It may also be noted that on the whole females give rather higher ratings than males, a feature that is apparent in other studies using the test.

In the various studies using this test a moderate degree of correlation (r = 0.28 –0.60) has been found with other scales related to hypnotic susceptibility. The study of Hilgard et al. (1981) indicated that two separate factors accounted for the response to this test, a hypnotic factor and an imagery factor.

As noted previously, the therapist is interested in gaining understanding of what sort of experiences the patient can imagine most easily, as well as the total score on the test. The same information could be gained by employing one of the other scales, such as the Stanford Hypnotic Clinical Scale for Adults, or the Children's Scale (Morgan & Hilgard, 1978a,b), which are longer scales and better predictors of the total response to hypnotic induction. However, the CIS has been described in detail because it is relatively short, simple and easily administered by beginners who are gaining experience of the basic principles of adapting one's methods to the individual characteristics of each patient.

AGE AND SEX DIFFERENCES RELATED TO HYPNOTISABILITY

Age Differences

That children are more susceptible to hypnosis than adults has been found since the time of Bernheim in the 1880s, and he stated that "As soon as they are able to understand, children are as a rule very quickly and very easily hypnotised" (see Bernheim, 1886/1973, p. 2). The question of their being able to understand is important, and hence maximum susceptibility is not reached until about the age of 9 years. A total of 1232 subjects ranging from 5 to over 44 years of age were tested by Morgan and Hilgard (1973), and the results of this study show a peak of susceptibility between the ages of 9 and 12 years, the level afterwards declining steadily with age. On the Stanford Scale, Form A (Weitzenhoffer & Hilgard, 1959) an average score of between 7 and 8 points was reached in the group aged between 9 and 12 years, and this dropped to just under 5 points in the 40-year-old group. That susceptibility declines slowly with age is significant and teaches us something about the nature of hypnosis. As children grow older, particularly in a technologically based culture, they develop more and more in the direction of testing reality and separating fact from fantasy. Wordsworth in his poem *Intimations of immortality* recalls that in childhood he had a very special vision of the world having "the glory and freshness of a dream", but in adulthood this vision had passed away and "The things which I have seen I now can see no more."

Hartmann (1984) refers to the perceiving of the world about us in a peculiarly vivid and imaginative way in terms of "permeable boundaries", children having boundaries between subjective experience and mundane reality that are less definite. Josephine Hilgard (1970, 1974) conducted a long series of interviews with young adults in order to relate their developmental histories to their later hypnotic susceptibility, and supplemented her research with an investigation of the fantasy life of children who were in the process of growing up. Her investigations give us an impressive picture of how the early talent for imagination tends to decline as the individual has to succumb to a greater or lesser degree to the pressures from the environment.

The greater hypnotisability of children is most manifest when the hypnotist selects a technique that is appropriate to the child's age (see Chapter 12). Thus in the study of Morgan and Hilgard (1973) referred to, although children in the 5- to 8-year age group were not quite as susceptible as older children, it should be remembered that the test that was used was the original Stanford Adult Scale. Had the children been tested on a more suitable scale they would undoubtedly have displayed more hypnotic talent. This is taken into account by therapists who work with children. Hilgard and LeBaron (1984) used special fantasy inductions for the younger children in their therapeutic group, but formal inductions for the older children and adolescents.

Sex Differences

In examining reported sex differences in susceptibility to hypnosis we come across the result of common prejudices affecting attitudes and beliefs. Liébault, as reported by Bramwell (1903), found that females were slightly more susceptible than males, and this has been manifest in subsequent studies, although it is often denied. Hull (1933) estimated that females exceeded males in susceptibility, on average, by one-fifteenth of the degree to which men are taller than women. Thus, according to Hull, the difference in susceptibility is very slight, but it is a very reliable difference, as in the case of height.

Weitzenhoffer (1953) reviewed a number of studies of sex differences in susceptibility and noted a regular slight superiority for females. In view of this widespread evidence we may wonder why so many authors deny the difference as though equality between the sexes in this matter were an established fact. Thus Barber (1969) states: "The sexes are equally responsive to standardised test suggestions". This statement is strangely at variance with the finding that very large sex differences were later to be shown on his Creative Imagination Scale.

Many studies have been published, each showing a slight superiority of females over males for hypnotic susceptibility, but reluctance to admit this sex difference is understandable because of the outmoded popular stereotype of women being more "submissive" and more "suggestible" in the opprobrious meaning of the latter term. This negative stereotype of women is reminiscent of the experiments of Charcot at the Salpêtrière Hospital which implied a relationship between hypnotisability and female hysteria. When more modern writers rejected this stereotype they were at pains to play down any sex differences in susceptibility.

Gibson (1977) points out that many experimental studies report that there was no *significant* difference between the two sexes, but this simply reflects the fact that as experimenters typically use as small a total sample of subjects as they can for reasons of economy of effort, the absolute numbers in the male and female groups were simply not large enough. With double the numbers the sex difference might be seen to be statistically significant.

In 1965 Hilgard (1965, p.317), usually a most accurate writer and a reliable authority on individual differences, denied that there was any sex difference with regard to hypnotic susceptibility. He went on to report that "attitudes to hypnosis, as measured by rather simple tests, correlate with hypnotic susceptibility for female college students but not for male ones. Why this sex difference should be found is an intriguing question to which we do not have conclusive answers". This latter point became the focus for a good deal of research. The slightly greater susceptibility of females, which was found again and again, was not in itself of importance; of greater interest was the fact that the relationship of hypnotisability to other factors was found to be different for the two sexes. Thus researches into everyday experiences showed that people who experienced things more intensely were more easily hypnotised, but here sex differences appeared to act as a moderator variable. Bowers (1971) found that in 12 women highly susceptible to hypnosis an index of "experiential intensity" was strongly predictive of hypnotisability. With the men in his sample, however, there was no such relationship. This finding may be compared with that of Ås (1962, 1963) who found that with women it was proneness to mystical and illogical experiences, and to changes in mental condition due to outside influences, that predicted hypnotisability. With men this was not the case. The more hypnotisable men reported experiences relating to impulsivity and aggression. Thus the women appeared to be reacting to external stimuli that came from the environment, but the men were reacting to internal, drive-related stimuli. Sex differences in brain organisation have also been noted with respect to hypnotic susceptibility. Several investigators have found that hypnosis produces more activation of the right hemisphere of the brain than the left (see Sackheim, 1982). Both Gur and Gur (1974) and Birkett (1979) found that right-handed subjects who were male exhibited a tendency to move their eyes to the left under hypnosis, but this tendency was not shown by right-handed females. The tendency to move the eyes to the left is shown by left-handed females under hypnosis. These findings are complicated by the fact that left-handed males and right-handed females exhibit no preferred direction of movement of the eyes under hypnosis. No one has yet suggested a convincing explanation for this complex relationship between sex and handedness in relation to hypnosis. It is merely noted as an example of one of the many indications that males and females are not the same with regard to the lateralisation of the functions of the brain (see Benton, 1985), nor are they quite the same in the way in which they respond to hypnosis. Research studies which do not report the findings on the two sexes separately may lead to erroneous conclusions. From a clinical point of view it is of little importance that female patients are a little more susceptible than males, but what may be relevant is that susceptibility is related to different sorts of characteristics in the two sexes. Thus the clinician may find that experience gained with female patients cannot necessarily be generalised to male patients.

HYPNOTISABILITY AND PERSONALITY

It might be thought that psychologists studying differences in personality would have been able to predict fairly accurately which people would be specially susceptible to hypnosis, and which would show little talent for it. Psychologists have indeed produced a great variety of personality tests, some of them quite objective, that have proved very useful in various areas of research. It is disappointing, therefore, to find that they have not proved of much use in predicting hypnotic susceptibility. Shor (1972) lists 27 psychological tests that have been employed in hypnotic research, but he admits that very little has been achieved. For instance, Furneaux and Gibson (1961), using the Maudsley Personality Inventory found that among the more susceptible subjects two contrasting personality types predominated to a significant extent, "stable extraverts" and "neurotic introverts". In an attempt to replicate this work Hilgard and Bentler (1963) used the same test and again got significant results, but in the opposite direction! A number of subsequent studies using the extraversion and neuroticism scales of the Eysenck Personality Inventory have confirmed the earlier study, but they have also shown that although such research may be of interest to personality theorists, it does not tell us much about hypnotic susceptibility, nor does it provide a very useful tool for predicting people's reaction to attempted hypnotic induction (see Gibson, 1981).

It appears that although it was reasonable to expect personality tests to predict susceptibility to hypnosis, and a good deal of research in the 1960s was directed to such investigation, clear-cut trends did not emerge either for the objectively applied test or for the vaguer tests such as the Rorschach and the Thematic Apperception Test and other projective techniques. It was not the case that susceptibility did not correlate with a particular personality trait or dimension; frequently it did, but not reliably. Different studies gave different results and led to the disheartening conclusion that any apparently definite relationship that had been established in one research study was subject to so many Ifs and Buts that prediction in a future study was very hazardous. We have already seen how sex differences can act as a moderator variable in that an apparently clear-cut relationship between one personality characteristic and hypnotisability might hold for one sex but not for the other. Similar moderator variables bedevil research with the personality correlates of susceptibility.

The complexity of the picture revealed with personality tests indicates that there is no simple answer to the question: "What kind of person can be hypnotised most easily?". The answer lies not in describing a number of the most obvious personality traits, but rather in the unique experiences of the individual that predisposes him or her to react in an appropriate way in the hypnotic situation. This has led some theorists such as Barber (1964, p.313) to argue that "we should look for factors other than 'personality traits' that might account for interindividual variability and intraindividual consistency in response to suggestions". He goes on to suggest that we should focus on variables that are less enduring than personality traits and more situationally variable than the characteristics that are measured by personality tests. He suggests that among the variables of prime importance are the subjects' attitude towards the relationship with the hypnotist, their attitudes and goals in the test situation, and their degree of motivation to perform well. In criticism of Barber's view it may be said that everyone would agree that the situational factors he mentions are of importance, but this does not take us far enough. They are the *necessary* pre-conditions for hypnosis to take place, but they are not *sufficient* to account for the high inter-person variability of response among people who are already empathic with the hypnotist, highly co-operative and strongly motivated. Attitudes and motivation are easily motified, but we have seen that the degree of hypnotic susceptibility is extremely stable for any given person and rather resistant to attempts to modify it.

A better understanding of the nature of personality traits may be achieved by considering the following. When lay people learn that psychologists have developed tests that identify personality traits they are rather apt to get an over-simple picture of what is being attempted and perhaps achieved. It is easy to define a personality trait such as extraversion by describing the "ideal type" of the extreme extravert, and our own experience of people tells us that some people do in fact approach this ideal type, whereas others approach the "ideal type" of the introvert. But no individual is like this all the time in all situations. Personality traits such as extraversion, acquiescence, dominance, tendermindedness, and aggressiveness are highly meaningful in understanding human behaviour, but the same trait may be expressed to a greater or lesser degree according to the situation. The generally aggressive person may be very yielding and timorous in certain situations, and one can multiply examples of the complexity of interaction among various personality traits according to the situation. Such considerations are highly relevant to the study of personality traits in relation to hypnotic susceptibility.

A consideration of moderator variables brings us to what is the most confusing moderator of all, the individual's experience of and level of talent for hypnosis. People who encounter hypnosis for the first time are likely to have their performance determined to some extent by all sorts of attitudinal factors. Their *apprehensiveness* may mask what real talent they have for experiencing hypnosis, so it will be the personality traits associated with apprehensiveness that appear to be the chief ones determining susceptibility. But with experienced subjects who have no apprehension associated with the situation, such traits may be irrelevant, and quite other personality traits may show up as being associated with hypnotic susceptibility. We have already referred to a study by Bowers (1971) in which sex differences acted as a moderator variable, and it should be noted that *the level of susceptibility* was also a moderator variable. Performance on tests of creativity were strongly predictive of hypnotic response in the more susceptible half of the population studied but not in the less susceptible half.

The situation of becoming hypnotised in response to suggestions given by another person may mean many different things to different people, and individuals of a rather similar personality may react entirely differently according to their past experience. This means that in the clinical situation the therapist has no sure means of predicting which patients will be readily hypnotised, and which will show little talent. The only way to find out is to try to hypnotise them, or as was discussed earlier in this chapter, to use a standard scale of measurement of susceptibility. It must be left to the therapist's clinical judgement *when* such an attempted induction or standard scale should be applied, for earlier we have seen that experience of hypnosis is a moderator variable, and some patients may not on the first or even the second interview be ready to employ their full talent for hypnosis. Even so mild a test as the Creative Imagination Scale may appear threatening initially to the very anxious patient.

INVESTIGATION BY INTERVIEW AND BY QUESTIONNAIRE

It has been suggested that people of very similar personality may nevertheless respond quite differently to attempted hypnotic induction, according to their own past experience. Investigation of the past experience of college students was carried out in two studies by Josephine Hilgard (1970, 1974). In the first, interviews focused on elucidating the students' developmental histories from early childhood, and it was found that certain types of experience heralded the development of a person who readily responded to hypnotism. Such experiences included becoming involved in aesthetic appreciation of nature, pleasure in music, having religious experiences, becoming absorbed in novels and plays, and enjoying adventurous pursuits such as mountain climbing and skin diving rather than team competitive games. The person who becomes very involved in such pursuits sets aside ordinary reality and becomes totally engrossed in the experience to the exclusion of all irrelevant stimuli. In the second study (Hilgard, 1974), the interviews were carried out with students who had already been tested for hypnotic susceptibility, and it largely confirmed the earlier findings.

Coe (Note 5) developed Hilgard's work by incorporating most of her points of significance in a 200-item questionnaire, The Coe Experience Inventory , which he administered to 285 university students, both males and females, whom he afterwards tested for hypnotic susceptibility. In general, Hilgard's findings were confirmed by Coe's study, but not entirely, and some significant sex differences were found. Most significantly, involvement in drama was predictive of susceptibility (especially for females), involvement in music (especially for males), and being active in outdoor adventurous pursuits. For females, being influenced by their fathers was slightly predictive of later susceptibility. In contrast to Hilgard's findings, Coe found no relationship between reported childhood fantasy and later hypnotic susceptibility, nor did involvement with religion, type of extent of parental discipline, and cross-sex identification with parents (for males) appear to be predictive.

This work of Josephine Hilgard and Coe was a continuation of work that had been carried out in the 1960s using questionnaires. Acting initially largely on hunch experimenters such as Ås (1962, 1963), Shor (1960), and Shor, Orne, and O'Connell (1962) developed inventories of experience which many people would regard as "uncanny", such as mystical experiences of feeling "at one with the universe", and events in which there was no certain division between fantasy and reality. These sort of events often have the quality of "visitations", that is, happening to a person without their clear volition or intention. This is of course typical of hypnotic experience in which the ideas suggested by the hypnotist just seem to happen as in a dream. The hypnotised subject has no sense of "obeying" the hypnotist, say, when a movement occurs in response to a suggestion. Such a movement appears to happen of its own accord, even to the surprise of the subject.

Two types of items in inventories were found to correlate with hypnotic susceptibility. First, the experience of becoming totally absorbed in some activity, and it was the *intensity* of such experience rather than its frequency that was significant. Second, the tolerance and acceptance of trance-like experiences, which many people would regard as quite bizarre and disturbing. Research findings of this nature have not always been replicated. Barber and Calverley (1965) found no evidence for an association with hypnotic susceptibility such as that found by the previous researchers, and in some other studies the association was found for one sex only (Bowers, 1971). Despite some conflicting evidence the early researches of this type built up a body of knowledge about experiences in waking life that led on to the more advanced researches with larger numbers such as those of Josephine Hilgard and Coe that have been described. Tellegen and Atkinson (1974, p.270) investigating the responses of 471 women, identified a factor they labelled "absorption" which in various samples showed a moderate correlation with hypnotic susceptibility. An example of a relevant item will illustrate the concept of "absorption": "If I wish, I can imagine (or daydream) some things so vividly that they hold my attention in a way a good movie or story does". There are many technical snags in measuring people's response tendencies by means of questionnaires, but this modest but reliable association between reported "absorption" and hypnotic susceptibility is probably the best predictive device we will get by this method. It should be noted that these researchers studied women only; their results might well have been less impressive if they had included the male sex also.

Such findings are of some significance for the clinician and the associations revealed are not wholly fortunate in their clinical implications. People who are apt to get "carried away" and experience events in the environment with overwhelming intensity are the very people who are most likely to develop phobic reactions if they have such experiences in unpropitious circumstances. We do not know enough about the acquisition of phobic disorders, but Frankel and Orne (1976) have proposed that the related mechanisms are akin to those responsible for entering hypnosis. Phobic conditions lend themselves readily to treatment by the various techniques of behaviour therapy, and such techniques may be facilitated by the adjunctive use of hypnosis to control anxiety and to enhance imagery (McKeegan, 1986; see also Chapter 5).

THE QUESTION OF SUGGESTIBILITY

The fact that people vary in the degree to which they respond to hypnotic techniques is apt to be acknowledged but shrugged off by some clinicians who make the observation that they can generally tell in advance who the most "suggestible" patients are. Here they run a risk of misleading themselves by not being clear what they mean by "suggestibility". It is therefore worthwhile examining its meaning .

It was noted earlier that psychologists have developed a large number of so-called "suggestibility tests", but only some of them predicted susceptibility to hypnosis. Hull (1933) advanced the theory that if a person gave a positive response to a suggestibility test and also responded well to hypnotism, it was because of a common factor of "prestige suggestibility". He thought that the perceived prestige of the operator was highly important. In practice this idea proved to be erroneous. Hull's well-known postural sway test will work just as well if the voice giving the suggestions comes from a tape recorder controlled by a technician who has no particular prestige. Similarly, hypnotic induction does not depend on the perceived prestige of the hypnotist. Extensive experiments by Hilgard (1965) and others have shown that provided the hypnotist is perceived as a reasonably responsible person, his or her degree of perceived prestige is irrelevant. The capacity for hypnosis lies with the subject and depends very little on the characteristics of the hypnotist.

An important series of experiments by Eysenck (1943) and Eysenck and Furneaux (1945) established that the term "suggestibility" was being applied to two basically different types of response. The first, which they called "primary" suggestibility, involves subjects being given an idea which acts upon them so that they make *unwilled* responses. Thus, in the postural sway test when people stand upright with their feet together and their eyes closed and are given suggestions of falling forwards they will tend to feel this happening independently of their own volition. Similarly, some people high in "primary" suggestibility may feel themselves blushing if they are told that they will blush; this is another *unwilled* response. The various tests of "primary" suggestibility are excellent predictors of hypnotic susceptibility. "Secondary" suggestibility, on the other hand, is rather a rag-bag category referring to various tendencies otherwise known as "gullibility", "credulity", "conformity to social pressure", and "compliance". These are social tendencies that have no relation to hypnotic susceptibility. This has been confirmed by a number of independent workers such as Stukát (1958), and the literature has been reviewed by Duke (1964). Such studies are important landmarks in the history of hypnotism, adding to our understanding of what goes on when a state of hypnosis is induced by verbal suggestion. Such experimental studies would not have been possible in earlier times before the development of modern research methods and the invention of statistical techniques such as intercorrelation and factor analysis.

All this is highly relevant in the clinical field. Growing up as we do in a society that has certain mistaken preconceptions about hypnosis, preconceptions that we have traced to the powerful influence of fictional writers, it is entirely natural that clinicians will start off with an intuitive feeling that they know who will respond well to hypnotism and perhaps overlook the fact that certain patients do not respond well to their suggestions. It is for this reason that very experienced clinicians regard their intuitive reactions to patients with caution, and seek to back intuition with the findings from empirical research .

CONCLUSION

Hypnotism in therapy has undoubtedly been oversold in some quarters, and because of this we get practitioners such as Kihlstrom (1985, p.402) writing as follows:

> The apparent stability of hypnotic susceptibility in the face of efforts to modify it has at least two implications for the clinical use of hypnosis: (a) Hypnotizability should be assessed in patients who are candidates for hypnotherapy; and (b) Claims that hypnosis is an active ingredient in therapy should be supported by a significant correlation between hypnotizability and outcome. If a person proves to be insusceptible, it would seem better for the clinician to try a nonhypnotic approach to the problem. Clinicians may try to capitalize on what might be called the placebo component of hypnosis, but this practice should be conceptually distinguished from the claim that something occurs beyond the social influence attendant on the hypnotic ritual.

The question remains, what role has hypnosis to play in therapy? The answer undoubtedly lies in recognition of the fact that it may have a greater or lesser part to play, or no part at all, according to the unique nature of the patient at the time he or she presents to the therapist. It is partly for this reason that we may strongly deplore the practice of people setting up as self-styled "hypnotherapists" and trying to treat all patients by hypnotic techniques whether or not they are appropriate to the individual or to the disorder (see Chapter 13). The professional person is qualified to treat patients in relation to his or her own discipline and is not dependent on a resort to hypnosis. When professional people are fully conversant with the facts about differential susceptibility to hypnosis, they will use hypnotic techniques with discretion and obtain the best results possible by using them as an adjunct to their normal therapeutic skills.

4 Hypnosis in Therapy: General Considerations

HYPNOSIS AS AN ADJUNCT TO THERAPY

A central tenet of this book is that hypnosis is not itself a therapy but is an adjunctive procedure, applicable to a wide range of therapies. That is, merely performing hypnotic induction and deepening procedures with a patient is not normally sufficient to enable an appreciable therapeutic change. Of course, there may be a significant placebo reaction to such a limited intervention (Gibson, 1987). Also, as will be reported in Chapter 7, some conditions, such as those of a psychosomatic nature, may occasionally respond very well to quite simple interventions involving regular sessions of hetero-hypnosis and self-hypnosis emphasising relaxation. For example, Alladin (1988) reported an excellent response to relaxation instructions, including home practice using a tape-recording, in patients with migraine, and Brattberg (1983) similarly obtained positive results in patients with tinnitus. However, it may be argued that the essential therapeutic ingredient in such cases is relaxation training, rather than the hypnotic experience of the patient (and here we emphasise our conviction that hypnosis is not equivalent to relaxation). The relation of hypnosis to relaxation is discussed below.

To return to the main point: if the reader is willing to accept that hypnosis is not a therapy but an adjunctive procedure in therapy, then several conclusions flow from this, some of which are concerned with professional and ethical matters and the requirements for training in hypnosis. These will be pursued in Chapter 13; for the moment let us observe that the professional contemplating a course of training in hypnosis will be asking several questions, most prominently: "In what ways is hypnosis applicable to the therapy or therapies which I practise?" and "For what problems and with what patients is hypnosis most useful?". It is hoped that this and the remaining chapters will provide some answers. Before these questions are addressed there is another important point to consider, namely the similarity of hypnosis to other therapeutic procedures. A common observation of trainees at hypnosis workshops is that hypnotic procedures resemble other techniques used in therapy — for example, progressive relaxation, autogenic training, meditation, biofeedback, and guided imagery. In what ways does hypnosis differ from these other procedures?

A comprehensive analysis of the available evidence on this question is not within the scope of this chapter, but some impressions will be given here. If we think of hypnosis just in terms of induction and deepening procedures, then from the point of view of the subject's own experience there is probably not a great deal of difference between hypnosis and the above relaxation procedures (Edmonston, 1981; Humphreys, 1984; Wadden & Anderton, 1982; Wagstaff, 1981). In most instances the subject is mentally and physically deeply relaxed; attention is focused inwardly on sensations, feelings, and images; there is the implicit or explicit use of suggestion (principally that the subject will gradually relax more deeply); he or she is encouraged to adopt a non-analytical acceptance of what is taking place, and so on. Indeed, while therapists have ingeniously contrived a wide range of procedures aimed at relaxing their patients, the range of subjective experiences available to the latter is probably modest by comparison. It is inevitable therefore that the experiences of people undergoing the various procedures listed above will tend to be similar. Where hypnosis differs from the others is probably in the emphasis on verbal suggestion and imagery as a means of directly altering the subjects' mode of responding to and experience of both their inner and external worlds. This characteristic applies not only to the induction and deepening phases of hypnosis but also, and very importantly, to what the therapist proceeds to do *after* these phases are complete.

THE THERAPEUTIC BENEFITS OF HYPNOSIS

Some writers have listed what they regard as the benefits to psychological therapy conferred by hypnosis. For example, Holroyd (1987) lists nine ways in which hypnosis may potentiate psychotherapy; these include increase in suggestibility, imagery enhancement, improved therapist-patient rapport, and decrease in reality orientation. Hart (1988) presents a similar list of equal length.

One obvious benefit is that patients do experience often quite profound depths of mental and physical relaxation, even though the same may be obtained by other means; likewise greater vividness and involvement with imagery and fantasy, and an enhanced disposition to respond automatically to suggestions administered by the hypnotist. How these characteristics of hypnosis may be utilised in the behavioural treatment of psychological problems will be outlined in Chapter 5. We shall also explore in Chapter 7 the evidence for the influence of suggestion on more basic physiological functions and how this may be harnessed in the treatment of psychosomatic illnesses.

It is also assumed that the hypnotic state enables easier access to unconscious material of relevance to the patient's presenting problems (Barnett, 1981; Hart, 1988). This is not to be confused with the notion that hypnosis improves memory, a matter which was discussed in Chapter 1. Rather, it is held that hypnotic procedures may enable the patient to become aware of unacceptable or disturbing memories, ideas, impulses, conflicts, and so on and to resolve them in a satisfactory manner. This application of hypnosis will be further explored in Chapter 6.

THE THERAPEUTIC APPLICATION OF HYPNOSIS

The Symptom-oriented versus the Analytical Approach

When one is overviewing the therapeutic applications of hypnosis it is useful to make the distinction between therapy which is aimed directly at helping patients control, alleviate or overcome their symptoms or disorder, and therapy aimed at helping patients gain insight into and resolve the problems which are presumed to underlie their symptoms, such as hidden fears, repressed memories and feelings, and emotional conflicts. For example, a therapist may treat a patient complaining of migraine headaches by techniques of relaxation and pain relief, using direct therapeutic suggestions and teaching self-hypnosis; or the therapist may explore whether the migraine is a symptom of some underlying emotional difficulty—perhaps the manifestation of unexpressed or unacceptable anger—which the therapist will help the patient to acknowledge and resolve.

This distinction between the two types of therapy was, of course, long ago crystallised in the debate between behaviour therapy and psychoanalytic therapy (see e.g. Eysenck, 1952). The distinction in question is probably more apparent in theory than in practice; many therapists are not committed exclusively to one school; for instance many clinical psychologists will describe their approach as "eclectic", meaning they will use whatever techniques appear to be most appropriate at the time, and the development of cognitively oriented therapies has helped bridge the gap between the two sides (see Heap, 1984a, and Chapter 5). The impression of the authors is that practitioners of hypnosis very often combine the symptom-oriented and exploratory methods in their practice, often with the same patient and sometimes in the same session. Maybe one reason for this is that many hypnotic practitioners are drawn from the field of medicine and perhaps they are less inclined than psychologists to have an ideological commitment to one school or another.

What Sort of Problems may be Treated by Hypnosis?

This question is one which the practitioner of hypnosis is often asked, along with more specific questions such as "Is hypnosis used for agoraphobia?", "Can hypnosis help a patient with obsessional rituals?", "Can you treat alcoholic people with hypnosis?" and, all too frequently, the dreaded request "I have a very difficult patient I've been seeing for five years...(etc.) Will hypnosis help?" Such questions often place the respondent in the awkward position of having to disappoint the interrogator by appearing to be imprecise and evasive.

The reason for this is first that, as we have emphasised, hypnosis is best viewed as an adjunctive procedure in therapy, so it makes more sense to ask questions of the sort "How can hypnosis be assimilated into psychodynamic therapy, behaviour therapy, cognitive therapy, anxiety management?" rather than addressing particular problems. Second, the labels used to define psychiatric and psychological problems do not indicate as clearly as, say, medical diagnoses, what the appropriate treatment should be. This decision can only be made with any degree of conviction when a full assessment is made of the patient's history and the particular details of his or her problem. Thus patients given the same diagnostic label, say "agoraphobia", may receive quite different treatments: one patient may undertake assertiveness training, another may be offered exposure therapy, and yet another may receive marital counselling with his or her spouse.

Therefore, the answer to the question posed above is that hypnosis may be used in the treatment of a considerable number of psychological and medical problems, depending on the personal characteristics of the patient, the exact nature of the problem, and the therapeutic approach which has been selected. In addition to this broad statement we may add the following guidelines:

1. *Controlling anxiety.* Hypnosis may prove useful in most problems in which the control of excessive anxiety and tension has been identified as an important goal. Obviously this covers a large proportion of the problems encountered by therapists, but as was mentioned previously, there exist a number of relaxation procedures similar to hypnosis and it is not clear that hypnosis has any definite overall advantage. Probably the relaxation and anxiety-control techniques adopted need to be tailored to the individual patient; some patients may respond better to hypnotic procedures whereas others may show a preference for the other methods available. Likewise it may be important for therapists themselves to select those methods best suited to their own personal style and approach.

2. *Psychosomatic disorders.* Hypnosis is an effective procedure in the treatment of many problems commonly termed "psychosomatic", such as migraine and asthma, dermatological ailments such as eczema, and gastrointestinal problems, such as irritable bowel (see Chapter 7). This may be due solely to the benefits of

relaxation, but additionally it is conceivable that hypnotic suggestions can be effective in promoting therapeutic change in specific autonomic functions including cardiovascular, respiratory, and gastrointestinal activity, as well as altering the experience of pain and discomfort. Wadden and Anderton (1982) concluded from their review of clinical studies that hypnosis is a significant component in the treatment of warts, pain, and asthma, as distinct from "self-initiated" problems such as obesity and smoking. In this area of application we may also include the use of hypnosis with patients recovering from burns and in patients with haemorrhagic disorders such as haemophilia (see Chapter 7).

3. *Stressful treatment procedures.* Hypnosis may similarly prove useful as a means of helping patients cope with procedures in medicine and dentistry which may occasion anxiety, discomfort, pain, and bleeding, such as surgical operations and chemotherapy in cancer patients (see Chapter 9), dental extractions (see Chapter 11), and in childbirth (see Chapter 10).

4. *Modifying patients' attitudes and reactions.* Hypnotic (including post-hypnotic) suggestions are presumed to be useful in augmenting certain therapeutic maneouvres directly aimed at altering the manner in which the patient habitually thinks, feels or behaves in a given situation. Examples of this include the range of behavioural procedures which are undertaken at the covert level — covert densensitisation, sensitisation, rehearsal, modelling, and so on. For example, in the case of the covert sensitisation treatment of a smoker, the post-hypnotic suggestion may be given that as soon as the patient feels a cigarette on the lips he or she will experience an overwhelming feeling of nausea. Similarly a patient's use of cognitive rehearsal strategies may be reinforced by post-hypnotic suggestions. These applications are discussed in Chapter 5.

5. *Hypnosis in psychodynamic treatment.* Hypnosis may be a useful adjunct in the psychodynamic treatment of those problems which are the manifestation of emotional conflicts and repressed feelings and memories (see Chapter 6).

6. *Obsessive-compulsive disorders and phobias.* Although, as was stated earlier, the diagnostic label assigned to a problem often in itself does not provide the therapist with a definite indication of the treatment to be pursued, there are certain types of problem for which a particular treatment has been demonstrated to be especially effective. In such cases hypnosis may not necessarily be a useful adjunct. A good example of this is an obsessive-compulsive disorder, where the treatment of choice is a programme of response prevention (Rachman & Hodgson, 1978) in which hypnosis has little part to play. Of course, there are covert methods applicable to this problem (Cautela & McCullough, 1978), there may be a role for hypnosis in anxiety control and thought-stopping techniques, and in some cases there may be scope for hypno-analytical methods, but the therapist should carefully consider whether hypnosis would really be useful or merely an unnecessary distraction in the conventional behavioural approach to this problem. Incidentally, Hoogduin (1988) has demonstrated that obsessive-compulsive patients are generally low in hypnotic susceptibility.

A similar argument applies to the treatment of phobic anxiety (including agoraphobia and social phobias). Popular expositions of hypnosis frequently cite hypnosis as therapy of choice for phobias, but this is inaccurate and misleading. Hypnosis may indeed have a productive role, but again the therapist must be satisfied that this is so and not be distracted from more important therapeutic procedures. For example, for many phobics, exposure both to situations which precipitate phobic anxiety and to the panic state itself is often the essential ingredient in a behavioural approach. The therapist should therefore think carefully when, say, confronted by an agoraphobic patient asking for "hypnotherapy"; he or she would be unwise to embark on a potentially lengthy and unproductive course of analytical or covert behaviour therapy when simple exposure or confrontation may be the most pressing requirement of the patient. Nevertheless, hypnosis is still often used with phobic anxiety, and there is evidence that people with phobias, unlike obsessional patients, have a tendency to higher-than-average hypnotic susceptibility (Frankel & Orne, 1976). A fuller presentation of the use of hypnosis in behavioural and cognitive treatments of these problems is reserved for Chapter 5.

7. *The depressed patient.* Patients who are clinically depressed pose special problems for therapists of all persuasions (Gilbert, 1984; Storr, 1979), and it is stated by some (e.g. Hartland, 1971) that hypnosis is contraindicated in the suicidal depressed patient. Such caution appears to rest on the assumption that the interaction of hypnosis and depression carries its own dangers and may precipitate a suicide attempt, perhaps as a result of some elevation in mood sufficient to mobilise the patient to carry out this act (Burrows, 1980). There may be more likely explanations. Heap (1984b) described a depressed patient who after a course of 11 sessions of hypnosis with ego-strengthening (not with the author!) made a serious suicide bid out of sheer frustration and despair with his therapy. It is unlikely that a simple and direct approach such as ego-strengthening (see Chapter 5) would have any significant beneficial impact on the depressed state. Also, depressed people often have impaired concentration and for this reason may make poor hypnotic subjects which again may compound their feelings of failure and desperation. Another source of danger may present itself with the hypnotist engaged in uncovering techniques (Chapter 6). A depressed patient leaving a session in which painful and upsetting material has been brought to awareness may be especially vulnerable, particularly if he or she has to return to an unsympathetic family or stressful home environment.

Notwithstanding these difficulties, renewed interest and hope in the potential benefits of hypnosis for depressed patients has come with the rise of cognitive therapies (Beck, 1976; Ellis, 1962) which have been demonstrated to have a significant impact in the case of depression (e.g. Rush, Beck, Kovacs, & Hollon, 1977) and which may be augmented by the use of hypnosis (Alladin, 1989; Alladin & Heap, in press). Robinson (1977) and Matheson (1979) have also reported the successful use of certain covert behavioural techniques with depressed patients. Again the reader will find a more comprehensive discussion of these topics in Chapter 6.

It is always important for the therapist to be alert to the possibility that his or her patient may be suffering from an affective disorder and whether a course of medication may be desirable before any psychological therapy is embarked upon. This is certainly the case for manic-depressive illness, for which traditionally hypnosis does not appear to have had much of a role. Recently, however, Feinstein and Morgan (1986) have described the use of self-hypnosis and imagery and suggestions pertaining to the notion of a "balance in brain chemistry" in patients with bipolar affective disorder.

8. *The psychotic patient.* Perhaps a more negative outlook for hypnosis emerges in the case of the psychotic patient who traditionally has been considered unsuitable. Obvious reasons are the difficulties of gaining rapport with the patient and his or her inability to give sufficient sustained attention (Vingoe & Kramer, 1966). There may also be a risk using imaginal procedures of exacerbating the patient's involvement with hallucinatory or delusional experiences (Rosen, 1960) and the question of whether he or she is able to assimilate constructively material elicited by uncovering techniques. Some workers, however, particularly those of the psychoanalytical tradition, have developed approaches to the hypnotic treatment of psychotic patients (see Baker, 1981; Scagnelli, 1975), but unless one is highly skilled both in analytical methods and in working with psychotic patients, one would be best advised to avoid this area of application.

9. *Psychopathic personality disorders.* Traditionally, individuals with psychopathic personality disorders have not been responsive to psychological therapies and hypnosis does not appear to add any leverage to the treatment of their major problems.

10. *Dissociative states.* The efficacy of hypnosis in the treatment of dissociative states such as multiple personality has been reported in North America (Braun, 1984b; Gruenwald, 1984).

These general areas of application have been outlined with the individual adult patient in mind, but hypnosis also has behavioural, cognitive, and analytical applications in therapy with children (see Chapter 12) and therapy with groups, couples, and families (Araoz, 1978; Braun, 1984a; Ritterman, 1983; Ross, 1988). It is also important to bear in mind that the hypnotic part of a treatment programme may represent a small component of the therapy. In, for example, the treatment of an anxiety complaint nearly every session may involve the use of hypnotic procedures, or it may be that only occasionally in the treatment programme does the therapist resort to hypnosis.

It may be seen then that, rather than listing every problem for which hypnosis has a conceivable application, it has been more apposite to speak of general areas of usage and the ways in which hypnosis may augment therapy of one sort or another, regardless of the problem being treated.

THE INFLUENCE OF HYPNOTIC SUSCEPTIBILITY

It is a reasonable conjecture that the more hypnotically susceptible a patient is the more successful the outcome of any hypnotherapeutic intervention. The evidence so far paints a more complex picture. In their influential review of the clinical research literature, Wadden and Anderton (1982) concluded that on balance hypnotic susceptibility is positively related to outcome in the treatment of pain, warts, and asthma. However, for the "self-initiated" problems—obesity and smoking—there is no clear relationship. Some caution is required in the interpretation of these observations. The studies reviewed often used hypnosis in a straightforward way with the aim of direct symptom alleviation. Experimental studies naturally require that the administration of the treatment be undertaken in a standard and prescribed manner (indeed in some clinical studies, therapy is delivered via a tape recorder). In the clinic the therapist must design the treatment, and the whole way in which it is to be conducted, around the needs and characteristics of the individual patient. Also, as was stated earlier, a hypnotic intervention may be but one component in a range of therapeutic procedures forming part of the whole treatment programme. Furthermore, the research reviewed by Wadden and Anderton (1982) does not address the relationship of susceptibility to outcome where hypnosis is used adjunctively in analytical psychotherapy, regardless of the problem being treated; it again seems reasonable to presume that one limiting factor in the success of this kind of hypnotic intervention is the extent to which the patient is able to become involved in or respond to the uncovering techniques employed—age regression, dream suggestion, ideo-motor signalling, and so on (see Chapter 6).

Let us make some tentative conclusions relating to hypnotic susceptibility and the therapeutic effectiveness of hypnosis generally:

1. When used in a direct symptom-oriented fashion hypnosis can be significantly effective in the treatment of "involuntary" problems such as warts, asthma, and conditions of pain (and various other psychosomatic conditions, although the evidence is less clearly documented) and hypnotic susceptibility is a significant determinant of outcome. This conclusion accords with the earlier stated assertion that hypnotic suggestion may have a specific effect on certain involuntary functions and may also directly alter the subject's experience of pain.

2. When used in this manner for "self-initiated" problems such as obesity and smoking, hypnotic procedures appear to have a largely ceremonial function, regardless of susceptibility, and a favourable outcome probably depends on non-hypnotic aspects of treatment. As Wadden and Anderton (1982) state, these problems involve complex emotions and behaviours which are probably unlikely to be modifiable by direct hypnotic suggestion.

3. When hypnosis is an adjunctive component in a broader therapeutic framework such as behaviour therapy, cognitive therapy or psychodynamic therapy, then it is a matter of further research to elucidate in what circumstances and for what

reasons it potentiates that therapy. It seems inevitable that where it does have a significant positive effect, the hypnotic susceptibility of the patient is a determining factor.

IS HYPNOSIS A PLACEBO?

All treatments, whether with drugs, physical manipulations, behavioural programmes, or intended psychotherapy, have a placebo component in addition to whatever intrinsic effectiveness they may have. Hypnosis used therapeutically is no exception to this general rule. Strangely enough the psychological mechanisms that are put into operation in the placebo effect have little relevance to the mechanisms involved in hypnosis and those people who are specially likely to be placebo-reactors in a given situation are not necessarily very susceptible to hypnosis. This fact, which some lay people may find surprising, was elegantly demonstrated in an experimental study by McGlashan, Evans, and Orne (1969) and has been further discussed by Evans and McGlashan (1987). However, some people have suggested that when hypnosis is used therapeutically and patients benefit from the treatment, the improvement is *entirely* a placebo effect; that is, the patients improve because they know that hypnotism is reputed to be beneficial. Such a case is argued by Wagstaff (1987a).

The whole matter is discussed by Gibson (1987) who reviews much of the related literature. He concedes that while much of what passes for "hypnotherapy" in the hands of unskilled and non-professional people has only a placebo effect when it does any good at all, hypnosis in the hands of properly qualified therapists is like any other therapeutic treatment; it has a placebo component, but all the beneficial results cannot be attributed to the placebo effect. This paper is discussed by five clinicians in the same issue of the journal, and although they write from different viewpoints and make different criticisms of the main paper, they are all agreed that the wide range of clinical evidence that is now available makes it quite clear that hypnosis is not *only* a placebo. The paper is also commented on by Wagstaff (1987b), who reiterates his own original standpoint.

The placebo effect has now been widely studied and documented (see White, Tursky, & Schwartz, 1985), and it is important that clinicians should not regard hypnosis just as a placebo measure, as if they do they may tend to maximise its "hocus pocus" aspects and fail to use it intelligently as an adjunctive technique that can potentiate many existing therapeutic procedures

MYTHS ABOUT "HYPNOTHERAPY"

In Chapter 1 it was mentioned that some of the most common myths about hypnosis concern its use in therapy. Having discussed the placebo effect in therapy, we may now consider the chief myth that largely flourishes on the basis of the placebo mechanism. As discussed earlier in the present chapter, it is believed by many people that hypnosis in itself has a generally therapeutic value for all sorts of disorders, both psychological and physical. This has led to quite a number of unqualified people advertising themselves as "hypnotherapists" and charging fees for their services. The basic techniques of hypnotism can easily be learnt by anyone, but of course the necessary therapeutic skills of doctors, psychologists, and other professional people take many years of training, and without these skills a "hypnotherapist" can neither diagnose a patient's ills nor provide an appropriate programme of treatment.

"Hypnotherapy" is an ambiguous term having several meanings. Used by professional people it merely refers to the use of hypnosis in a programme of therapy. Vingoe (1987) writes: "I believe that the use of the term hypnotherapy without further elucidation of what is involved in the treatment package should be quite unacceptable to responsible clinicians and experimentalists alike". The same point is made by Spiegel (1987), who notes that "hypnotherapy is a somewhat misleading term". But as the lay public generally understand the term, and as they are encouraged to do so by various lay therapists, it implies that hypnosis *in itself* has some therapeutic value. This is not the case. Patients cannot be cured of their ills by "hypnotherapists" who simply hypnotise their troubles away. Apart from the placebo effect that has been mentioned, little good can be achieved just by hypnosis. Some lay "hypnotherapists" use a sort of pop Freudianism and claim that they use hypnosis to delve into their patients' "unconscious" and dig out the alleged hidden complex of factors that is causing all the trouble and, hey presto, the patient is cured! (see Chapter 6). In reality, therapy is not so easy.

Heap (1984b) describes the cases of four people who underwent treatment by various lay "hypnotherapists". His account makes depressing reading, and it is clear that anyone, no matter how ignorant and unqualified, can set up in practice and make a living as a "hypnotherapist", as the myth of the magic properties of hypnosis is so widespread. It is important that this myth should be dispelled and that people should understand that the only proper use of hypnosis in the therapeutic context is as an adjunctive procedure employed by properly trained health professionals who understand what they are doing and why hypnosis may be useful in a particular case. This is what this book is all about.

5 Hypnosis in Behaviour Therapy

This chapter will examine the application of hypnosis and hypnotic procedures to those therapeutic approaches which attempt to modify directly and systematically the patient's behaviour or thoughts. Such approaches have usually been subsumed under the heading of "Behaviour Therapy", but more recently we have seen the growth and development of cognitive therapies and their amalgamation with behavioural procedures, allowing us to speak of "cognitive behavioural methods" (see Chapter 4).

A number of texts and reviews have appeared in recent years which present and discuss behavioural applications of hypnosis from various standpoints. Dengrove (1976) has produced a useful book of edited readings which include some original manuscripts and a review paper by Weitzenhoffer which earlier appeared as a journal article (Weitzenhoffer, 1972). Other useful books on this topic are those by Kroger and Fezler (1976), Clarke and Jackson (1983), and although not specifically on behaviour therapy, Edmonston (1981). Recent review papers have appeared by Daniels (1980), Humphreys (1986), Spinhoven (1987), and Vingoe (1981).

The reader may wish to take issue with the authors' approach of considering *hypnosis as applied to behaviour therapy*. Could we not just as validly speak of *behaviour therapy as applied to hypnosis*? As Weitzenhoffer (1972) points out, those practitioners who call themselves "hypnotherapists" appear to have been using learning principles in their work *before* the development of behaviour therapy. This point may well be true, but we must concede that, whereas behaviour therapists have been comparatively successful in developing theoretical models which provide possible aetiological bases for many of the problems they treat and at the same time generate effective treatment methods, the same is not true of hypnosis. Moreover, just from a pragmatic standpoint, it is much more likely that the trainee in clinical hypnosis will (and arguably should) already have a firm grounding in behaviour therapy and therefore will be asking how he or she may augment this therapy using hypnotic procedures.

This presentation then will be directed from the above standpoint and will accordingly have a practical bias in its scope. It will also be noted that we have tended to focus on applications to common therapeutic procedures rather than to the specific problems (sexual difficulties, smoking, obesity, and so on) to which these procedures are applied. To the authors, at least, this seems the more logical approach.

TECHNIQUES OF BEHAVIOUR THERAPY

Behaviour therapy is the application of procedures based on principles of learning theory to the management and alleviation of problematical behaviour, cognitions, and feelings. There are a number of such procedures, amongst the more important of which are the following:

Verbal Instruction. Because important active procedures for changing behaviour have been developed and refined, the potency of simple verbal instructions may tend to be overlooked by behaviour therapists. Verbal instruction is indeed not always the best way to learn, and in many cases, such as learning a skill like riding a bicycle, it has a very limited role. Nevertheless, in everyday life it is a common and potent means of producing desirable and lasting behavioural change. Therefore, one way of helping patients learn desirable behaviours may simply to be instruct them what to do. In fact, it is surprising how much patients value simple instructions about how to handle a particular situation; often they will report back and say, for example, "I remembered what you said about keeping my breathing under control and not rushing things...etc., and it seemed to work".

Rehearsal and Practice. New or amended responses such as those mediated by instruction, often need to be rehearsed and practised before they are easily incorporated into the subject's behavioural repertoire. Of importance here is *feedback:* the behaviour is modified appropriately by, say, further verbal instruction or audio/visual feedback or merely by the patient's awareness of having executed a correct or an incorrect response. This is similar to:

Shaping. The patient's behaviour is "shaped" by contingencies of positive or negative reinforcement. The reinforcing stimuli may be primary rewards such as food and drink, but more often they will be verbalisations such as praise, tokens which may be exchanged for other rewards, pictures of pleasant scenes and so on.

Aversion. An undesirable response such as performing, or the urge to perform, an unacceptable act is extinguished by the administration of a noxious stimulus—e.g. a verbal rebuke, a sudden noise, or a mild electric shock. This procedure is obviously useful in the treatment of habit disorder, deviant behaviours, and with obsessive ruminations.

Desensitisation. A stimulus which arouses a negative emotional response such as fear is systematically paired with a feeling incompatible with that emotion, such as relaxation. The potency of the stimulus in eliciting the original negative response is thereby progressively weakened. This procedure is obviously useful in the treatment of phobic anxiety.

Sensitisation. This is very similar to aversion therapy; a stimulus which arouses a positive but undesired emotional response is systematically paired with an incompatible response such as fear or nausea. Again the potency of the stimulus to elicit the pleasureable response is progressively weakened and the negative response may replace the latter. The obvious areas of application are with addictive problems and deviant behaviours such as antisocial sexual preferences.

Exposure, Flooding, and Response Prevention. The common denominator in these procedures is that the patient is exposed to whatever situation he or she fears (in the case of an obsessional illness this may be *not* executing the ritual or decontaminating responses) until the anxiety diminishes by habituation and the escape or avoidance responses are extinguished.

Modelling. The patient observes another person either successfully carrying out the desired behaviour, and in some applications being suitably rewarded, or behaving inappropriately and being duly punished. Modelling has a wide area of application, particularly in social skills training and with children.

Covert Procedures

While all of the above procedures have been described in the overt or *"in vivo"* form, they may also be employed covertly or *"in vitro"*. One of the most widely used covert procedures is systematic desensitisation for phobic anxiety described by Wolpe (1958). As in most covert methods, the patient is first taken through a relaxation procedure, then asked to imagine situations which in reality evoke increasing degrees of anxiety. The effectiveness of this therapy was originally explained in terms of counter-conditioning ("reciprocal inhibition") but other explanations may be more appropriate (Bandura, 1971).

Other covert methods (covert reinforcement, covert modelling, covert sensitisation, and so on) have been described by Cautela (1978). In the case of covert aversive therapy and covert sensitisation, the noxious stimulus is self-generated—say, the memory or image of some unpleasant scene or state of nausea or actual physical illness; pleasant imagery may be used for positive reinforcing purposes. A special form of flooding in imagery was developed by Stampfl (Stampfl & Lewis, 1967, 1968); termed "implosive therapy", this involves symbolic descriptions of a psychoanalytic nature. In fact where there is a choice, *in vivo* exposure to the feared situation is probably preferable to imaginary exposure (Marks, 1969), although some preliminary rehearsal in imagination may be beneficial.

Finally, a covert method, termed "thought stopping", may be useful in cases of obsessional thinking. The patient rehearses covertly saying the word "Stop!" immediately he or she is aware of an undesirable thought or chain of thinking, and then switches attention to neutral or pleasant imagery.

COGNITIVE TECHNIQUES

Cognitive therapists such as Ellis (1962) and Beck (1976), although accepting the thrust and philosophy of behavioural methods, have emphasised the role of thinking in mediating emotional states such as anxiety, depression, guilt, and anger (as well as feelings such as elation and excitement). Therefore, in order to change the feeling one must alter the cognition. Psychopathological states such as chronic anxiety and depression arise from the patients' cognitive distortions which create representations of their world which are fearful, hopeless, depressing, and so on. The therapist aims to help patients recognise their maladaptive cognitions and habits of thinking, acknowledge their inappropriateness, and substitute more realistic ways of interpreting their world.

APPLICATIONS OF HYPNOSIS: GENERAL CONSIDERATIONS

The reader will probably realise that it is in the area of covert applications where hypnosis is most likely to be used; if a treatment programme is based mainly on active *in vivo* exposure then the role of hypnosis may be more limited although it may serve a purpose in the preparatory stages of therapy—say, in anxiety management training. In what ways, then, may hypnosis be used to augment these problems and what exactly is it that defines this contribution as "hypnotic"? Let us first illustrate the application of one of the most commonly used hypnotic techniques, namely post-hypnotic suggestion.

The Use of Post-hypnotic Suggestion in Behaviour Therapy

It was stated previously that simple verbal instructions are a potent, though limited, means of effecting therapeutic change. Often they will be employed as a back-up to the main learning procedure employed. Post-hypnotic suggestions may be similarly utilised in most covert paradigms, and the format of the suggestions resemble the usual verbal instructions (Spanos, Demoor, & Barber, 1973). Generally they take a form such as "Whenever/As soon as you do/think/feel X you will immediately do/think/feel Y". Some examples will serve to illustrate.

In the successful treatment of three out of four cases of trichotillomania, Barabasz (1987, p.149) used the following permissive post-hypnotic suggestion: "You will be acutely aware whenever you put your hand to your head, then it is entirely up to you, you have the power, the control, no one else, no habit controls you. You can pull your hair if you want to or you can choose to control the habit".

In relaxation therapy with a patient suffering from chronic headaches, Todd and Kelly (1976, p.221) administered the post-hypnotic suggestion: "After you wake from the trance... you will take a deep breath, and when I say 'relax' you will think 'relax', exhale and relax *just as you are now, just as you are now*".

Wright and Humphreys (1984) describe the use of hypnotic procedures in the covert sensitisation treatment of two cases of sexual deviance, namely an exhibitionist and a transvestite who stole female clothing. One component of the treatment was that a cue word spoken by the therapist (e.g. "police") was paired with the aversive scene (the patient's arrest) and the suggestion was given that each time the therapist uttered that word the aversive scene would be vividly brought to mind by the patient, thus facilitating the conditioning process. Post-hypnotic suggestions were given, that in the future, each time the patient thought of performing the undesirable act, the aversive scene would immediately spring to mind and its emotional consequence.

The last two examples illustrate how hypnotic and post-hypnotic suggestions may be augmented (in theory at least) by the use of a cue stimulus. This ploy will be elaborated upon shortly when we consider the procedure referred to as "anchoring". For the moment let us return to the question of what it is about the methods we are describing which define them as "hypnotic".

The answer seems to be that hypnosis involves the use of suggestions which *automatically* bring about changes in the subject's behaviour, thoughts, feelings, sensations, and physiological processes. So, when we administer a post-hypnotic suggestion of the kind described above, we are assuming that the patient will respond to that suggestion automatically and involuntarily on the specified occasion. The sexual deviant, for example, will not have to deliberately try to recall his arrest when he experiences the undesirable impulses; the image of the scene will come automatically, along with the bad feelings associated with it. We further assume that the induction of hypnosis will increase the responsiveness of patients to these kinds of suggestions, whereas merely telling them in the waking state that the particular responses or experiences will occur will not have the same effect.[1] Finally we assume that the extent to which the patient will response automatically to these suggestions will be correlated with his or her measured hypnotic susceptibility. In other words, when using hypnosis we are exploiting the subject's capacity to respond automatically to therapeutic suggestions made by the hypnotist.

---

[1] It has always been taken for granted by practitioners of hypnosis that such suggestions have a greater potency than the equivalent non-hypnotic instructions (e.g. Meyer & Tilker, 1969). The underlying mechanisms are in need of elucidation. Accounts have been presented in terms of conditioned responding (e.g. Barrios, 1973) and the vaguer and less scientific notions of the unconscious or subconscious mind. The latter description may be useful in everyday work with patients, but outside this it has little explanatory value (see Chapter 6).

Hypnosis in Cognitive Therapy

Keeping these considerations in mind, the reader familiar with some of the major techniques of cognitive therapy will perhaps have an idea of how post-hypnotic suggestion may be used to augment the process of cognitive restructuring. This involves altering the manner in which the patient construes certain situations in his or her life by replacing habitual irrational and maladaptive cognitions with realistic and adaptive ways of thinking. Patients are required to monitor their thoughts carefully whenever they are experiencing feelings of undue anxiety, anger, jealousy, guilt, depression, and so on. We shall see that the technique of revivification may be useful here, but, once the process of cognitive reconstruction has been undertaken, post-hypnotic suggestions may be employed to reinforce the cognitive changes prescribed. Alladin (1989; see also Alladin & Heap, in press) has described an extensive account of the use of "cognitive-hypnotherapy" for depression (see also Tosi & Baisden, 1984).

"Ego-strengthening"

Hartland (1971) presented a set of standard suggestions which are aimed at enhancing the patient's self-confidence, self-image, sense of well-being, and so on. He described these suggestions as "ego-strengthening" (sometimes they are termed "ego-boosting") and they are often reported (either in original or amended form) in accounts of clinical work as being an augmentative technique in a range of therapeutic paradigms. Heap (1985a) and Ross (1985) have criticised them on account of their generality and the absence of any imagery-evoking instructions. For example, suggestions such as "you will think more clearly", "you will become much less easily worried", "your memory will improve", "your nerves will become stronger and steadier", and "you will feel much happier", all involve very complex experiences and processes, and it seems unlikely that subjects will respond to them in the same way as a suggestion of arm levitation, a pleasant image, a specified thought or act, and so on. Moreover, they do not reveal to patients precisely *how* they are to achieve these desirable feelings and states of mind. In short, the ego-strengthening routine has too much of the air of a magic incantation about it.

The experience of hypnosis itself can be a pleasant and uplifting one, particularly when the patient has the sense of being in some kind of altered state. More likely, this and the patient's confidence, trust, and hopeful expectation concerning the therapy are being exploited in Hartland's type of ego-strengthening ritual, rather than the patient's suggestibility *per se*. If these ingredients are absent, then the ego-strengthening routine will fall decidedly flat, even with a suggestible subject.

Accordingly, Heap (1985a) has recommended that, when using positive suggestions in the above manner, the therapist should be more precise about the behavioural, cognitive, and physiological responses which are presumed to mediate the desired feelings of strength, optimism, self-confidence, and calmness. These include the kind of specific post-hypnotic suggestions described in the present chapter. Another technique, outlined later, is to elicit recollections of events and situations when the patient actually has experienced the desired feelings. The use of symbolic imagery may also facilitate this. In Chapter 12, for example, an ego-strengthening routine for children is described in which the child imagines eating some "magic biscuits", the ingredients of which contain all the good things that have happened in his or her life. Fromm (1968) describes some useful ego-strengthening imagery (e.g imagining being a tree and feeling the sap rising, filling the tree with new life) and the "hyperempiric" routines presented by Gibbons (1979) may also be appropriate (e.g. imagining ascending the steps inside a magnificent cathedral or riding through a rainbow). Therapists may also make up their own imagery material, tailored to individual clients. Finally, "anchoring" techniques, described later, may also be incorporated into an ego-strengthening routine.

THE USE OF HYPNOTIC PROCEDURES IN ANXIETY AND STRESS MANAGEMENT

A number of behaviourally oriented procedures have been developed by practitioners of hypnosis to help patients forestall, control or alleviate feelings of tension, anxiety, and panic. Nearly all of these methods include the use of suggestion and post-hypnotic suggestion as well as imagery.

Self-hypnosis

The hypnotic induction itself is a relaxing experience; however, most practitioners are keen that their patients should not be entirely dependent on the therapist to achieve this relaxed state, and they teach self-hypnosis for regular use. The basic procedure is to suggest to hypnotised subjects that they may relax, enter the hypnotic state, hypnotise themselves, or whatever terms are preferred, by going through the same procedures on their own (e.g. fixating a point, counting down or imagining being in a safe place). One may specify the exact duration of the period of self-hypnosis or one may use a suggestion such as: "As soon as you wish to alert yourself and come out of your self-hypnosis, you will count down, to yourself, from five to one, preparing to open your eyes at the count of one when you will feel fully alert, fully oriented, and ready to face the rest of the day feeling relaxed, calm, confident, etc."

It is important to incorporate certain assurances and safeguards in the suggestions for self-hypnosis: first, the assurance that it is quite safe and that self-hypnotised subjects are in full control, so if for any reason they are required to take immediate action—e.g. there is a knock on the door or the telephone rings—then they will open their eyes immediately and be fully alert, fully oriented and ready to take the appropriate action. Second, again as a safeguard, it is important to emphasise that patients will only ever practise their self-hypnosis when it is absolutely safe and convenient to do so.

Research has shown that a 20-minute period of simple relaxation each day is beneficial as a means of allaying the effects of the numerous potential stresses of everyday life (Benson, 1975). Sometimes, however, it may be desirable to incorporate into the self-hypnosis routine imagery which has a bearing on the patient's problem. Symbolic ego-strengthening imagery and fantasy of the type described above may be a useful addition to a basic self-hypnosis procedure. Mantras or simple suggestions in the manner described by Emile Coué have been recommended by some (see Stanton, 1979a). Wilkinson (1988a) has described the combination of self-hypnosis and remedial breathing exercises, including diaphragmatic breathing, for patients prone to hyperventilation. It is becoming increasingly recognised that one predisposing factor in the occurrence of anxiety and panic attacks may be chronic overbreathing (Wolpe & Rowan,1988), and a consequent lowering of carbon dioxide levels in the bloodstream. This manner of breathing tends to be more rapid and shallow than normal respiration, with an overuse of the chest muscles. Patients who hyperventilate need to be educated to understand the mechanisms of overbreathing and may be taught compensatory breathing exercises which make greater use of the diaphragm and follow a slow rhythmical pattern (see Wilkinson 1988a). The suggestion may be given that carbon dioxide acts as a relaxant and as the patients are breathing in the manner prescribed, they are replenishing the carbon dioxide in the bloodstream, thus reducing the likelihood that they will experience panicky feelings.

In fact, most tense and anxious patients may benefit from relaxation procedures which combine slow diaphragmatic breathing with a key word or phrase connoting feelings of calmness and well-being (e.g. the words "relax", "calm", or "peace"). One may also suggest that the patients give some emphasis to the outward breath by thinking of "letting go" as they release the breath and prolonging the outward breath; they are then informed that their body automatically relaxes while breathing out, and they can add to this effect by thinking of a word such as "relax" or "calm" (imagined visually and/or spoken) on the outward breath. They also imagine "holding the relaxation steady" as they breathe in, thus accumulating relaxation on each outward breath. This and other breathing exercises may be accompanied by the patients' placing their hand on their abdomen over or just above the navel and following the rhythmical movements of the hand.

An additional technique is for the patients to locate any tension in their body (e.g. in the shoulders or stomach) and to give that tension a colour. As they breathe out they are to imagine breathing out the tension in the form of a vapour of that colour; the vapour dissipates into the air around them leaving their body relaxed.

Imaginal rehearsal of coping strategies may also be incorporated into the patient's self-hypnosis. Such strategies—for instance, imagining successfully coping with a situation which has hitherto caused the patient undue anxiety—are described in more detail below. As the self-hypnosis thus becomes more complicated in terms of imaginal material, it may be useful to provide the patient with a tape-recording of the whole sequence. Indeed, in the authors' experience, many patients seem to prefer to follow a recording, even for simple self-hypnosis instructions; they appear to find it easier to work through the procedures under the direction of a recorded voice than with no external guidance at all.

However, not all patients seem to be able to set 20 minutes or so aside to perform their self-hypnosis, and the danger then arises that it becomes a chore to be performed at the behest of the therapist. In fact, it may be at least as beneficial to suggest several brief sessions of self-hypnosis throughout the day—say of between 2 and 5 minutes' duration. This may be useful in any case, because the patient may need these periods of time-out to unwind and forestall the build-up of tension throughout the day, in preference to waiting until the end of the day to relax.

Post-hypnotic Suggestion in Anxiety and Stress Management

As always, the above methods and others to be described may be reinforced by post-hypnotic suggestion. The use of "cued" post-hypnotic suggestion (mentioned earlier) in anxiety and stress management is discussed by Humphreys (1988). In such cases the cue may be a word ("relax", for instance) which the patients say to themselves and the response may be relaxed breathing or relaxation of some part of the body prone to tension such as the forehead or neck muscles. Thus, the post-hypnotic suggestion may be "As soon as you start to notice these feelings of tension in your stomach the word 'relax' will immediately come to mind and you will start to breathe in this calm steady manner, etc." Where the patient has been taught to think of a relaxing scene or event in his or her life associated with a positive self-image (see later), a cue word may itself be used elicit the recall of that scene when appropriate. When these kinds of post-hypnotic suggestion are employed, it is important to ascertain carefully the triggers for the anxious feelings. Often the most potent triggers are internal—a sensation in the stomach, an increase in heart rate, a catastrophic thought or image, and so on. Such triggers may then be specified in the post-hypnotic suggestion "As soon as you experience X, etc."

The "Clenched Fist" Technique and Variations

This is a widely used anxiety management technique which involves suggestion and the use of a cue of sorts—the clenched fist. One common version is to ask patients to focus attention on any tense feelings in their body. They are then instructed to slowly make a fist with, say, the left hand and as they are doing that to imagine all the tension in their body streaming down into that hand so that as the fist is becoming more and more tense, the rest of the body is becoming more and more relaxed. They then either take in a deep breath and slowly breathe out, or count from five down to one. As they are breathing out or counting they are to release the fist slowly so the hand becomes loose and comfortable again, and they imagine the tension evaporating into the air around them, leaving the hand and body relaxed. This exercise is practised several times in the clinic and reinforced with post-hypnotic suggestions concerning its use in everyday situations in which the patient experiences undue tension.

An additional instruction, which may also be used with similar techniques, is to ask patients to rate their tension on a 0–10 scale before and after the exercise. A score of 0 means complete relaxation and 10 means extreme tension or panic. After making the first rating, they may also be asked to try to increase their anxiety or tension on the scale—say by one point. They are to do this by "will power", not by merely consciously clenching the muscles. One rationale for these instructions is that if the patient does succeed in increasing the anxiety then one can draw their attention to the fact that they can control this anxiety by increasing it and so should be able to control it by *reducing* it. Nothing is lost if they do not succeed in increasing their subjective anxiety—perhaps they can even take some comfort from this. The patient is then instructed to reduce the tension using the clenched fist or some other technique.

Another variation is to place the hand over the part of the body which experiences the most severe tension—often the stomach or forehead. As the fist is tightening the patient imagines all the tension being drawn from that part of the body and accumulating in the fist. The tension is then symbolically discarded in the manner described above.

Stein's (1963) technique involves the clenching of both fists separately. One hand (usually the non-dominant) is reserved for bad feelings and the other for good feelings. To elicit the latter, the patients recall as vividly as possible an event in their life when they felt strong, in control, confident, and so on. As they are doing this they gradually make a fist with the dominant hand and imagine associating all those good feelings with that fist. They are then instructed in real-life situations to dissipate the bad feelings using the non-dominant fist and replace them with the good feelings using the dominant fist. It is, of course, important to practise the technique regularly in order to derive any benefit. Basker (1979) describes the use of this method in the successful treatment of agoraphobic patients, and Stanton (1988) claims it is a very rapid and effective treatment for phobic anxiety, with 76 out of 103 of his patients showing a good response.

Anchoring

The above techniques involving the use of cues to trigger desired feelings, antagonistic to anxiety, are very similar to some of the ideas of "anchoring" described by Bandler and Grinder (1979) amongst others. "An anchor is any stimulus that evokes a consistent response pattern from a person" (Lankton, 1980, p.55). Most often we are interested in anchors for particular feelings, everyday examples being a souvenir of a holiday, a favourite melody, a pat on the back, and a particular perfume. Anchors may be internal (images) and the may elicit negative as well as positive feelings.

Bandler and Grinder (1979, p.82) describe ways of setting up anchors; for example, a positive anchor may be established by instructing the patient to imagine vividly a situation in which he or she possessed the desired feelings, strengths, and resources to cope with his or her problems, and the therapist then touches the patient, say on the wrist or knee. It is claimed that touching the same place is now an "anchor" for the elicitation of those positive feelings and resources. A negative anchor may likewise be established for those feelings associated with a situation in which the patient has need for those same resources. Bandler and Grinder (1979) describe a routine which involves, amongst other things, simultaneously touching the patient on those parts of the body associated with positive and negative anchors. It is alleged that the problem can be very quickly resolved with these methods, although claims of one-session cures have not been substantiated in controlled trials (Allen, 1982; Krugman et al., 1985). There will be some elaboration of the above procedure later when we discuss techniques for "transferring resources".

"Ego-shrinking"

This technique was described by Heap (1985a) and is appropriate for some socially anxious people. Such individuals are extremely self-conscious and believe that other people are paying far more attention to them than they are in reality. Thus, when experiencing strong feelings of anxiety they tend to assume that other people are aware of their state of discomfort and are thinking ill of them on that account. These patients may be very embarrassed by some visible aspect of their anxiety—e.g. their sweating or blushing (Edelmann, 1987). Some will also have a fixation on a particular feature of their appearance, such as the size of their nose or their body shape generally, and will again believe this to be the special focus of other people's critical attention.

The aim of the "ego-shrinking"[2] routine is to help patients have a more realistic perception of just how little they themselves and their self-perceived difficulties and shortcomings figure in the concerns of others. A case report will illustrate.

Case Study. Mr J had suffered from torticollis for a number of year and, despite treatment from many orthodox and alternative doctors and therapists, his head was turned to the right much of the time particularly when he was feeling anxious. He was forced to endure considerable discomfort at times and was very self-conscious about this problem, and on account of this had experienced a period of being virtually housebound. At the time that he sought hypnosis (he had received hypnosis previously from both a lay practitioner and a clinical psychologist) he was going out

[2] The term "ego-shrinking" was chosen as a counteraction against the all-pervasive vogue for "ego-strengthening" or "ego-boosting" methods. The choice was also influenced by the discussion of Skynner and Cleese (1983) of the role of the psychotherapist in "shrinking the patient's ego"—hence perhaps the not-too-inappropriate nickname for the former, namely "shrink"! "Ego-shrinking" may also be conceived as a necessary progression from the earliest Piagetian developmental stage of complete egocentricity (see Inhelder, 1962).

but avoided the High Street, busy shops, public transport, and various crowded places. His torticollis acted as a "positive feedback loop" for his anxiety because the more anxious he became about his appearance, the more his muscles would tense and turn his head. The focus of therapy was his anxiety and self-consciousness, exploratory methods having been unproductive.

One of Mr J's outstanding attributes was his skill as painter, particularly of landscapes, and when painting these he would feel relaxed and his head would be straight. He was therefore asked to imagine that he was painting his favourite landscape, feeling relaxed and at ease. It was emphasised to him that all his attention was absorbed in the scene around him, the colours, shapes, and textures, the sounds and smells, etc., and that *he was having no effect on the scene; the scene would be exactly the same if he were not there.* Next he was asked to imagine walking down the High Street, thronging with people, and the suggestion was given that he would bring into this situation the same mental set as in the landscape image. That is, he was asked to view the scene as though he were painting it, with all his attention focused outwards on the people, the shops, the traffic, and so on. Forceful suggestions were given that he was having no effect on the scene—the situation would be just the same if he were not there and the people would be seeing, thinking, saying, and doing exactly the same things and paying no attention to him. He was then asked to rise above the whole scene and, looking down, see himself amongst the crowd, inconspicuous and just like everyone else. This routine was repeated several times each session and was reinforced with post-hypnotic suggestions (e.g. "Each and every time you become aware of these feelings of self-consciousness you will immediately switch your attention away from yourself to the scene around you, etc."). Although Mr J.'s torticollis remained, his anxiety and self-consciousness in social situations diminished and he was able to extend significantly the range of his social activities. He attributed his increased self-confidence to the imagery and suggestions described.

THE USE OF AGE-REGRESSION AND REVIVIFICATION IN BEHAVIOUR AND COGNITIVE THERAPY

Although hypnotic age regression is commonly thought of in terms of psychodynamic psychotherapy it is sometimes a useful procedure in behaviour therapy. Age-regression and revivification suggestions typically require the subject to imagine going back in time and to relive an incident as vividly as possible. (When referring to the re-enactment of those incidents which occurred in the recent past without regression to a radically earlier stage of the person's development, we shall simply employ the term "revivification".)

A discussion of techniques of age-regression is reserved for Chapter 6, where we will address the issue of the authenticity of "memories" elicited by these methods, and where one particularly useful procedure, the affect or somatic bridge (Watkins, 1971) is described in detail. This method is very useful where there is an acute affective or somatic component to the problem, as in phobias, anxiety states, and psychosomatic disorders.

There are a number of reasons why the therapist should require the patient to relive some significant incident in the recent or distant past.

Age-regression or Revivification to Elicit Further Information

This application is of particular value in cognitive-behavioural treatments in which the therapist is helping the patient to identify the maladaptive behaviour and cognitions which precipitate inappropriate negative feelings such as anxiety and depression. The therapist will often ask the patient to monitor and record thoughts and reactions in critical situations and bring the records to the session for analysis. However, records are often incomplete and the patient may require considerable assistance in accurately identifying relevant cognitions and automatic thoughts. The use of revivification procedures in the session may prove valuable in eliciting further relevant information.

Age-regression and Revivification for Facilitating Access to Positive Feelings such as Self-confidence, Calmness, and Assertiveness

Simply asking patients to relive vividly a pleasant experience can be very therapeutic in itself. Matheson (1979), for example, has described the use of age-regression to happy experiences in the treatment of four depressed patients. These experiences served as imaginal stimuli for the elicitation, via post-hypnotic suggestion, of appropriate positive feelings.

The transfer of positive feelings and cognitions from past experiences into present problematical situations is the basis of a number of therapeutic paradigms. The anchoring techniques of Bandler and Grinder (1979) and the use of the "landscape" image in the case of Mr J, both described previously, are examples of this approach.

Another example is the case (seen by M. Heap) of a man, Mr P, with multiple sclerosis, who asked for hypnosis to help him maintain his self-confidence in his struggle with the disease. From his life history it was ascertained that in his teens he was a great sportsman and had won medals for swimming. Accordingly he was age-regressed to a time when he swam for his county and he was asked to re-experience the will-power, strength, and confidence he felt while swimming through the water. Post-hypnotic suggestions were given of accessing these positive feelings via this and other images, in situations where he would require them. These situations were also rehearsed in fantasy in which he would imagine transferring the good feelings from the original event into the new situation. Mr P found such imagery very useful, particularly on awakening in the morning when he required great mental effort and perseverence to mobilise himself for the day. In fact, he requested a cassette tape of the suggestions to work from for that purpose.

Cladder (Note 4) reports that he and his colleagues prefer to use "good strong feelings from the past" for the counter-conditioning of anxiety, rather than traditional relaxation instructions in the desensitisation of phobic patients. They also use only a four-step hierarchy of situations eliciting 20, 40, 60, and 80 degrees of anxiety.

Age-regression and Revivification to Enable the Patient to Re-interpret or Reconstruct a Significant Event or to Imagine Coping with it More Effectively

In this particular application of age-regression or revivification the two general approaches, the symptom-oriented and the psychodynamically oriented, tend to merge. On the far side of the symptom-oriented approach, one may be asking the patient to imagine using relevant skills to cope with a past situation which was not handled to his or her satisfaction. An assertiveness training or anxiety management programme may employ such a procedure. One may simply ask the patient to replay an experience in imagination in such a way as to bring about a more satisfactory resolution (cf. Ahsen & Lazarus, 1972; Lamb, 1985). In some cases this will be an appropriate instruction; in others some skills training (e.g. in such anxiety management approaches as described earlier) will be necessary if the patient lacks good coping responses. In yet other cases the instruction will be inappropriate: the patient may have had no choice as to how he or she responded. More psychodynamically oriented ploys such as the use of ego states (see p.85) may be worthwhile here.

Cladder and his co-workers (Cladder, Note 4) favour the paradigm described by Bandler and Grinder (1979) for anchoring good and bad feelings, in their treatment of phobic patients. A recent fearful incident is relived in imagination and the corresponding bad feelings are anchored. This is followed by a search backwards in time for another five or so similar incidents, including the earliest one recollected. The patient is then asked to recall what resources were needed in order to feel as well as possible in all these situations, then to think about where to find such resources. Usually these may be obtained in the form of memories as described earlier or from observations of others known to possess those resources. These are also anchored and the patient again relives the past incidents in chronological order, this time bringing those resources to bear in each situation. The patient is also asked to rehearse imaginally a future situation again using those coping strategies. Posthypnotic suggestions are given that the anchor (e.g. a particular gesture) will elicit the required resources in future problem situations.

Another approach to the reconstruction of past traumatic experiences, particularly those associated with early life, lies more within the psychodynamic framework and involves helping the patients to work through the unresolved emotional ramifications of certain critical events in their life. We must postpone discussion of such applications until Chapter 6; however, we should like to underline here that it is quite acceptable and indeed often desirable for therapists to be flexible in how they choose to utilise the material elicited using age-regression and revivification techniques and to feel free to adopt either a behavioural or psychodynamic approach, according to their own judgement.

Age-regression to Uncover Memories which may Underlie the Presenting Problem

This application is again more commonly the domain of psychodynamically oriented therapy and is discussed in Chapter 6. Nevertheless, a cognitive-behavioural treatment programme may sometimes be usefully augmented by an exploratory investigation of some early memories which may be of importance in the development of maladaptive cognitions underlying the patient's problem. Such habits of thinking may, and often do, extend far back in the person's life, and recognising their origins may help the patient acknowledge their inappropriateness in adult life. Such information is of course usually elicited without hypnosis, but sometimes the use of hypnotic techniques, such as the affect bridge (see Chapter 6), may serve to facilitate this process.

In many of these uses of age-regression and revivification the therapist may choose to suggest to patients, provided their imagery is sufficiently vivid, that they are reliving the memory in the dissociated state—i.e. observing themselves from a detached viewpoint. This may ease the reliving of the incident if it is emotionally demanding. In the case of a reconstructed memory it may likewise be useful for patients to first imagine observing themselves coping effectively with the situation. This may prove easier than first attempting to imagine coping "live", when anxieties and irrational cognitions may be too intrusive, and it may literally enhance their self-regard to imagine viewing themselves as coping. Mairs (1988) describes the use of hypnosis to enhance the performance of a sportsman—an archer—whereby he was trained to imagine observing himself going through the motions of loading, aiming, and firing as though he were coaching himself. A variation of this is the covert modelling procedure in which the patient imagines another person, perhaps one with similar anxieties, coping effectively with the situation—say, asserting himself or herself at work.

AGE-PROGRESSION

Age progression is simply the suggestion that the patient is moving ahead in time in order to fantasise a future situation. From a behavioural standpoint it is useful to have patients mentally rehearse coping effectively with future as well as past situations. It is the authors' contention that once patients are able to do this and to feel that that way of coping is realistic for them, then they are a long way towards overcoming their problem. Many anxious and phobic patients at the outset of therapy are heard to exclaim, "I just can't imagine doing that!" and they mean this quite literally; or they may say "Whenever I imagine myself in that situation all I think of is me panicking and running out!". Therefore, mentally rehearsing coping effectively but realistically with future situations—and this includes using newly taught skills such as the anxiety management strategies described earlier and cognitive restructuring—may be an important component of self-hypnosis for many patients. It is not sufficient to rely solely on post-hypnotic suggestion.

A second reason for rehearsing future situations is to test out whether the chosen means of coping are indeed workable. There may be hidden penalities (real or imagined) for making the desired changes: for example, marital disharmony may ensue as a husband or wife becomes more assertive and independent; or if an anorexic person's weight gain means becoming sexually more attractive, hidden anxieties may be thus brought to the fore. If such problems are not addressed in therapy then it is quite possible, though not inevitable, that any change will be short-lived. One of the authors (M. Heap) recalls a patient who stopped smoking, then discovered one drawback: one day he was involved in a heated discussion with his colleagues over some issue at work and found his customary manner of coping with the tension, namely picking up his cigarettes and going out for a smoke,was no longer available. Fortunately he realised he had other means of dealing with the situation—he remained in the office and stood his ground!

Of course, a behavioural analysis will reveal many of these obstacles to progress (or secondary gains in maintaining the *status quo*) but a careful imaginal rehearsal of a future situation may elicit useful information. Grinder and Bandler (1981) describe a "reframing" routine which, amongst other things, acknowledges that the "problem" may be a means of coping and asks the patient to fantasise using alternative coping strategies in future situations and to give an ideo-motor or ideo-sensory signal (see Chapter 6) if any part of him or her objects to these new arrangements.

One may also instruct patients to progress to a time when they no longer have the presenting problem. It is again possible that such a manoeuvre will reveal anxieties about changing, but the benefits of being rid of the problem may also be rehearsed. For example, in a treatment programme for weight reduction, the patient may be progressed to a target date and asked to imagine vividly the feelings of being slim, fit, and healthy, wearing a favourite outfit once more, lying on the beach in a bathing costume again, or whatever the patient perceives as the benefits of weight reduction. A similar procedure may be used with smoking cessation: the patient may be progressed to one year after the abstention date and may be asked to imagine, amongst other benefits of not smoking, how much extra money is now available (this often runs into hundreds of pounds) and then to imagine enjoying the benefits of alternative purchases, such as a holiday or some new furniture—again whatever the patient has stipulated. Such imagery helps to bolster the patient's motivation to succeed, which is an essential ingredient in all such cases. For further ideas on these methods, the paper by van Dyck (1988) is recommended.

METAPHORICAL AND ANECDOTAL METHODS

Although the notion of influencing people by telling them some story or fable is not new (cf. the parables of Jesus), there has recently been an upsurge of interest in their employment in formal therapy as a means of creating therapeutic change. This is largely a result of the popularising of the works of Milton H. Erickson, the late American psychiatrist (Erickson & Rossi, 1979; Erickson, Rossi, & Rossi, 1976). The approach typically involves relating an anecdote to the patient (with or without hypnosis—though the idea is that the patient is in some kind of "trance" state, may be by being absorbed in the story). The anecdote is chosen by the therapist to contain ingredients, at an allegorical level, which may be used by the patient to solve his or her problem but it is not made explicit what the connections are. For example, Erickson (see Erickson & Rossi, 1979) in his treatment of a patient with tinnitus, told the patient how he himself had once deliberately slept the night in a noisy factory and on waking the next day appeared to have learned to shut out the din of the machinery.

The theoretical rationale for such methods is rather shaky; it is assumed that it is the patient's "unconscious mind" which is receptive to the therapeutic message and thereby locates the appropriate resources possessed by the patient to deal with the problem. Such explanations and other aspects of Erickson's work have been subject to criticism from a number of quarters (Heap, 1980, 1988c; Gibson, 1984; Hilgard, 1984; McCue, 1987; 1988a,b). Nevertheless, any good therapist will be flexible enough to incorporate new methods into his or her repertoire and no harm can come from including some timely metaphorical communications in a therapeutic programme. The interested reader may consult Lankton's (1983) volume on such procedures.

SUMMARY AND CONCLUSIONS

We have attempted in this chapter to describe important hypnotic approaches which practitioners of behaviour and cognitive therapy may incorporate into their work. These have included the use of the hypnotic induction itself and self-hypnosis as techniques of relaxation; the use of suggestion to reinforce behavioural and cognitive changes; the augmentation of suggestion by cues or anchors; the use of ego-strengthening suggestions (with certain provisos); the techniques of age-regression and revivification to access relevant memories and the cognitions and feelings associated with them; the use of age-progression or future rehearsal to enable the patient to try out new ways of coping; and the use of metaphorical ideas and imagery.

Both Humphreys (1986) and Spinhoven (1987) have remarked on the possibility that any therapeutic enhancement due to the use of hypnosis may be non-specific and arise from the increased expectations of success on the part of the patient (and indeed the therapist). If this were the case then the benefits of hypnosis would depend on public beliefs concerning hypnosis and these may not necessarily always be positive. We have mentioned, however, that the "hypnotic" nature of the methods described in this chapter relies on the degree to which they are experienced as having an automatic and dissociative quality, rather than being active efforts of will, an assertion also emphasised by Spinhoven (1987). Accordingly, we have given prominence to the role of the therapist's suggestions in directly producing discrete changes at the behavioural, cognitive, and physiological level. In support of this emphasis is the evidence that when such suggestions are used with "involuntary problems" (pain and psychosomatic complaints) they do have a specific effect (see Chapter 7). Moreover, just as with such problems the hypnotic susceptibility of the patient is a significant factor (Wadden & Anderton, 1982), so the same should apply to behavioural and cognitive applications (see also the discussion by Kihlstrom, 1985, quoted in Chapter 3 of this book). It is still unclear whether or not this is the case (Wadden & Anderton, 1982). Either the specific effects of hypnosis in such therapies are weak, or, as Spinhoven (1987) suggests, researchers have not focused the hypnotic suggestions on directly altering the subject's behaviour and experience at an involuntary level.

In accordance with the conclusions of Wadden and Anderton (1982), Humphreys (1986), and Spinhoven (1987) we urge that methodologically sound investigations be undertaken, calculated to elucidate the specific effects of hypnotic suggestions in behavioural and cognitive interventions which are aimed at facilitating automatic and dissociative responding, and which owe their effect to the measured hypnotic susceptibility of the subject. If and when such investigations produce evidence of a specific adjunctive effect due to hypnosis, then perhaps more behavioural and cognitive psychotherapists will be keen to incorporate hypnosis in their work.

6 Hypnosis and Psychodynamic Therapy

In the present chapter we will consider the application of hypnosis in those therapies, generally referred to as "psychodynamic", which seek to promote greater awareness on the part of the patient of those feelings, conflicts, memories, and so on that may underly the presenting problems. It is assumed that once the patient has been helped to acknowledge these feelings, conflicts, and memories, and, very importantly, to re-evaluate them appropriately, then the associated distress and hence the presenting symptoms, will be alleviated. The role of hypnosis in psychodynamic therapy may therefore be described as augmenting this process of identifying and re-evaluating material relevant to the patient's problems.

In other words, the assumption is that hypnosis facilitates access to "the unconscious", a notion which we will later explore in further detail. For these purposes, various procedures, termed "exploratory" or "uncovering", have been developed. The use of hypnosis in this way is also referred to as "hypnoanalysis", but as hypnosis is only a component part of the therapy, and other methods not unique to hypnosis are employed, this label may be rather unsatisfactory.

EXPLORATORY AND UNCOVERING TECHNIQUES

There are a number of standard exploratory and uncovering techniques at the disposal of the hypnoanalyst, who may also develop his or her own according to intuition and style. For further information on these methods, summaries of hypnoanalytical procedures are to be found in standard texts such as Cheek and Le Cron (1968), Crasilneck and Hall (1985), Hartland (1971), Karle and Boys (1987), and Kroger (1977). More comprehensive presentations are exemplified in volumes by Barnett (1981) and Wolberg (1964). Karle (1988) also gives an excellent overview of methods. Several North American writers have contributed to both theory and practice in studies of the analysis of patients with specific psychopathological conditions including psychotic and borderline patients (Baker, 1981; Copeland 1986; Fromm, 1984; Scagnelli, 1975), multiple personality (Ross, 1984; Kline, 1984) and post-traumatic stress disorders (Brende & Benedict, 1980; Spiegel, 1981; 1986).

Age-regression in Psychodynamic Therapy

In Chapter 5 we discussed age-regression and revivification of memories and outlined a number of reasons why a therapist may wish to age-regress his or her patient. For hypno-analytical purposes, the usual aim of age-regression is to enable patients to re-experience and re-evaluate in imagination an event or events in the past which in some way relate to the presenting problems and their resolution. The event may be one which the patient is able to recall without hypnosis, or he or she may only have partial or even no recall at all until regressed, when a fuller recollection emerges or seems to emerge.

Age-regression may be effected in a number of ways. Hartland (1971) describes a very direct procedure by which the therapist counts down from the patient's present age to the target age. Another method uses Yes-No ideo-motor signals to identify the age at which a significant event occurred, and both this and yet another method, the affect bridge, are described later.

The patient's response to age-regression may be dramatic and convincing, with behaviour and speech assuming child-like characteristics in the case of a regression to childhood. Often, however, the regression will appear less profound with no obvious alterations in the patient's manner, and the recalled experiences may still be related in the past rather than the present tense. This should not necessarily cause the therapist to be disconcerted, as the material elicited may still prove to be of great therapeutic value. Also, if the therapist prompts the patient to give his or her account in the present tense (e.g. "I am sitting at home with my sister....") and speaks as one would to a child of the age in question, the patient may gradually become more absorbed in the imagery and experience more vivid recollections. Indeed, Hilgard (1986) reports that unhypnotised, highly susceptible individuals will age-regress quite easily in a role-playing interaction with their therapist.

The technique of dissociation may be useful with patients who are resistant to re-experiencing a critical period in their life, maybe because of the distress associated with it. For example, they may be asked to view the regression on an imaginary cinema or TV screen, while they remain in the "adult state". Now that home video-recorders are in everyday use, one can also ask patients to imagine selecting a video-tape of their life at the target age and viewing it on their imaginary TV screen. The aim here is to enable the patient to dissociate the emotional part of the memory or fantasy from its content. More illustrations of this technique are given later.

At this point it might be pertinent to raise the questions of how far back one can usefully regress a person and of how reliable the reported memories are, particularly those of very early experiences. First, let us emphasise that contrary to some popular ideas there is no known part of the human brain which faithfully records every single event of its owner's life. This is a common public assumption (Loftus & Loftus, 1980) and is not infrequently made in the hypnotic literature (e.g. Barnett, 1981). In support of this contention, the work of the neurosurgeon Wilder Penfield is often cited. Penfield (Penfield & Roberts, 1959) electrically stimulated the exposed cortex of epileptic patients on whom he was operating in order to establish the neuroanatomical focus of the epileptic seizure. Stimulation of certain areas of the temporal lobes appeared to elicit vivid memories, sometimes of quite distant and long-forgotten events in the patient's past. However, Loftus and Loftus (1980) have pointed out that these observations were made in only 40 of the 1132 patients tested, and close examination of the reported "memories" suggested these were probably reconstructed events, rather than faithful reproductions of the original experience. Neisser (1967, pp.167–170) arrived at the same conclusion.

Even if there were such a mechanism which faithfully recorded the minutiae of our experiences, it is clear that it is not accessed when patients are hypnotically age-regressed. Rather, the memories elicited under hypnosis, like any other memories, are the result of an active, creative process, and are therefore subjected to distortions due to forgetting, interference,confabulation, expectancy, emotional state, and so on (see Chapter 1 of this volume and the thorough review by Nash, 1987).

To the question how far one can usefully regress a person, it must be said that there appears to be no limit to this and quite dramatic performances may occasionally be elicited when people are regressed to their birth and even to the fetal state, not to mention regression to previous lives, a topic which has periodically aroused public interest over the past 50 years or more. Here we stress that we do not accept that the material elicited by birth, pre-birth and past-life regression is anything other than a product of the subject's expectations and fantasies. (Orne, Note 14, has remarked that equally compelling past-life regressions may be enacted by motivated unhypnotised subjects.) Nevertheless, the fact that the material may be inaccurate, or even, from a factual point of view, wholly fabricated, does not imply that it is useless for therapeutic purposes. The fantasy elicited may be symbolic in some important way or represent a condensation of similar incidents. For example, a recalled parental assault may represent several such assaults, or may incorporate fantasies concerning the assault which the patient had at the time, or indeed may be a fantasy of an assault that never really occurred. A re-enactment of the birth experience may symbolise how patients feel about their being in this world now (do they ever say "I wish I had never been born"?) or being independent of their parents; similarly their fantasies of being in their mother's womb may symbolise their relationship with her in some profound way. Even a past-life regression may evoke material from real life which the patient finds too difficult or traumatic to acknowledge and which he or she finds easier to confront by locating in a previous-life fantasy (compare this with the dissociation method mentioned previously and again below). These suggestions are speculative and more research is required in this area.

One important message, therefore, which will be re-emphasised later, is for the therapist to be cautious about interpreting the events of regression literally and simplistically. Otherwise, he or she will be led into making unjustified and unsupportable inferences about the patient's experience and behaviour. Case 2, later, illustrates a very straightforward age-regression, and further discussion of the nature and problems of this procedure are taken up later in this chapter.

Other Imagery Techniques

There are other exploratory techniques involving imagery which are less directive; one such procedure is to ask hypnotised patients to imagine a blank screen on which an image will shortly appear which will reveal important information about their problem, perhaps to do with its origin, development, and solution. It may be a scene from the past, a significant person or word or phrase, and it may be symbolic or not immediately obvious in meaning, so that some elaboration of the material may be necessary before the message becomes clear. The screen may be that of a television or a cinema and the therapist may suggest that the image is gradually coming into focus. A variant is Wolberg's (1964) "Theatre Visualisation Technique" in which the scene appears on an imaginary theatre stage. Finally, it may be suggested that the patient will have a dream which will be relevant to the problem and its resolution. The dream may be suggested to appear immediately or sometime before the next appointment. In the latter case, the patient is instructed to write down the dream and bring the account to the next session (Degun & Degun, 1988).

Once the material is elicited by the above methods, it may only be necessary to suggest that the patient will become aware of its significance. Otherwise, further elaboration and development of the imagery or dream will be necessary. Appropriate methods include free association and free fantasy, guided fantasy based on the original material, and the gestalt techniques of "being" each element in the dream or fantasy and interrogating each element (Fagan & Shepherd, 1971; Perls, Hefferline, & Goodman, 1973).

The advantage of all these methods is that the material is elicited gradually and in symbolic, disguised or fragmented form, thus enabling patients to assimilate their experiences at their own pace without being emotionally overwhelmed or, on the other hand, totally resisting the probings of the therapist.

Ideo-motor Responses

The ideo-motor response (imr) provides another very useful procedure whereby the patient is enabled to communicate information to the therapist which often may not be obtainable by direct questioning. The information is conveyed by means of simple movements, usually by the fingers, which correspond to the messages "Yes" and "No". One may also include a response to indicate the message "I don't know", and sometimes a fourth response indicating "I don't want to tell you". Such signals may be established by the suggestion that the patient think very deeply and honestly about the word "Yes" and that whilst this is happening the unconscious mind will choose one of the fingers on one of the hands to convey this message by slowly, and without conscious effort, lifting this finger. The other messages may be established likewise via other fingers. Having established the signals,the therapist may proceed to interrogate the patient by asking questions which demand the answer "Yes" or "No". It is assumed that the patient's answers are "unconscious"—that is, he or she need not consciously know what the answer is but the unconscious mind does. Typical questions may be: "Is your problem associated with an experience you have had in the past?", "Was this experience before the age of 10....8....6.....(and so on)?", "Is there any important reason why you need to have this pain now?"

If it is assumed that the method is valid, then we have one way of assessing whether regression to a significant experience is indicated, or whether a more symptom-oriented approach is more appropriate. It is also a useful safeguard when broaching material which may be distressing for the patient, say, by asking the question "Is it acceptable for you to recall this right now?" If the negative is given, then further information may be elicited by the imr without the patient's having to fully confront the material.

One way of interpreting the imr technique is by reference to the everyday phenomenon of how we convey messages, particularly concerning the way we feel, via automatic movements of hands and face, body posture, and other non-verbal cues. To convey "Yes" and "No" we nod and shake our heads, usually quite involuntarily. Such non-verbal messages may provide the observer with information about the person's emotional state, personality, what he or she is thinking, and so on. Sometimes this information is contrary to the message being spoken; the person may say "I am not angry", "I am very interested", or "I am telling the truth", while non-verbal cues are conveying the opposite message.

Such an account may provide the therapist and the patient with a model on which to base their interactions using imr signals. Of course, more explaining needs to be done to understand how such cues can be accessed in such a direct and dissociated manner by the therapist. The sceptical reader will demand to know whether imr signals are truly "unconscious" and whether they are any more valid or informative than more obvious ways of communicating. There is unfortunately a lack of serious research into these questions. Notwithstanding this, the imr is a widely used method amongst practitioners of hypnosis and this attests to its useful application in therapy. Similar procedures using ideo-sensory responding (e.g. an intensification of a particular feeling may be a "Yes" signal and a diminuation a "No" signal) have been proposed by some authors (e.g. Bandler & Grinder, 1979).

The Affect Bridge

This is a very useful regression method described by Watkins (1971) whose paper should be consulted for a complete description of the steps involved. The main procedural component is the suggestion that the patient regress to the very first occasion when the affect associated with this problem was experienced (e.g. a feeling of anxiety or rage, a craving or impulse to indulge in a destructive habit, or a somatic experience such as a migraine—in which case, the procedure is sometimes called the somatic bridge). The affective or somatic component is first elicited by having the patient vividly recall the most recent occasion when it was strongly experienced. The patient is then asked to focus solely on the feeling part of the experience and to allow it to become intensified by a factor of 2...3...4..., and so on. The regression to the earliest experience is then elicited; suitable imagery may be employed such as going down a road or a bridge surrounded by mist and receding further and further back in time accompanied only by that intense feeling.

The affect bridge can be used in a simplified form, either prior to or as part of the hypnotic induction, both as a means of eliciting important material and as a way of handling resistance to the induction as the following case studies (from Heap, 1985b) illustrate.

Case 1: Mrs D was referred for help with her fear of darkness and confined spaces. A behavioural approach was planned and hypnosis was chosen as a method of relaxation and anxiety control. She was first asked to close her eyes and breathe comfortably but a little deeper than usual and to emphasise the outward breath, imagining the feeling of "letting go" as she breathed out. She was then asked to focus her attention on the physical sensations in her body and to allow any feelings or thoughts to enter her mind as and when they occurred. After a short time, the therapist noticed her eyes flickering and that her forehead seemed tense. These observations were confirmed on questioning and she was then asked to focus on them to the exclusion of everything else and to allow the rest of her body to relax. It was further suggested that she imagined the feeling becoming more and more intense.

We have here the ingredients of a hypnotic induction, with the subject focusing on one stimulus or a range of stimuli (albeit an uncomfortable one) and some suggestions to "let go" and relax. The above method of breathing, incidentally, seems conducive to the expression of any emotion which may be present at the time.

Mrs D was then asked if she associated the sensation with any particular feeling or emotion and her eyes began to water as she said: "Yes, I feel that I shouldn't be here. I don't think I deserve all your attention when there must be other people far worse off than me". She was then asked to focus on that feeling to the exclusion of everything else and to imagine it increasing. She was then asked if she could now connect that feeling with any other experience in her life (it is not necessary for these particular purposes to regress to the earliest experience). She cried a little more and said that she had never been able to go to her mother with a problem. Her mother had always been unsympathetic and had made her feel guilty and unworthy. A specific memory or fantasy was then elicited to enable her to work on these feelings a little more (methods for this are discussed later). After this work a more conventional deepening technique was used, followed by suggestions of relaxation and anxiety control.

The advantage of building up from the somatic and affective components (particularly, as in this case, when these are already in the here and now) is that the information elicited is less likely to be contaminated by the patient's intellectualising or need to comply with the demands of the therapist, problems to which methods such as the screen and theatre visualisation techniques may well be susceptible. In the case just described the material may not have been central to the patient's problem or therapy, but it was clearly affecting her and by coming to some resolution it is likely that the hypnotic induction was facilitated by the removal of the associated tension or "resistance". In conclusion, it should be pointed out that similar procedures of focusing on and intensifying feelings have been described by gestalt therapists (see earlier references).

TECHNIQUES OF RE-EVALUATION AND RESOLUTION

It may sometimes be the case that merely eliciting a vivid recollection or recollections of a relevant past event may be instrumental in promoting therapeutic changes. For example, patients may gain insight by becoming more aware of how their habitual ways of responding in the past are still causing problems in the present. More often than not, however, they will require some help from their therapist in enabling them to re-evaluate these memories in a therapeutic way. Sometimes behavioural and cognitive methods may be employed as outlined in the previous chapter.

With a traumatic incident the patient may abreact and methods for dealing with this are described further on. Another useful re-evaluation procedure in psychotherapy (which may also be interpreted in cognitive terms) is ego-state therapy which again is described further on. An excellent review of these procedures is presented by Karle (1988).

Abreaction

It is a common experience that the release of an emotion can be very therapeutic. Naturally, this is so for a joyful feeling but the same is often true of sadness and anger, particularly if the emotion has been held in check for some time and its expression does not invoke feelings of guilt and shame on the part of the person concerned. In psychotherapy one is often gently encouraging patients to be aware of their feelings of the moment and to give expression to those feelings in any appropriate way that they wish. In the case of the methods of age-regression and fantasy discussed above, it is not uncommon for patients to become spontaneously intensely emotional. Often they will cry, out of grief, sadness or fear as a distressing incident is recalled or fantasised. Should patients not immediately reveal any emotion it is still important to encourage them to explore and develop any feelings they may have concerning the material. They can, for example, be asked to attend to any physical sensations—perhaps some tension or some alteration in their breathing rhythm. The technique of suggesting an enhancement of the sensation (see the discussion of the affect bridge) may be useful. The associated affect may then be explored by simple probing, for example by asking the question "What is this tension concerned with?" Finally, the appropriate behavioural responses may be developed by asking "What do you feel you want to do now?" For example, the patient may be recalling an incident when he or she was provoked by one of his or her parents, but was not allowed to be angry. In the reconstruction of this scene, however, the patient can be encouraged to give expression to this anger in a suitable way.

Intuitively, there seems little point in asking patients to relive an upsetting incident if they were able to express their feelings adequately at the time. Also, such methods should be employed with great sensitivity in the case of depressed patients. One can imagine the dangers of sending such a patient away from a session in which sad memories have been stirred up in this way, particularly if there is no one to provide understanding and support when the patient arrives home.

As a rule, one associates abreaction with an emotion which the patient was unwilling or unable to ventilate at the time—maybe through guilt, fear of punishment, or fear of losing control. As we will discuss later, however, one should beware of being over-reliant on a too simplistic hydraulic model of therapy—that is the idea that one blocked emotion on one single occasion will result for evermore in some psychological or psychosomatic disorder until that emotion is discharged and the associated "pressure" released. First and foremost the fact that the patients are sharing their feelings with another person—their therapist—is of crucial significance. As in any system of psychotherapy, the message of the therapist, delivered with calm acceptance and empathy, should be that the patient has every right to express this feeling without any loss of dignity or any need to feel guilty or ashamed. If this is achieved in the abreaction, the patient may then begin to be able to feel secure about expressing such emotions but may still need to work on this. For example, an angry abreaction in fantasy against the parents may facilitate the patient's learning to be assertive with authority figures in his or her present circumstances but this may require further development. Another therapeutic outcome may be that if the emotion is one which the patient has difficulty expressing, then, as a result of a successful abreaction, his or her self-image as "a person who (say) *cannot* cry" changes to "a person who *can* cry". In other words, although one is dealing with emotional experiences in the past, the main focus for therapeutic change may actually be how the patient handles these emotions in the here and now.

Another important point to consider is whether, in different cases, distressing emotional conditions are better resolved by abreaction methods or by rational discussion aimed at changing the patient's perception of the situation. Beck, Rush, Shaw, and Emery (1979) point out that although a patient may feel transiently better after an emotional outburst, such unrestrained expression of feeling may have little lasting effect on the progress of therapy. Obviously, patients will differ in their individual needs. For example, when a patient is troubled by strong feelings of anger—say concerning his or her upbringing—but is able to acknowledge such feelings without guilt, then a cognitive restructuring procedure may be a better means of effecting a therapeutic change of outlook.

Ego-state Therapy

Berne (1967) presented a theory of human personality development, upon which the therapy Transactional Analysis is based. He proposed the existence of three ego states, which represent different individual states of mind with their own characteristic pattern of thinking, experiencing, and behaving. These ego states (which are not dissimilar to Freud's concepts of the id, ego, and superego) are present within each person, and the extent to which they exist in harmony will determine his or her degree of adjustment and fulfilment. The child ego state results from the experiences of the person during early development; the parent ego state represents the internalisation of the real parents and parent-like figures; and the adult ego state represents the part of the self which has matured, mainly from the child state, as a result of interactions with the world, the knowledge, wisdom and learning gained, and so on. Although ego states are believed by transactional analysts to be separate entities which are observable through the individual's overt behaviour, the preference here is to view this system as a hypothetical model on which to base one's therapeutic strategies. A popular procedure for helping the patient resolve traumatic and disturbing childhood memories using the concept of ego states is, in simplified form, as follows: the patient is regressed to any such incident and any abreaction is allowed to take place; the therapist then takes the patient through a kind of psychodrama in fantasy in which it is suggested that the patient's adult ego state, possessed of all the resources, knowledge, and learning accumulated since that incident, goes back in time and provides the child ego state with all the reassurance, comfort, and resources with which to cope with and resolve that memory so that it no longer causes problems for the patient. This procedure is demonstrated in the following case illustration:

Case 2: This is an unusually uncomplicated case. It concerns Deborah, a stable and happily married secretary in her thirties. Her problem was that since a child she had had a nervous stammer in a number of situations, such as giving her name in front of people, reading to people, asking for a train ticket, or giving any kind of specific information such as ordering a meal, and instructing and directing people.

She did not always stammer in these circumstances, but would still be very anxious. She was also anxious but still fluent on the telephone.

Deborah received three sessions of therapy over a period of six weeks, plus a follow-up at three months. The second and third sessions consisted of anxiety management training using techniques described in Chapter 5. However in the first session the therapist felt that it might prove useful for Deborah to review her earliest recalled experience of stammering as this seemed to have been very upsetting for her and she felt it had unnerved her in subsequent similar situations. Following a hypnotic induction and the establishment of "Yes","No", and "Don't Know" imr signals, the affect bridge method was employed to facilitate regression to the critical experience; the anxiety was initially elicited by having her recall the most recent incident in which she experienced the tension and anxiety associated with her speech difficulty. Permission to have this and all subsequent experiences was sought via the imr.

The patient regressed to the age of seven on her first day at her new school. She used the present tense, speaking in a child-like voice and said her name was Debbie — (using her maiden name). She said that she was in class and her new teacher was asking the pupils to say their names in turn. She said she was very nervous and worried about saying her name. Deborah's adult ego state was then addressed by reminding her that she was now an adult woman who had many more experiences and resources than seven-year-old Debbie, that she herself had children and knew how to help them and give them confidence when they were afraid and upset. In imagination adult Deborah was instructed to go back to seven-year-old Debbie and give her all the reassurance, comfort, and strength that she needed to cope with this difficult situation. She was allowed as long as she required to do this and to signal with an imr when this was done. Seven-year-old Debbie was then asked if she needed anything more from adult Deborah to help her feel OK about this situation and she signalled "No". She also signalled "No" to the question whether there were any other memories which it was important to deal with. Deborah was then progressed to her present age.

The patient was seen three weeks later. She reported that since her appointment she had experienced a feeling of "warmth and well-being"; she felt calmed and uplifted by the session, and she was most surprised to find that these feelings were still present. She had found herself spontaneously reading aloud to people, and, what was quite new, she had actually enjoyed doing this. This progress was maintained and furthered in the subsequent sessions using behavioural procedures.

Resolution by Ideo-motor Responses

Is it possible for the uncovering and resolution phases of therapy to be undertaken entirely covertly without the patient's disclosing any material at all to the therapist? This is the claim of some practitioners of the Ericksonian and NLP schools (e.g.

Grinder & Bandler, 1981). For example, the patient, having signalled that a problem has been identified, may be completely unwilling to share this with therapist. The therapist may then continue by asking the patient consciously or unconsciously to consider ways in which the problem may be resolved, and, having thus identified one or more possible solutions, to signal a "Yes" response.

These methods have been elaborated into a "reframing" ritual which was described by Grinder and Bandler (1981) and outlined in Chapter 5. It has also been suggested that the resolution phase may be accomplished at an unconscious level so that patients may themselves be unaware of the manner in which they are to work towards solving some problem; their unconscious mind has made the decision indicated by the execution of some ideo-motor response.

What are we to make of these apparently magical and simplistic procedures? Can pervasive and long-lasting psychological problems really be solved by such techniques of digital levitation, which seem a far cry from established procedures such as psychodynamic therapy, behaviour therapy, or even everyday ways in which we set about counselling a person in distress? Let us first present an actual case in which this type of intervention was employed. We will then make some observations and interpretations concerning the rationale of these procedures and of hypno-analytical methods in general.

Case 3: Simon was a 13-year-old boy with a life-long history of nocturnal enuresis, wetting most nights of the week. He responded to direct hypnotic suggestions (see Chapter 12 for enuresis in children) in so far as he became dry most nights, but he would frequently relapse. These relapses were eventually contained by recourse to an enuresis alarm whenever he resumed wetting, in preference to a visit to the therapist. Although Simon denied it, his mother felt that there were reasons for the relapses and the occasional isolated instance of wetting. They often occurred after an argument with a sibling, at the start of the school term, or after contact with his natural father (his mother and father were divorced).

On his final follow-up appointment, Simon underwent his usual hypnotic induction and "Yes" and "No" imr finger signals were established. Then he was asked to think very deeply and honestly about all the important things happening in his life—people, places, memories, things he does, experiences, and so on—and if there was anything there that might be connected in some way with his wetting then his finger would signal "Yes"; if there was not, his "No" finger would signal. After some time the "Yes" finger lifted. Simon was then asked if he knew what it was in his life that might be connected with his wetting, and then if he could share it with his therapist. First a "Yes" then a "No" signal were observed. Simon was then asked to think very deeply about whether there was anything he might be able to do about this so that he was less likely to wet his bed. After a while a "Yes" signal was observed. The next question was whether Simon would undertake such action for a while to see if it reduced his wetting. The "Yes" signal was observed. Finally Simon was asked to imagine taking such action in future and to signal "Yes" or "No" according to whether he felt able to carry it out or whether there were some serious problems in the way. The "Yes" signal (i.e. no serious problem) was observed.

Some months later his mother called in to see the therapist and said that although Simon was now hardly wetting at all she was a little concerned because he had of late been losing his temper with members of his family and was at times being rather obstinate and self-willed. She was not concerned about this behaviour as such, but it was very much out of character and she wondered how to handle it and whether it was indicative that there was something troubling her son. The therapist assured her that this behaviour was quite normal in a young person moving towards independence.

SOME CAUTIONS, CRITICISMS, AND INTERPRETATIONS

It will be clear from the above presentation of hypnotic techniques in psychotherapy that many practitioners and writers lean heavily on the concept of "the unconscious mind" in order to formulate therapeutic strategies. We wish now to examine this concept in greater detail as we feel there has been in the literature on hypnosis an over-reliance on simplistic notions of the unconscious mind. This has led to much loose thinking and practice, and to the perpetration of certain myths and misconceptions about hypnosis which have probably served to repel many prospective trainees.

The Concept of the Unconscious Mind

The notion of the unconscious mind is common to many systems of psychotherapy. In Freudian terms the "unconscious" is associated with the repression of undesired impulses, although these may be manifested in artistic, creative, and otherwise socially acceptable spheres of activity through the mechanism of sublimation. Generally, then, in this formulation, the contents of the unconscious are held to be troublesome and potentially destructive, but there is also a tradition (albeit considerably less well elaborated) which portrays the unconscious as a somewhat mysterious and almost paranormal source of mental energy and creativity. We have, for example, already commented on the prevalent notion that the memory of every event in our lives resides in our unconscious mind. In terms of this model also, creative and artistic inspirations and intuitions are often ascribed to the workings of the unconscious mind and we have recently witnessed interest (or perhaps a revival of interest, since these ideas ebb and flow) in problem-solving during sleep (inspired in part by the story of Kekule whose solution to the problem of the structure of the benzene molecule was revealed in a dream about snakes forming rings). There is also now an unfortunate vogue for trying to interpret as much as possible about human psychology in terms of the functional differences between the cerebral hemispheres, the right hemisphere being identified as concerned with unconscious processes both in traditional psychoanalytical terms (Galin, 1974) and in formulations of the unconscious as a creative resource (Blakeslee, 1980; Erickson & Rossi, 1979). Just as in the case of the conscious–unconscious mind split, writers tend to dramatise and oversimplify the nature of left–right brain differences[1] (Springer and Deutsch, 1985). In fact, if one felt so inclined, one could develop a similar framework of ideas around the anterior–posterior division of the cortex (anterior subserving more abstract, expressive and enactive functions, posterior more concrete, receptive, and passive). The fascination with right–left brain distinctions has probably much to do with the extraordinary studies of Sperry and others (Gazzaniga, 1970; Sperry, 1968) on patients whose cerebral hemispheres have been disconnected by sectioning the corpus callosum. Nevertheless, we acknowledge that there are reasons for identifying the unconscious more with the right hemisphere, if only because of the specialisation of the left hemisphere for language and verbal skills which are more concerned with conscious expression. Moreover, as was indicated in Chapter 3, there is psychological and psychophysiological evidence of increased right hemisphere activation during hypnosis (see also Gruzelier, 1988; Pagano, Akots, & Wall, 1988).

We do not deny that the concept of the unconscious mind is a useful one in therapy and it is one to which people can readily refer their everyday experiences. We know what people mean when they say they did something "unconsciously" and patients themselves spontaneously volunteer the idea of the unconscious mind as a way of interpreting their problems. They may say "There is something at the back of my mind that is causing me to feel like this", or those engaged in some compulsive habit will readily attribute their behaviour to some "unconscious" urge which they do not comprehend. Yet the simple idea of the unconscious mind is of very little value in the scientific analysis and understanding of human behaviour and mental processes. It is far too superficial and simplistic a notion to be anything otherwise.

---

[1] The reader may discern a process at work in the development of such formulations. First, a distinction is defined—e.g. the conscious–unconscious mind or the left–right brain. Second, the tendency grows to interpret as much as possible in terms of this distinction, often at the expense of objectivity and logical discipline. In the present context we can do no better than quote William James's (1880, p.163) pronouncement on the concept of the unconscious as: "the sovereign means for believing what one likes in psychology and of turning what might become a science into a tumbling ground for whimsies". The third stage involves a kind of hallowing or mystification of one member of the dichotomy, usually that which is less orthodox or understood. This seems most evident when the idea becomes popularised and commercially exploited, and we witness a further abandoning of scientific standards.

We readily perceive these three phases in the development and popularisation of the "unconscious mind" and "right brain"; the same fate appears to have befallen other concepts and phenomena—e.g. the notion of "hypnotic trance" (versus the "waking state"); "direct" versus "indirect suggestions" appears to have gone this way too and perhaps, further afield, "convergent" versus "divergent thinking" and "orthodox" versus "alternative medicine". We leave the reader to think of others.

Hypnosis and the Unconscious Mind

We perceive at least three areas in hypnotherapy where the concept of the unconscious may prove useful but where an over-reliance leads to the inappropriate application of hypnosis, not merely by the lay practitioner:

1. It is useful to speak of "implanting suggestions in the unconscious mind" of the patient as a way of conveying the idea that the responses have an automatic and involuntary quality as distinct from being deliberate acts of compliance. However, the simple idea that patients' problems arise because the unconscious mind is at fault and can be reprogrammed by appropriate hypnotic suggestions can, as we remarked in Chapter 5, tempt therapists into trying to treat quite severe and complex problems such as depression using suggestion and ego-strengthening rituals. Moreover, we also discern a curious assumption that instructions not received or comprehended at a conscious level must *ipso facto* have an especially potent effect on the unconscious mind. In this regard, we may mention the use of subliminal perception tapes and indirect or metaphorical techniques (see Chapters 5 and 7, and Heap, 1987; 1988d). True, an instruction or request may in some circumstances be more likely to be acted upon if the recipient is not given the opportunity to examine its consequences critically and maybe offer some resistance. We question how much one can realistically build, in the manner of some of the Ericksonians, an entire treatment strategy based on this one idea (see also Kirmayer, 1988).

2. It may at times prove useful to convey to patients the idea that the unconscious mind is a sort of repository of all the skills, knowledge, and learning that they have acquired throughout life, including the resources to overcome the presenting problems. Many patients worry incessantly about circumstances which, when they do arise, they have the means to cope with quite effectively. Their conscious effort and energy appears to be useless and wasteful. A good example to cite is the tip-of-the-tongue phenomenon, when *not* trying to find the answer appears to be at least as productive as trying. However, as Hammond (1988) remarks, the assumption that the patient's unconscious mind has all the answers and that the principle therapeutic manouevre is to hypnotise patients and inform them that their unconscious mind will solve the problem ("Trust your unconscious" being a current cliché) is a tempting invitation for therapists to abandon their own conscious efforts to understand and help their patients. At best, this metaphor of the unconscious mind should be used sparingly and incidentally to the main therapeutic programme.

3. The notion that the source of the problem lies repressed in the patient's unconscious mind and that via hypnosis this may be brought into conscious awareness is again a useful but limited model of therapy. We have earlier discussed

the various exploratory procedures which have been devised with this paradigm in mind. However, again by taking the model literally and simplistically, we can over-extend it into areas of theorising and practice in which its application is quite inappropriate and misleading. There appear, for instance, to be some practitioners who age-regress their patients as a matter of course on the premise that for every psychological difficulty there is an associated incident possibly of a traumatic nature, the memory of which the patient has repressed in his or her unconscious mind, and that recovery of this memory is essential to resolve the problem.

There are indeed reports in the literature which suggest convincingly that a patient's problems may occasionally be referable to the dissociated memory of a traumatic incident, the uncovering of which may be facilitated by hypnosis and lead to symptom remission. For example, Hart (1984) describes two long-standing phobic patients whom he regressed to childhood and in whom satisfactory therapeutic changes were observed after only two sessions. He admits, however, that such rapid results are atypical. Degun and Degun (1977) report the spontaneous regression and abreaction of an agoraphobic and claustrophobic patient; the traumatic incident was his being locked in the lavatory at the age of three. Both sets of symptoms disappeared after this one session. Less dramatic than these is the case of Deborah described earlier; however, it did not seem that in this instance recovery of the painful memory itself was a critical ingredient since the patient was fully aware of it prior to hypnosis.

In reality, the experiences of clinicians, clinical researchers, and patients alike indicate that it is relatively rare for a psychological problem to be clearly linked with one incident in the patient's life. It is more likely to be associated with a combination of factors in the patient's past and present circumstances. This point was made in the earlier discussion on abreaction. Consequently, adherence to naïve formulations concerning the unconscious mind may lead the therapist down false avenues in the theory and application of hypnosis.

The Question of Compliance and Collusion

Consider these two case reports, typical of the writings which appear in books popularising hypnosis. The first one is taken from *Superpsych: the power of hypnosis* by T. Hall and G. Grant (London: Abacus, 1978).

> A man in his sixties presented with a tic whereby his head was drawn to his chest and twisted sideways. The therapist regressed him to the age of five and uncovered the memory of his mother taking him into his grandmother's bedroom and pulling back the sheet to reveal her lying there dead. The therapist concluded that "The spasm was nothing more than an unconscious attempt by the boy to turn away from the bed". Fortunately, the condition was improved by the use of ego-strengthening.

The following case report is taken from *I heard every word: hypnotherapy explained* by D. Lesser (The Curative Hypnotherapy Examination Committee, 1986).

> A sixty-two year old lady was concerned to reduce weight because of a heart condition, but she was quite unable to do so. Hypnosis revealed that, as a child, she was very ill with diphtheria and her mother had told her "You must eat, Mummy knows best, it will take away the pain. It will make you better." The therapist believed that the mother's remarks were an unconscious trigger for the patient's continuing to overeat. After treatment, she was able to reduce weight.

These tales have a certain fascination and no doubt this is enhanced by the fact that the patients were reported to improve, although whether this improvement was related to their recalling the events is open to question. As accounts or how the problems were acquired, they are, given a little thought, thoroughly unconvincing. Consider that in the lives of all of us, there must nave been times when we have wanted to turn away from some unhappy or frightening scene; or that there can be few of us who on one or more occasions were not given some dire parental warning about not eating our food. So, if the therapist and patient set out in search of such specious explanations for the presenting problems one can safely bet on their coming up with something that will fit the requirements. Collusion of this nature is familiar to anyone who has surveyed the field of forensic hypnosis; here the propensity of the hypnotised eye-witness to provide the interrogator with some useful evidence, and the eagerness of the interrogator to receive it, may result in an unproductive and time-wasting interaction for both parties (see Chapter 1, and Mingay, 1988).

In fact Wagstaff (1981) argues that the phenomena of hypnosis may largely be explained as the subject's way of complying with the demands and expectations of the hypnotist and do not entail being in an altered state. We do not subscribe to this interpretation of hypnosis but there is no reason to suppose that such processes cannot characterise some interactions labelled (wrongly, in our formulation) "hypnotic". Finally, we note a similar phenomenon in experimental psychology known as the "experimenter effect" whereby the desired results of an experiment are anticipated by the implicit collusion of the subject and experimenter. This has been well documented (Rosenthal, 1963) but corresponding research in psychological therapy is lacking.

This problem is not insurmountable if therapists adopt a more client-centred stance (as was recommended in our discussion of the affect bridge technique) and recognise that the paradigm they have chosen on which to base their communications with their patients may not necessarily be the one most suitable for the patients themselves.

Hypnotic Techniques as Aids to Communication

To understand this line of thinking consider the case of Simon, presented earlier. One likely explanation of the reported changes in his behaviour (the virtual disappearance of bed-wetting and his increased assertiveness) is that they were normal developmental signs and were unrelated to his therapy. Also, as we have discussed above, his responses to the imr procedures described in his final session of therapy may well have merely been his endeavour to comply with the demands and expectations of his therapist. But if any therapeutic value did accrue from this session, what kind of processes might have been involved?

Certainly the notion that the hypnoanalytical techniques described in this chapter enable one to communicate with a separate part of the patient's mind, termed "the unconscious", does not advance us very far. Perhaps a more tangible and realistic interpretation is that such manoeuvres as age-regression, imaginary screen and theatre fantasies, ego states, and imr signalling facilitate the patients' ability to *communicate within themselves*—that is, to become more aware of dissociated thoughts, feelings, memories, and fantasies—and second, to *communicate to the therapist* (or anyone else they may choose) whatever they discover from these inner explorations. In Simon's case, for example, it may have been that the kind of interaction constructed by the therapist enabled him to do what he possibly had not done before (maybe out of anxiety or guilt), namely to explore his own thoughts and feelings for any conceivable association of his bed-wetting with the rest of his life—his daily experiences, conflicts, his way of handling his emotions, and so on. Moreover, he was enabled to share this with another person, even in so limited a way as lifting a finger, and to start to think how he might behave differently. The therapist's task, then, is principally to facilitate the above lines of communication by way of *his or her own* communications with the patient—warmth, empathy, and acceptance—and by selecting appropriate contexts, of which hypnosis and the hypnotic procedures discussed are examples. This, after all, is the goal of any system of psychotherapy, and indeed in everyday situations when one person endeavours to help another.

7 Hypnosis in Psychosomatic Medicine

This chapter examines the role of hypnosis in the treatment and management of problems which are, for various reasons, labelled "physical" or "medical" rather than "psychological". It is debatable to what degree such a distinction holds up under scrutiny. Problems of a "psychogenic" nature, such as anxiety states, give rise to physical symptoms, some of which may acquire a chronic status (such as cardiovascular or gastrointestinal problems) and complaints generally referred to as "medical" may precipitate or be aggravated by psychological problems. Indeed, the distinction may sometimes be a hindrance. Some patients will construe as pejorative any interpretation of their condition as "psychological" and will only be satisfied with a diagnosis which they perceive as "organic". These attitudes may be seen in current preoccupations with alternative explanations for mental and behavioural disturbances, such as food allergies and dietary deficiencies. The authors' impression, however, is that where a "medical" condition has been formally identified, the notion of psychological treatment is quite acceptable to the patient.

Returning to the scope of this chapter, we can define several areas of application of hypnosis in the medical context.

AREAS OF APPLICATION IN MEDICINE

Overcoming Destructive Habits

When the patient's condition arises from, or is exacerbated by, a destructive habit (e.g. alcohol abuse leading to liver disease, or smoking aggravating bronchitis) hypnosis may be part of a programme of therapy intended to help the patient overcome that habit. Also, the evidence for the deleterious effects of a stressful lifestyle on immunity to illness (see later) speaks in favour of a role for hypnosis in preventive medicine. These applications are not discussed here and the reader is referred to Chapters 5 and 6 for applications to behaviour therapy and psychotherapy.

The Alleviation and Management of Medical Complaints

Hypnosis may be incorporated into the treatment and management of a wide range of medical complaints. In some of these conditions, such as those loosely described as "psychosomatic", there may be good evidence of contributory psychological factors in the aetiology and maintenance of the symptoms, and the literature usually acknowledges the value of psychological approaches to treatment. There are, however, certain other conditions which, although not often regarded as having significant psychological predisposing factors, nevertheless appear to respond to hypnotic procedures aimed at symptom alleviation. The use of hypnosis in the healing of burns and the control of bleeding are two examples to be discussed in this chapter. We may also mention that, to a limited degree, psychological approaches such as hypnosis and imagery are being employed as possible healing strategies in the treatment of diseases such as the cancers (Meares, 1982/83; Newton, 1982/83; Simonton, Matthews-Simonton, & Creighton, 1978), although this is a rather more controversial application.

Hypnosis may also be used to help patients cope with the pain, discomfort, and distress of illness; that is, their perception of their symptoms and the way they react to them may benefit significantly even if there is no alteration at the somatic level. Hence hypnosis may be applied effectively in the relief of chronic pain (see Chapter 8). In other chronic illnesses, hypnosis may help the patient adopt a positive attitude to coping and to live as independent and normal a life as is realistic within the constraints imposed by the illness. For example, the use of confidence-boosting suggestions and imagery in the case of a patient with multiple sclerosis is described in Chapter 5.

Alleviating the Pain and Distress of Medical Treatment

Hypnosis may help patients to cope with certain medical interventions which give rise to pain, discomfort, and anxiety. It may therefore be useful as an alternative or supplement to analgesic and tranquilising medication. Such interventions include dental procedures discussed in Chapter 11, and surgical procedures, chemotherapy for cancer patients, renal dialysis, and gynaecological examination, which are all discussed in Chapter 9. The use of hypnosis in obstetrics is reviewed in Chapter 10.

This chapter will consider the second of the areas of application listed above. Some general points will first be addressed and the application of hypnosis in a number of specific conditions will be briefly presented.

GENERAL CONSIDERATIONS

Whereas the use of hypnosis as an augmentative procedure in behaviour therapy and psychotherapy presents the reader with a rather confused picture in terms of definition and efficacy (Chapters 5 and 6), the application of hypnosis in the amelioration of psychosomatic illnesses is somewhat clearer. This is because for such problems hypnosis tends to be applied in a direct symptom-oriented fashion and practitioners have thereby been able to generate a set of procedures which may be administered with a reasonable degree of standardisation and replicability. Thus, as we shall see later, it has been possible to conduct, for specific problems such as asthma and migraine, clinical trials which endeavour to meet satisfactory criteria of scientific rigour and objectivity. Such work has proved extremely promising. It has been noted in Chapter 4 that surveys of the literature, such as that of Wadden and Anderton (1982) have concluded that hypnosis *is* an effective component in at least some conditions with an "involuntary" somatic component (e.g. asthma, organic pain, and warts) and in support of this is the impression that hypnotic susceptibility is a significant determining factor in response to treatment. This evidence and that of studies to be mentioned later, indicate that hypnotic suggestion may have specific effects at the somatic level. The mechanisms underlying such effects and their scope and limitations remain to be explicated, and this is an important field for the researcher, as is the question why some people respond better than others.

General and Specific Effects of Hypnotic Treatment

Before we outline the various types of hypnotic suggestion that may be employed in the alleviation of psychosomatic disorders it is useful to distinguish between the *general* effects of hypnotic treatment on a particular condition and the *specific* effects. This is a loose distinction and is not intended as a clear dichotomy. General effects include the placebo value of the treatment and the effectiveness of hypnosis as a relaxation procedure which it shares with other techniques (see Chapter 4). For many conditions such as migraine, asthma, and gastrointestinal complaints, which may be mediated or aggravated by over-arousal of the autonomic nervous system (ANS), relaxation training and stress reduction may be the main ingredient of the therapeutic programme. Other general effects, possibly potentiated by relaxation training, may include a renewed commitment on the part of the patient to a healthier lifestyle and to any other treatments which have been recommended. For example, the asthmatic patient may make a more determined effort to reduce smoking, the eczema sufferer may resume applying creams and ointments previously abandoned and be extra vigilant for any impulse to scratch, while the patient with an irritable bowel may resolve to be more selective in his or her diet. These therapeutic changes are not unique to hypnosis and they indicate the importance of a theraputic relationship based upon good rapport, mutual trust, and confidence, an expectation of success by both parties, and a high degree of commitment, again on both sides[1].

It is also believed that stress and undue anxiety impair the functioning of the body's immune system and render the individual more likely to succumb to ill-health through infection (see Bowers & Kelly, 1979). Consequently, the encouragement of a positive attitude as well as the adoption of a more relaxed lifestyle may strengthen the body's resistance to illness, and this may be another non-specific effect of hypnotic treatment. A large common denominator of hypnotic approaches to psychosomatic conditions does indeed consist of basic relaxation techniques and non-specific positive suggestions including ego-strengthening; self-hypnosis is practised daily, often using a cassette tape of the whole hypnotic session. Such general methods, which use many of the techniques outlined in Chapter 5, may be quite effective. However, as well as general effects such as placebo and relaxation, we also need to consider specific effects, namely those attributable to the therapeutic suggestions selectively focused on the symptoms particular to the patient's complaint. In Chapter 4 we discussed the nature of therapeutic suggestions and agreed that where possible these should be directed at basic levels of responding—i.e. discrete bodily reactions, cognitions,and behaviours, rather than higher level processes such as complex feelings and attitudes of mind (happiness, confidence, etc.)

Such therapeutic suggestions usually indicate to the patient the processes and changes which result in some allevation of the pathological condition. A scan of the literature reveals that practitioners have employed a number of different types of suggestion and whether all are effective to the same degree is not clear. Nearly all may be accompanied by relevant imagery, but again the extent to which this is contributory to outcome remains to be demonstrated.

Types of Suggestion and Imagery

Suggestions that the Affected Somatic Area or Organ is Healing. Here no attempt is made to describe to the patient the process whereby healing will be effected. There are obviously limitless applications of this type of suggestion; in the literature it is commonly used in the treatment of dermatological conditions such as warts, burns, and eczema (see later). Appropriate imagery may be employed—e.g. lying in the sun or being immersed in the sea or a lake, in the case of eczema. Sometimes age-regression to a premorbid stage may be used. For example, in the

[1] If such is the case, then the utility of commercially prepared cassette tapes for the treatment of such conditions as asthma and eczema is called into question, because no therapist is actively involved.

rehabilitative treatment of a stroke patient, Manganiello (1986) regressed the patient to the age of 10 years with suggestions of recovery of motor function.

This is obviously a controversial area of application and brings us into the realms of faith healing. What mechanisms are involved, what the limits of such suggestion and imagery are, and whether there is indeed a true specific effect, are matters for further investigation. Nevertheless, dramatic improvements are sometimes reported, as in Mason's (1952) case of congenital multiple warts, referred to later.

Suggestion and Imagery Describing Organic Processes that may bring about Remediation of the Condition. Such suggestions are often directed at specific autonomic processes such as vascular, bronchial or gastrointestinal activity. Examples are, in the case of asthma, imagining the bronchial pathways allowing the smooth and uninterrupted passage of air to and from the lungs and, in the case of irritable bowel, imagery of a quiet, resting bowel. Often, such suggestions require the therapist to first educate the patient on the nature of the disorder. Also, as with the first type of suggestion, age-regression to a premorbid period may augment such imagery.

Consideration of this type of approach now brings us back to the issue of the general versus specific effects of hypnosis and hypnotic suggestion, and we need to examine two further questions. The first is "What kinds of involuntary functions may be selectively influenced by suggestion?", and second "To what extent does the patient's response to such suggestions mediate therapeutic change?"

Everyday experience confirms that in an attentive subject we may intentionally influence selective involuntary functions by simple verbal communication. For example, salivation may be increased by suggesting that the person is eating a sour-tasting fruit; other examples are blushing (dilation of the facial blood vessels) and vomiting. In the hypnotic literature there is evidence for the selective effects of suggestion on hand temperature and peripheral circulation (Barabasz & McGeorge, 1978; Bishay & Lee, 1984; Grabowska, 1971) and, as we shall see, practitioners have attempted to exploit this in the treatment of certain vascular conditions.

Such suggestions may involve the use of imagery, either of the circumstances in which the change would occur (e.g. eating a lemon in the case of salivation) or of the actual changes themselves (e.g. imagining the blood vessels dilating in the case of hand-warming). Olness and Conroy (1985) remark on the apparent proficiency which children demonstrate in acquiring and maintaining voluntary control of autonomic activity. In their experiment, reported in more detail in Chapter 12, children learned to increase tissue oxygen by imagining the process actually taking place. Likewise, Olness, Culbert, and Uden (1989) have demonstrated the ability of children to elevate their salivary immunoglobulin A concentrations. These are known to be lowered in subjects when they are experiencing stress (Jemmott et al., 1983) but the control conditions in Olness et al.'s study indicated that the changes were not simply due to relaxation. There have been quite a number of studies now on the influence of imagery and suggestion on immunological activity, and these and their possible significance have been reviewed by several authors (e.g. Bowers & Kelly, 1979; Hall 1982/83; Jemmott & Locke, 1984).

As yet no significant therapeutic advantage is evident for these types of imagery, which brings us to the second question—whether the suggested physiological changes do in fact mediate recovery. If this were so we should expect that those patients who most successfully modify the targeted autonomic functions would show the greatest therapeutic benefits. Limited evidence from clinical studies, to be reported later, involving suggested peripheral temperature changes (e.g. Dane, Note 6; Friedman & Taub, 1985) does not bear out this prediction. This is somewhat paradoxical in that those patients who are higher in measured hypnotic susceptibility usually show a more favourable outcome (Wadden & Anderton, 1982). Probably the physiological models on which the hypnotic treatments are based are too simplistic, and the determinants of a good therapeutic response are rather more complex than merely modifying the autonomic function presumed to underly the particular disorder. Some of the findings on the clinical efficacy of biofeedback (Andrasik & Holroyd, 1980; Blanchard & Andrasik, 1982; Epstein & Abel, 1977) have presented a similar picture.

Post-hypnotic Suggestion of Appropriate Responses in Specific Situations. Examples of these are hyperventilation control in asthma (Wilkinson, 1988a,b), the extinction of the scratching response in eczema, and appropriate eliminatory behaviour in the case of urinary incontinence. For instance a post-hypnotic suggestion for a patient with eczema may be, to quote Hartland, (1971, p.295): "If...at any time...unknowingly, you *do* begin to scratch...*the moment your fingers touch your skin...you will immediately know what you are about to do...and you will be able to exercise sufficient self-control to stop yourself...before you have done any damage at all*".

The Use of Hypnotic Phenomena as a Means of Demonstrating Autonomic Control. Occasionally, therapists have elicited common hypnotic phenomena in their patients and used this experience to suggest that they will be able to control other physiological functions such as those pertaining to their problem. Golan (1986) illustrates how four hypnotic phenomena (relaxation, glove anaesthesia, hand temperature change, and arm catalepsy) may thus be utilised. For example, a patient had bad breath for no apparent physical reason, and it was therefore presumed to be the result of excessive gastric secretions associated with anxiety. She was first taught to control her hand temperature and it was then explained that as she was able to control the flow of blood in her hand, so she would be able to control the gastric secretions which were giving rise to her bad breath.

Indirect Suggestions and the Use of Metaphor. Some practitioners have extolled the use of indirect, metaphorical or anecdotal imagery and suggestions. For instance, mention was made in Chapter 5 of a case of tinnitus, described by Erickson and Rossi (1979) in which the therapist (Erickson) recounts to the patient the story of how he himself had naturally adjusted to the din of machinery in a factory where he slept the night. An example of a suggestion for asthma sufferers used by one of the authors (M. Heap) is to remind them (if appropriate) of how they use a bicycle pump to inflate a tyre. (They adjust the rhythm and force; too strong and they meet with resistance, but not too weak either—just right to get an efficient rhythmical flow of air, etc.) This example illustrates the use of material from the patient's relevant learning experiences to construct the metaphor. Further examples are given in Chapter 12 in the treatment of children.

The Problems of Need and Secondary Gain

We have centred much of our discussion thus far on methods which are concerned with directly alleviating the symptoms of psychosomatic and other medical disorders. The reader may rightly enquire as to whether these methods are not limited when the disorder may perhaps serve some purpose in the life of the patient. Such purposes may be construed from a behavioural standpoint, as in the case of a disorder which is reinforced by the reactions of others; perhaps having it results in the sufferer gaining more attention and consideration from his or her family than would otherwise be received, or allows the sufferer to avoid irksome responsibilities. It would be easy, however, for the therapist to interpret a patient's *gain* from having the symptoms as a *need* for them; the gain may represent poor compensation for the suffering involved. Clearly, much depends on the balance between the negative and positive consequences of having the problem, and whether the positive consequences may be realised by other readily available means. Another possibility is that the original gains are no longer operative but the patient's condition has persisted, perhaps almost through habit. For instance, a patient's asthma may at one time have exerted a very desirable controlling influence on the family, and therefore may have proved resistant to direct treatment, but with the patient now having moved away from home, the secondary rewards may be weaker and the condition more amenable to therapy.

From the psychodynamic standpoint some authors have reported that in certain cases psychosomatic disorders may be linked to some past, and often unrecalled, traumatic incident or incidents and the emotional conflicts—anxiety, anger,and guilt—associated therewith (e.g. Barnett, 1981). Perhaps more common is the assertion that the habitual failure to express certain emotions may result in various psychosomatic conditions, for example that migraine may be associated with unexpressed anger and hostility (Alpers & Mancall, 1971). Such formulations are not entirely incompatible with behavioural or cognitive schools; the patient may lack the skills of self-assertiveness or may have distorted cognitions of the catastrophic sort regarding the consequences of displaying emotions (e.g. "I must never upset anyone"). Again it may be that patients will, during the course of therapy, discover for themselves more satisfactory ways of handling such emotions, but it may also be desirable for the therapist to help them become more aware of and resolve such feelings more constructively from whatever standpoint adopted—behavioural, cognitive or psychodynamic.

It may therefore be useful, though by no means always necessary, for the therapist to explore more thoroughly the role of the symptoms in the patient's life. One straightforward method is to ask the patient to monitor the symptoms and the circumstances in which they occur, on a daily basis. Scrutiny of these records may indicate strong associations between the occurrence of the symptoms and incidents in the emotional, cognitive or behavioural life of the individual. If such associations appear to be particularly compelling, the therapist may consider that a specialised therapeutic approach (e.g. family therapy, relationships counselling, cognitive therapy or assertiveness training) may be required, with or without the adjunctive use of hypnosis. Another common exploratory method is to ask the hypnotised patient for a "Yes" or "No" ideo-motor signal (see Chapter 6) to questions such as "Is your problem concerned with some event in the past which is still troubling you?", "Is there any reason for your having your problem now?", or "Is there any part of you which would find it difficult to do without your problem?". A regression technique which is very useful in this kind of exploratory work with psychosomatic disorders is the somatic bridge, derived from the affect bridge and discussed in Chapter 6.

Finally, it has been suggested by some psychoanalytically oriented therapists (e.g. Hand & Lamontagne, 1976) that if patients are "robbed of a symptom" they will develop others. In fact, as was pointed out by Clarke and Jackson (1983), there is very little evidence for this; more likely, if patients "need" a disorder they will not relinquish it when a direct symptom-oriented approach is adopted.

Precautions and Contra-indications

Hypnosis is a relatively benign procedure and usually the most unfortunate outcome is that the patient does not respond to treatment and is understandably upset and disappointed. One may forestall a catastrophic reaction to this by not offering the patient an unrealistic goal; it does not help to speak in terms of "cure", but rather of helping to alleviate the symptoms and the patient's reaction to them. Non-medical therapists are advised to consult fully with the patient's general practitioner particularly in potentially life-threatening conditions such as asthma. It is often rightly stated that the practitioner should not attempt to treat a condition with hypnosis before the appropriate medical investigations have been performed. This of course applies to all psychological treatments, but in reality it does not amount to much of an issue; it is almost invariably the case that the patient will already have consulted his or her GP and possibly other medical specialists, and it is their responsibility to ensure that the patient's condition is given the proper medical attention. Also, within our Health Service the referral system and the practice of multidisciplinary teamwork ensure that patients are medically screened before psychological therapy is undertaken. In fact, in the opinion of the authors, much more common is the unfortunate case of the individual with a fundamentally psychological difficulty or life problem being treated entirely as a medical patient.

Although it is quite possible for psychosomatic and other medical conditions to be treated hypnotically without the hypnotist's having much understanding of the disorder in question, it is desirable that the non-medically qualified practitioner should be familiar with the pathology of the condition. Although it is easy to make too much of the "dangers" of hypnosis (which may be no more than any other psychological technique or treatment) nothing short of the utmost concern for the safety and well-being of the patient will suffice. Precautions need to be taken in the treatment of asthmatic patients, where the non-medical practitioner would be well advised to see them in a medical setting. Only those well experienced in the treatment of asthma should contemplate any interventions, such as regressive work, which may provoke an asthmatic attack, and the patient's medication should be readily accessible to him or her at all times. Wilkinson (1988b) has warned against attempting direct symptom removal by suggestion, which may encourage the patient to reduce the force of the respiratory flow below a safe level. Also with asthma, as with other disorders, patients should not be made to feel obliged to withhold medication for fear of experiencing a sense of failure should medical treatment be required. Likewise, care should be taken to ensure that those patients whose activities are curtailed by their condition should not attempt to extend themselves beyond what is reasonably within their capabilities. It is much better to proceed too slowly than to try to exceed what is realistic for the patient.

Indications for a Positive Outcome

Our impression from an overview of the literature and actual clinical experience is that if patients are going to respond positively to a symptom-oriented approach they will start to do so fairly early in treatment, and if no improvement is evident after the first few sessions the therapist may need to reconsider his or her approach. Generally the practitioner will find that those patients respond best who are well motivated and committed to the regular practice of self-hypnosis, who have, in conditions such as asthma, clear psychological concomitants to their disorder, and who are at least capable of a light state of hypnosis. The practitioner with enough time may consider performing an initial assessment of hypnotic susceptibility (see Chapter 3); this often yields useful information concerning the subject's ability to visualise, relax, concentrate, and so on; these data may contribute to a data pool which in time may provide indications for patient and treatment selection.

Group Treatment

In a busy general practice, clinic or specialised unit, lack of time and resources may preclude many of the preparatory procedures and refinements discussed here. Nevertheless, even the most restricted intervention may be better than none at all, and most of the procedures discussed may be, and indeed often are, conducted in groups, provided rapport is not too adversely compromised and the therapist is sufficiently attentive to individual requirements.

The Importance of Follow-up

In many studies reviewed, patients have been offered follow-up appointments after periods of months and even years. This may prove useful in the individual case in order to check on the maintenance of progress and perhaps to provide booster treatment at times of relapse.

SPECIFIC DISORDERS

Headaches

By and large, the behavioural treatment of both migraine and non-migraine headaches has comprised the regular practice of relaxation and tension reduction procedures using, amongst other techniques, progressive relaxation, muscle tension (EMG) biofeedback (tension headaches), thermal biofeedback (migraine headaches), hypnosis, and autogenic training (Blanchard & Andrasik, 1985; Drummond, 1981; Edmonston, 1981). Blanchard and Andrasik (1985) also describe a cognitive therapeutic approach to the treatment of headaches and have a useful discussion on assessment procedures including a "headache diary".

The benefits of hypnotic relaxation and suggestion for headache patients have been reported by Cedercreutz, Lähteenmäki, and Tulikoura (1976a,b) and Carasso, Kleinhauz, Peded, and Yehuda (1985). In the former study, three or four group sessions were usually sufficient, while in the latter, nine group and individual sessions were used and patients performed self-relaxation twice daily.

The treatment of migraine headache may be conducted along similar lines and the reader may consult Chapter 5 for ideas on tension reduction. However, certain refinements may be incorporated which are specific to the pathology of this type of headache. It has been suggested (Adams, Feuerstein, & Fowler, 1980; Bakal, 1975; Graham & Wolff, 1938) that in the prodromal phase of migraine there is a constriction of the cranial blood vessels immediately followed by a compensatory dilation which is responsible for symptoms such as pain, nausea, and dizziness. Therefore, as well as suggestions of relaxation and the regular practice of self-hypnosis, suggestions may be given, with suitable imagery, for redistribution of the blood supply. Although, as was noted earlier, peripheral vasodilation may occur anyway during hypnosis and relaxation, Edmonston (1981) in his review has concluded that specific suggestions may be an active component in the treatment of migraine. The changes may be suggested directly by asking the patient to imagine the process of constriction of the cranial arteries (Anderson, Basker, & Dalton, 1975) or by imagining the hands becoming warmer using imagery such as immersing them in warm water (Alladin, 1988). This presumably leads to peripheral vasodilation and redistribution of the blood supply away from the head region. Hand-warming via biofeedback is another technique often used in the treatment of migraine, and there does not appear to be much difference in the effectiveness of these two procedures (Andreychuk & Skriver, 1975; Friedman & Taub, 1984, 1985; Graham, 1975). Graham (1975) found no clinical advantage in combining these two methods, although this did lead to more rapid hand-warming.

Alladin (1988) has remarked on some discrepancies in the literature, namely between those authors who use hand-warming and those who suggest anaesthesia. In his study he found that a group of migraine patients trained in hypnotic relaxation, hand-warming and ego-strengthening improved more than patients who underwent the same treatment except that the suggestions were for glove anaesthesia, using imagery of immersion of the hand in cold, as opposed to warm, water. These suggestions appeared to compromise the main theraputic ingredient, namely relaxation. Alladin's explanation is that cooling is a sympathetic response, resulting from vasoconstriction, and this is antagonistic to the relaxation response, whereas warming is directly associated with relaxation. In fact, in Alladin's study, a group trained in progressive and selective muscular relaxation, without suggestions of thermal control, did as well at 13-month follow-up as those who received hypnosis and suggestions of warmth. A fourth treatment group who received hypnosis and direct suggestion of symptom removal did significantly less well than either the relaxation or the hand-warming group on measures of duration, frequency, and intensity of headache, and use of medication. These results indicate that suggestion and imagery of hand-warming, and by implication peripheral vasodilation, may indeed be effective in the alleviation of migraine, but perhaps this may be achieved just as well by a programme of training in progressive and selective relaxation. But we must also await the results of further physiological studies: Friedman and Taub (1985) found no relationship between outcome of therapy and peripheral temperature change during treatment.

In general, procedures described as "hypnotic" appear to give good results (Alladin, 1988; Anderson et al., 1975; Andreychuk & Skriver, 1975; Basker, 1970; Berlin & Erdmann, 1987; Daniels, 1977; Davidson, 1987; Friedman & Taub, 1985; Graham, 1975). The practitioner, then, may be confidently advised when treating migraine, to use a hypnotic procedure emphasising both general relaxation and hand-warming and perhaps appropriate vascular changes. Ego-strengthening suggestions may also be incorporated into the hypnotic script, and the hypnotic session may be recorded on tape for daily (or even more frequent) use by the patient. Inspection of Alladin's data (Alladin, 1984) indicates that improvement may have reached a plateau by the sixth session. Friedman and Taub (1985) recommend at least yearly follow-ups; at a three year follow-up, while 78% of patients rated their headaches as "better", their headache diaries indicated that frequency and intensity of attacks had returned to baseline. And while all of Alladin's (1988) hand-warming group were greatly improved, some studies (e.g. Andreychuk & Skriver, 1975; Cedercreutz, 1978) have found a better outcome for those higher in hypnotic susceptibility. One final recommendation (Alladin, personal communication) is that patients should be advised that their treatment is prophylactic and that, as well as practising their self-hypnosis regularly, they should take action at the first sign of an attack.

Hypertension

Quite a number of therapeutic programmes have been described for the management of hypertensive patients and these invariably require them to practise some sort of relaxation or self-control technique such as Jacobson's progressive relaxation (Deabler, Fidel, Dillenkoffer, & Elder, 1973), yoga (Patel, 1973, 1975), biofeedback (Blanchard & Young, 1974; Patel, 1973, 1975), autogenic training (Luthe, 1972), and meditation (Benson, Rosner, Marzetta, & Klemchuk, 1974).

Many of the hypnotic procedures described in Chapter 5 may be appropriately applied in this context. For example, Milne (1985) evaluated the efficacy of hetero-hypnosis and a twice-daily session of self-hypnosis in 30 patients with essential hypertension. Patients were seen at weekly intervals for the first month, then once every four weeks. The total number of sessions ranged from 8 to 18. There were follow-ups at 18 months and three years, when only 15 of the original 30 patients were contactable. Of these, five were considered to be successful. Those who were well-motivated and had initially relatively high blood pressure and anxiety appeared to be more likely to benefit. Friedman and Taub (1977, 1978) have reported a more favourable outcome for hypnosis compared to biofeedback in hypertensive patients. Each patient received seven treatment sessions and reductions were evident for both systolic and diastolic pressure. Similar results were found on a six-month follow-up. As in Graham's (1975) study of migraine, no advantage was incurred by combining hypnosis and biofeedback. The practitioner should be wary of doing this as in some contexts the two procedures may involve incompatible processes (see Sigman, 1988), although we shall see in Chapter 8 that they may sometimes be usefully combined in the treatment of pain.

Haemophilia

The use of hypnotic procedures in the management of haemophilia again raises questions about the general and specific effects of hypnosis. It has been noted (Agle & Mattson, 1976; Mattson & Agle, 1979) that episodes of spontaneous bleeding may occur at times of stress or emotional upheaval, and it may be that clotting factor levels, platelet function, and other blood constituents can be likewise affected (Clemenow, King, & Brantley, 1984). Therefore a programme aimed at general stress reduction and relaxation training may be all that is required. This is essentially the procedure adopted by Swirsky-Sacchetti & Margolis (1986) with a group of 15 haemophiliac patients compared with an equivalent control group. The treatment group underwent a six-week programme in small groups in which they were educated on the nature of stress and its possible involvement in their problem; they were also trained in self-hypnosis, with ego-strengthening and suggestions of decreased bleeding. Tape-recordings were prepared for daily usage and rapid inductions (one-to-two minutes) were taught as a means of coping with stressful experiences encountered during the day. There was an 18-week follow-up and it was found that the treatment group significantly reduced their usage of coagulant factor concentrate compared to the controls, while their measured levels of general distress also improved. One problem of interpretation in this study was that outcome did not correlate with hypnotic susceptibility, and as was argued in Chapter 4, this raises doubts as to whether hypnosis itself was an active ingredient in the therapy. Similar work has been reported by LaBaw (1975). It should be mentioned here that LeBaron and Zeltzer (1984) have pointed out the limitations of patients' reports of factor concentrate usage as an index of treatment outcome, since they may not actually correspond to any significant clinical changes.

Several writers have used more specific suggestions of bleeding control. It was noted earlier in this chapter that some vascular processes appear susceptible to hypnotic suggestion, so that some control of bleeding may be effected by direct hetereo- and auto-hypnotic suggestion, say via vasospasm or even by influencing the coagulation process itself (Hilgard & Hilgard, 1983). Illustrative examples of this approach for the control of bleeding in dentistry are given in Chapter 11, and later in this chapter in a case of gastrointestinal bleeding (Bishay, Stevens, & Lee, 1984).

It is not possible at present to say whether such specific suggestions add anything more to the general effects of hypnosis, particularly in the prophylactic management of haemophilia, although this is no reason for their conclusion from the hypnotic script. As LeBaron and Zeltzer (1984) have commented, more controlled investigations are required before the role of hypnosis in haemophilia can be adequately defined.

Asthma

There have fortunately been a number of quite extensive clinical trials of hypnosis in the treatment of asthma (see later) and, whereas they often do not allow one to distinguish clearly the relative contributions of the numerous procedures, it appears that the regular practice of various methods of relaxation, including self-hypnosis, plus the use of hetero-hypnosis, therapeutic suggestion, and ego-strengthening together have a beneficial effect with many asthma sufferers. In addition, other approaches, such as exploratory hypnotherapy or family counselling (if the sufferer is a child) may be adopted.

Wilkinson (1988b) recommends that self-hypnosis be employed once a firm diagnosis has been made and long-term maintenance treatment is indicated. He also emphasises the importance of anxiety control and the practice of slow diaphragmatic breathing to control for hyperventilation (see Chapter 5). He points out that wheezing itself may be a trigger for anxiety and a tendency to hyperventilate and thus further increase anxiety. Therefore, slow diaphragmatic breathing may be a useful prelude to the induction of hypnosis. Initially, hypnosis focuses on general relaxation, ego-strengthening, and the teaching of self-hypnosis. The immediate effects of hypnosis on asthma were demonstrated by Ben-Zvi, Spohn, Young, and Kattan (1982); prior to exercising on a treadmill, patients were hypnotised and given positive therapeutic suggestions. Under these conditions there was a 15.9% decrease in forced expiratory volume (FEV) compared with 31.8 % for no treatment and 29.8% for saline placebo. Pre-treatment with cromolyn resulted in a 7.6% decrease in FEV and was consistently superior to hypnosis. The authors concluded that hypnosis can therapeutically alter the bronchospasm after exercise in asthmatic patients.

Maher-Loughnan and his colleagues (Maher-Loughnan & Kinsley, 1968; Maher-Loughnan, Macdonald, Mason, & Fry, 1962) report that greater improvement appears to occur when self-hypnosis is practised for one year as opposed to six months. (This may of course be explained by patients who found self-hypnosis more useful when persisting with its practice.) Maher-Loughnan (1984) also reported that peak improvements tend to occur between the 7th and 12th weeks after the first hypnotic induction and Wilkinson (1988b) recommends that *daily* practice be continued for at least three months after peak improvement. This is to be regarded as prophylactic and not as a substitute for prescribed medication during an acute attack. Further precautions have been discussed earlier.

Other clinical trials have been reported by Collison (1975), Ewer and Stewart (1986), and Moore (1965). Taking all of these studies together, the picture emerges that the treatment of asthma by hypnosis and self-hypnosis leads to some significant improvement in the majority of cases; improvement is more probable for younger, less chronic cases, where there are emotional concomitants, where at least a light state of hypnosis is achieved, where the patient has a high level of commitment to self-hypnosis, and where he or she is not heavily dependent on steroids.

Gastrointestinal Problems

Irritable Bowel Syndrome. Walker (1988) has reviewed the use of hypnosis in the treatment of irritable bowel syndrome (spastic colon, irritable colon, mucous colitis or nervous diarrhoea). In 1984 he described two successful cases; treatment consisted of training in relaxation (practised on tape at home), positive suggestions of symptom relief and ego-strengthening, and imagining coping with situations which aroused anxiety concerning lack of immediate access to a lavatory. In one case the post-hypnotic suggestion was given that in such situations the patient would say to himself: "Stop! I am in control. I do not have to go to the lavatory at this moment. Relax!" The main treatment programmes for these two cases were of five and six sessions.

Successful cases using similar procedures have also been described by Byrne (1973) and Frankel (1975). Whorwell, Prior, and Faragher (1984) (see also

Whorwell, Prior, & Colgan, 1987) report results on 30 cases, in half of whom hypnosis was performed for seven half-hour sessions over a period of three months, with daily self-hypnosis. Outcome for the hypnosis group was superior to that for the controls (psychotherapy and placebo medication) and in all 15 symptoms were rated as "mild" or "absent" following treatment. Harvey, Hinton, Gunary, and Barry (1989) also report the results of 33 patients with refractory irritable bowel syndrome who had four 40-minute sessions of hypnosis over a seven-week period. Twenty were significantly improved, 11 of whom lost almost all of their symptoms. This improvement was maintained at three-month follow-up. Patients treated in groups did as well as those seen individually.

Additional techniques described in the above studies were visualising the smooth passage of stool through the bowels, with the appropriate sphincters in the gastrointestinal tract contracting gently and securely, and, with the patient's hand resting on his or her abdomen, imagining a soothing, penetrating warmth, relaxing and releasing any spasm and allowing the bowels to work smoothly and efficiently.

Walker (1988) advises that in these cases the presence of clinical depression should be considered and, if indicated, anti-depressant medication (with or without cognitive therapy) be prescribed. We should also add that the therapist be alert to the presence of obsessional thinking on the patient's part, which may be addressed by cognitive methods. Also, some patients may have developed considerable phobic anxiety and avoidance behaviour, and a more prolonged course of therapy involving desensitisation or exposure may then be necessary.

Duodenal Ulceration. Colgan, Faragher, and Whorwell (1988) have reported a controlled trial of hypnosis in 30 patients with rapidly relapsing duodenal ulceration. All patients were treated with ranitidine, which was continued for 10 weeks after the ulcer had healed, during which time 15 of the patients had hypnosis treatment. This consisted of seven sessions of hypnotic relaxation with suggestion of symptom alleviation, visualisation of healing, and the hand-on-abdomen method with suggestion of warmth and control of gastric secretion. Twenty-eight weeks following treatment all control patients had relapsed compared to 53% of the hypnotherapy group, who also showed no further relapse at one-year follow-up.

Bishay et al. (1984, p.23) report a single case of an anxious patient with upper gastrointestinal tract bleeding prior to oesophagoscopy and gastroscopy. The patient underwent hypnosis for twenty minutes, one hour before endoscopy under a local anaesthetic; this revealed "non-bleeding gastritis, no ulcer seen". No surgical intervention was deemed necessary. The techniques employed were relaxed breathing, imagining lying on a beach sipping an ice-cold drink while the unconscious mind is "controlling your pulse . . . your blood pressure . . . and your skin vessels . . . you can allow it to control your bleeding completely. It will cool down and close all the bleeding points in your stomach and oesophagus effectively and safely . . . as if it is healing you while you are slowly sipping this refreshing ice-cold drink in your hand . . . "

Nausea and Vomiting. The use of hypnosis to control nausea and vomiting attendant on certain medical procedures is widely reported and is discussed later in Chapter 9. Disorders associated with vomiting may be ameliorated by the use of hypnosis and self-hypnosis. Fuchs, Paldi, Abramovici, and Peretz (1980) present data on the use of hypnotic relaxation and positive suggestions in 138 pregnant women with hyperemesis gravidarum. Between one and three sessions of 45–60 minutes each were sufficient. Group hypnosis gave better results than individual sessions.

Urinary Incontinence

Urinary incontinence or enuresis is usually considered in the context of childhood problems and is discussed from that standpoint in Chapter 12. However, Freeman, and Baxby (1982) report the successful application of hypnosis in a sample of 50 incontinent women with proven detrusor instability. Treatment consisted of 12 sessions of hypnosis, namely relaxation, direct suggestion of symptom removal, and ego-strengthening, over one month. At the end of the 12 sessions, 29 patients were symptom-free and 14 had improved. A three-month follow-up of 44 of the patients revealed stable cystometrograms in 22 patients and a significant improvement in 16

Dermatological Complaints

Although most general texts on hypnosis speak favourably of the use of hypnosis in the amelioration of skin disorders (e.g. Crasilneck & Hall, 1985; Hartland, 1971; Karle & Boys, 1987; Kroger, 1977), with the exception of investigations of warts, there appear to be few, if any, major clinical trials.

There are a number of case reports in the literature involving various dermatological ailments treated both directly or by reference to some presumed underlying maladjustment. Sometimes the results are dramatic, and perhaps these reports collectively do not present the typical picture in everyday practice. For example, Mason (1952) reported obtaining very rapid results using direct hypnotic suggestion in a severe case of multiple warts (ichthyosiform erythrodermia) which, unknown to the hypnotist at the time of treatment, was congenital. Similarly, Bowers (1983) describes his very successful three-month treatment of a patient with a 20-year history of severe hidradenitis suppurative, whose body was covered in postules "the size of silver dollars". Treatment consisted of hypnosis and healing imagery.

There is a fairly substantial literature on hypnosis and warts, including both case reports (Clawson & Swade, 1975; Ewin, 1974; Morris, 1985) and clinical trials (Johnson & Barber, 1978; Sinclair-Gieben & Chalmers, 1959; Spanos, Note 15; Surman, Gottlieb, Hackett, & Silverberg, 1973). Wadden and Anderton (1982) concluded that hypnosis itself and hypnotic susceptibility are both significant factors in treatment. Hypnotic suggestions may be framed directly in terms of removal of the warts, and in fact the therapist probably has considerable leeway in his or her choice of suggestions. For example, Ewin (1974) in his treatment of four patients with genital and anal warts suggested that the patient imagine the affected areas becoming warmer and the blood vessels dilating, bringing a surge of white blood cells to fight the infection. Other practitioners (e.g. Clawson & Swade, 1975; Morris, 1985) have used suggestion and imagery of *vasoconstriction,* the warts being starved of nourishment via the blood supply, and crumbling away.

In the case of other common dermatological conditions such as pruritus, eczema, acne, and psoriasis, reports tend to be in the form of single case presentations or descriptions of common practice (e.g. Frankel & Misch, 1973, Goodman, 1962; Motodo, 1971; Waxman, 1973). As well as relaxation, ego-strengthening, and self-hypnosis, appropriate suggestions and imagery for symptom relief are administered. For example, patients may be asked to imagine lying on a beach feeling the gentle, soothing, warmth of the sun on their body, healing and making the skin smooth, comfortable, and healthy. Another image is that of wading into the sea, gradually going deeper and immersing oneself in the cooling, soothing water. The images chosen must be acceptable to the patient; a non-swimmer would not appreciate the previous suggestions, and if actual exposure to the sun invariably aggravates the condition one would avoid such imagery. On the other hand, where sun and water do prove beneficial to the condition, the patient may be instructed to practise self-suggestion and healing imagery while in the real-life situation. One may also use suggestions of appropriate vascular changes of the type adopted by Ewin (1974) above. Post-hypnotic suggestion of elimination of the scratching response may be forcefully repeated and in some patients transfer of glove anaesthesia to the affected area may be practised.

Shertzer and Lookingbill (1987) studied the effect of hypnotic relaxation in 15 patients with chronic urticaria. Both high and low hypnotisable patients improved; the former, however, had fewer hives and were more likely to regard stress as a causative factor. Five to 14 months later, six patients were free of hives and a further seven reported improvement.

Therapy for Burns

Quite widely documented now is the use of hypnosis with victims of burns (Crasilneck, Stirman, Wilson, McCranie, & Fogelman, 1955; Ewin, 1979, 1986a; 1986b; Schafer, 1975; Wakeman & Kaplan, 1978). Ewin (1986a, p.9) regards the mental state of the patient as a significant determinant in recovery from burns and recommends that hypnotic procedures be administered in the emergency room as soon as possible after trauma. The patient is reminded of the experience of blushing and blanching: "*What you think* is going to affect the blood supply to your skin, and that affects healing, and you can start right now". It is then suggested that the patient can go in imagination to a "laughing place" (e.g. a favourite beach) where he or she is at ease, free of responsibilities, and so on. Hypnotic induction consists of the upward eye-roll technique (Spiegel & Spiegel, 1987) with suggestion of relaxation. Further suggestions are made of feelings of calmness, coolness, comfort, etc.

Dobkin de Rios and Friedmann (1987) have described their hypnotherapeutic work with 27 burn patients of Hispanic origin. Three sets of tapes were constructed for consecutive use as the patient progressed through therapy. The first tape focused on pain control (glove anaesthesia) and sleep management. The authors also made use of culturally relevant symbolic and metaphorical imagery; for example a green jug was visualised "to signify plants, health, and growth", and images of animals, such as the eagle, suggested power and mastery. Suggestions of blood flowing once more to the extremities were communicated via images such as an irrigation canal providing a flow of water to the crops. The second and third tapes focused on the patients' successfully completing their programme of occupational therapy and regaining confidence to resume work.

Finer (1987) also reports on a number of burns victims, and, as with the previous authors, he prepares cassette tapes for use several times daily. He employs suggestions of body coolness, heaviness, tiredness, and numbness, and presents an image of "sponges in the head and body, which, [can] absorb bodily and mental disturbances, so that [the patient feels] calm and peaceful in the mind". Other recent reports include those of Margolis, Domangue, Ehleben, and Shrier (1983), van der Does, Spijker, and van Dyck (1988), and Wakeman and Kaplan (1978), who record significant reductions in the analgesic requirements of patients thus treated.

Reviews of this field have recently been undertaken by Patterson, Ouestad, and Boltwood (1987), and van der Does and van Dyck (1989). The latter define three areas of application: (1) in crisis intervention, to help patients cope with the acute distress of their trauma; (2) acceleration of healing; and (3) pain management. Their review leaves them doubtful as to whether hypnosis has yet been demonstrated to accelerate burn wound healing, and they call for better controlled clinical trials.

Insomnia

Though not usually regarded as a "medical" problem, insomnia may arise as a result of medical as well as psychological problems. In many cases it will be unnecessary to treat the insomnia directly, as improvement in sleep may be attendant upon improvements in the underlying medical or psychological complaint. If the patient is unable to sleep because of worrying thoughts, even when using self-hypnosis, the technique of Spiegel and Spiegel (1987) may prove useful. The patient imagines a screen on which are projected worries, memories, feelings, ideas, and so on. The worrying thoughts are then imagined as being drawn off to the left on a separate screen (the "sinister" screen) and the patient attends to the more creative thoughts, feelings, and resources, which likewise are drawn off to a third screen which emerges on the right. Thus, imagining the screens floating above, the patient allows natural sleep to take over, repeating the procedure each time he or she awakens.

In uncomplicated cases, the patient may simply be taught self-hypnosis to be practised daily, including immediately on retiring to bed. Suggestions are given of the self-hypnosis turning into deep and restful sleep. Often patients are able to use a cassette tape of the instructions; some recorders automatically switch off at the end of the tape, or the patient's partner can attend to this.

Various relaxation procedures have proved successful with insomnia (see Borkovec & Fowles, 1973; Mitchell & White, 1977) though the method of paradoxical intention (deliberately remaining awake) has also proved effective (Relinger & Borstein, 1979). Favourable results for hypnosis have been reported in a small controlled trial by Anderson, Dalton, and Basker (1979) and in two cases reports by Mangioni (1987) using standard hetero- and self-hypnosis procedures with Hartland's (1971) instructions for the preparation for sleep.

Tinnitus

Heap, in his Introduction to Karle (1988b), has summarised recent studies of psychological approaches to the treatment of this distressing problem. Results have been mixed. Crasilneck and Hall (1985) claim that in good subjects 50% symptom reduction may be achieved "Probably through blocking awareness at a cortical level", and Brattberg (1983) reported that 22 out of 32 patients, using a 15-minute relaxation tape daily for four weeks, learned to disregard the noise. However, Ireland, Wilson, Tonkin, & Platt-Hepworth (1985), in a controlled trial of progressive relaxation, observed no differences between treated and untreated groups; similar findings emerged in a study using frontalis EMG biofeedback (Haralambous et al., 1987). Marks, Karle, and Onisiphorou (1985) investigated the efficacy of hypnosis, self-hypnosis, ego-strengthening, and suggestions of either turning down the volume of the perceived noise or its total cessation (in both cases using appropriate imagery). Patients practised these procedures twice daily using a cassette tape. Therapeutic changes (observed in five patients) were mainly associated with improvements in mood and attitude to the tinnitus, rather than with ability to block awareness of the noise (which was claimed by one patient only).

Voice Disorders

Dunnet and Williams (1988) have outlined the application of hypnosis as an augmentative procedure in speech therapy with organic and functional voice disorders. In cases such as functional aphonia and dysphonia, standard relaxation and breathing techniques may be augmented by anxiety management methods such as the clenched-fist procedures outlined in Chapter 5. Post-hypnotic suggestions of relaxation of the throat and vocal apparatus, with feelings of "coolness and comfort" are repeated to encourage carry-over of voice improvement into everyday situations. For exploratory work, Dunnet and Williams recommend the affect bridge technique described in Chapter 6 of this book. We will make some further comments on the use of hypnosis in speech therapy when we discuss professional issues in Chapter 13.

Neurological Disorders

There have been a number of reports on the use of hypnosis in rehabilitative work with patients with neurological disorders including cerebrovascular and neuromuscular disturbances. Manganiello (1986) used five sessions of hypnosis in the treatment of a 57-year-old male who had sustained a left-hemisphere stroke two months previously. As described earlier, hypnotic suggestions targeted at symptom alleviation apparently led to improvements in speech to nearly normal capacity, some return of writing ability, return of full use of foot and arm, and greater control of facial musculature. Thompson, Hall, and Sison (1986) have also described the use of hypnosis and imagery training to improving naming ability in three cases of Broca's aphasia. Dunnet and Williams (1988) also discuss the use of hypnosis in acquired neurolinguistic disorders.

Ewing (1985) has reported the productive use of 11 sessions of hypnosis (emphasising relaxation and ego-strengthening) in a 45-year-old man who suffered a mild stroke following neurosurgery. Johnson and Korn (1980) have outlined hypnotic procedures in the rehabilitation of a 16-year-old head-injured female with contusion of the right frontoparietal lobe. In the days following emergency laparotomy for repair of liver damage, the patient was clinically comatose, but autonomic functions suggested "an undifferentiated anxiety response which was hindering her recovery". Hypnotic suggestions and imagery were compatible with relaxation and anxiety control (e.g the "safe place" technique) and recovery of various abilities. For example, the swallowing response was suggested via memories of ingesting favourite foods, recovery of limb function by imagery of a marionette with strings pulling at the left arm and leg (the patient had a marked left-sided hemiplegia), and the overcoming of dressing dyspraxia by imagery of clothing a life-size doll. The patient made an excellent recovery and was discharged 13 weeks after the injury.

Johnson (1987) has also described the use of hypnotic imagery and suggestions in a coma patient who, following a successful shunt implantation for hydrocephalus, showed no outward signs of cognition. Positive suggestions of relaxation, and gradual recovery were administered with imagery of "strong healthy blood, healing and restoring her body and brain". Signs of responding were gradually apparent and yes/no signalling was established using lateral eye movements. Images of favourite activities and diversions were suggested and eventually direct suggestions were given for return of speech and other functions. The patient made "remarkable" recovery with minimal residual neurological difficulties. The reader may already be familiar with the practice of playing tapes of the voices of loved ones and heroes to people in coma, and may be reminded of the work on cognitive processing under general anaesthesia (Goldmann, 1988). Mention will be made in Chapter 9 of some work on the use of positive suggestions during surgical operations on anaesthetised patients. For the moment let us bear in mind that, although the work on neurological and neuropsychological recovery is indeed exciting, much of it is presented in the form of case reports rather than clinical trials and therefore we cannot yet say with any certainty that the hypnotic treatment does indeed influence outcome in cases of this sort.

Various difficult physiotherapeutic procedures can be facilitated by combining hypnosis with manipulation. Kimura (1975) uses hypnosis in treating patients with spastic paralysis where the remedial therapy involves their executing movements that would be impossible for them in the normal waking state, and this practice is common in Japan. Similarly, Pajntar, Roskar, and Vodovnick (1985) in Yugoslavia use hypnosis extensively in the rehabilitation of patients suffering from various forms of spasticity and peripheral nerve lesions. Stein (1980) used self-hypnosis and imagery with an 82-year-old man with action myoclonus, and Finkelstein (1982) reports the successful treatment of a patient with disrupted flexor function after laceration of the fifth finger of her right hand. The patient was regressed to several months before the accident and all the fingers of her right hand were placed in the flexed position. It was suggested that she could retain the memory of closing all the fingers and could practise this when relaxed. Relaxation and ego-strengthening were rehearsed daily using a cassette tape. Spiegel and Chase (1980) also describe their successful use of self-hypnosis and daily flexing exercises with a male patient with severe post-traumatic contractures of the hand.

Dane (Note 6) presented encouraging results of nine cases of radicular sympathetic dystrophy (a sympathetically mediated vascular condition associated with peripheral nerve injury) treated with thermal biofeedback, hypnosis, and in some instances, psychotherapy. Severity of symptoms was related to inter-hand temperature difference but even though some substantial increases in temperature on the affected side were obtained, this was not necessarily the hallmark of successful therapy. Schneiderman, Leu, and Glazeski (1987) report a case of spasmodic torticollis treated by general relaxation and specific suggestions of control of the neck muscles. Conrad (1985) successfully treated a socially anxious female with a functional intention tremor and muscle spasm; procedures included cognitive restructuring, systematic desensitisation, direct and indirect therapeutic suggestions, and the use of an "anchor" (see Chapter 5), namely a foot-pressing response paired with imagined resources. Lucas, Stratis, and Deniz (1981) describe hypnotic procedures (relaxation, therapeutic suggestions, ego-strengthening, and self-hypnosis) as an adjunct to physiotherapy with a 21-year-old quadraplegic patient. Finally, van Strien and Weele (Note 16) have presented evidence for the effective application of hypnosis in the treatment of patients with hernia nuclei pulposi (disc prolapse). Of the 31 patients treated, 17 were described as "completely cured"; the rest either dropped out of treatment or, in two cases, were suspended from treatment owing to unfavourable progress.

The use of hypnosis by physiotherapists and other professions trained in physical manipulation will be discussed further in Chapter 13.

Reynaud's Disease

Brief reference to the use of hypnosis in the treatment of this problem is made in a number of texts (Crasilneck & Hall, 1985, Kroger, 1977); suggestions of hand-warming and vasodilation may be made as well as general relaxation (Grabowska, 1971; Greenleaf & Natali, 1987; Hofle, 1980). Thermal biofeedback has also been reported to be effective (Taub & Stroebel, 1978).

Menstrual Disorders

In problems such amenorrhea, dysmenorrhea, and premenstrual tension, hypnotic procedures, either aimed at direct symptom alleviation (relaxation, self-hypnosis, pain control, and so on) or uncovering possible sources of conflict, may be productive. Where there is abdominal pain, the hand-on-abdomen method with suggestions of symptom relief (see Chapter 5) may prove useful. Van der Hart (1985) has recently described the treatment of two cases of functional amenorrhea using metaphorical imagery.

Hyperhidrosis

This condition may respond to hypnotic suggestions of anxiety reduction and symptom relief. King and Stanley (1986) present a case illustration in which the suggestion of coldness was cued by the word "cold", augmented by a "conditioning" procedure whereby for two weeks the patient took daily cold showers while repeating the cue word.

Infertility

Several recent studies (Harrison, O'Moore, O'Moore, & McSweeney, 1981; Harrison, O'Moore, O'Moore, & Robb, 1984; see also the review by Edelmann & Connolly, 1986) have reported that couples with problems of unexplained infertility have measurably higher levels of anxiety than couples who have had no difficulty in conceiving. This heightened anxiety could be present in the first place or could arise from the failure to conceive (Edelmann & Golombok, 1989; Moghissi & Wallach, 1983).

Kroger (1977) speculates that stress reduction may bring about favourable biochemical changes in the secretions within the female reproductive tracts and release of tubal spasm. Fava and Guaraldi (1987) have summarised evidence demonstrating increased serum prolaction in females in situations such as medical interventions, which the patient perceives as stressful. Hyperprolactinaemia is associated with suppression of ovulation (in, for example, nursing mothers) and pathological hyperprolactinaemia with infertility (Robyn et al., 1977, 1981). O'Moore, O'Moore, Harrison, Murphy, and Carruthers (1983) have reported elevated plasma prolaction levels in women with ideopathic infertility, and Harper, Lenton, and Cooke (1985) have found, in the same population, a positive correlation between prolaction level and measures of (1) stress, and (2) state (but not trait) anxiety. O'Moore et al. (1983) obtained significant reductions in both state anxiety and plasma prolactin in infertile women who underwent a course of autogenic training.

These reports indicate that in cases of unexplained infertility, a stress-reduction approach may be productive. Mackett and Maden (1989) reported on four cases of female infertility which had failed to respond to hormone treatment. These women then received between three and six sessions of hypnotic relaxation and Hartland's (1971) ego-strengthening, and were taught self-hypnosis. They were also instructed to put all thoughts of becoming pregnant out of their mind. At the time of the report, all four patients had conceived naturally although one had aborted. In the discussion of this conference paper, other practitioners described the use of symbolic images in the hypnotic treatment of infertile women. These include the image of a river flowing through a meadow with the sun warm and relaxing, while the patient also visualises her womb, ovaries, fallopian tubes, and so on. The hand-on-abdomen technique may also be employed with suggestions of warmth and relaxation penetrating into the reproductive tract. Again we have here an example of specific images and suggestions in contrast to the more general relaxation approach of Mackett and Maden (1989). Hinton, Meadowcroft, Pike, and Wardle (Note 11) have also reported on the use of a hypnotic stress-reduction procedure in couples receiving *in vitro* fertilisation (see next chapter).

These reports should certainly encourage those working with infertile couples to use hypnosis in cases where anxiety appears to be a contributory factor and where other treatments have been unproductive or refused by the couple. (In fact, there is no reason why hypnosis should not be used *alongside* other treatments.) Hitherto, the emphasis has been on the infertile wife, and perhaps this is *not* entirely unconnected with the anxiety on the part of couples that it is not the husband who is responsible for their inability to conceive (Hinton et al., 1988). Yet psychological stress may impair the reproductive capabilities in men also (McGrady, 1984), and recent studies have linked stress with semen quality in healthy male volunteers (Giblin et al., 1988) and men involved in *in vitro* fertilisation and embryo transfer programmes (Harrison, Callan, & Hennessey, 1987). Clearly there is a need for some well-controlled clinical trials in this field.

GENERAL CONCLUSIONS

It is hoped that from this survey of the applications of hypnosis in the field of medicine the reader will gain an understanding of the principles and procedures involved, and of how these are adaptable to a diverse range of conditions and ailments. The main aims of such hypnotic procedures appear to be, via the use of suggestion and imagery: to promote physical and mental relaxation and control of tension and anxiety; to diminish self-destructive habits of behaving and thinking and encourage healthier practices; to bring about appropriate alterations in perception and awareness, particularly in the experience of pain; to facilitate therapeutic changes in autonomic and physiological activity; to enable patients to have an understanding of their illness whereby they may gain a sense of hope and mastery of their condition; to instil feelings of confidence and self-worth.

We must emphasise that hypnotic procedures are but one way of facilitating these goals. Indeed, the extent to which they are realised, whether hypnosis is employed or not, depends in great measure on the relationship of the patient with his or her doctor and other members of the medical team. The ritual delivery of, say, Hartland's ego-strengthening suggestions would be a poor substitute for the doctor's natural ability to instil trust, confidence, and hope, or for the sensitivity and empathy of other carers involved. These must be given priority before hypnotic or any other formalised psychological procedures are contemplated.

Regarding future developments, it is clear that, whereas single case reports are a very useful way of passing on ideas concerning techniques (Heap, 1984c), only by controlled clinical trials will the real efficacy of those techniques be reliably delineated. In such trials, the independent variable—that is, the therapeutic procedures—should be standardised for all subjects, but this does not imply that they should receive absolutely identical treatments. The principles used to generate the suggestions and images must be carefully specified, but their content may be determined by the unique personal characteristics of each subject. It may be that many clinical studies, particularly those employing auto-hypnotic tape-recordings, may have suffered from undue rigidity in this regard.

Such research will help determine those conditions to which hypnotic procedures may provide a significant therapeutic contribution. They will also assist in elucidating the kinds of suggestion and imagery which are especially potent; is their contribution simply on the level of general relaxation or is it possible to influence, by means of hypnosis, selected physiological processes in a manner which directly promotes healing or symptom alleviation?

A final point must be, but rarely is, given strong emphasis. There is little purpose in investing time, energy, and resources in refining theory and practice if, in the end, only a small minority of patients have access to the treatment. There is a real problem in the availability of hypnosis to its potential beneficiaries, and this is not helped by irrational and unfounded prejudices against hypnosis, nor by the all too prevalent notion that hypnosis is the private property of a restricted number of specialists. There is no place in this field for amateurs and self-styled "hypnotherapists" who have no professional qualifications relevant to their attempted area of practice, but the wider availability of hypnosis will only come about by opening up training to all health care professionals—speech therapists, physiotherapists, specialised nursing staff, midwives, and so on—who are able to apply hypnosis constructively as an adjunctive procedure in their own specialisms. This theme will be taken up again in Chapter 13.

8 Hypnosis in the Treatment of Pain

ATTITUDES TO HYPNOSIS

One of the most widely held beliefs about hypnosis is that it is particularly effective in the attenuation or abolition of pain. The general basis for this belief is connected with the confused history of mesmerism in the eighteenth and nineteenth centuries, when it was occasionally used in surgery to produce analgesia up to and beyond the time at which chemical anaesthesia was introduced. Furthermore, there is a general assumption that what we now know as "hypnotism" is none other than the practice known as "mesmerism" up to the time of James Braid who coined, or at least popularised, the new term in the 1840s (see Chapter 2). However, if we read contemporary accounts of how the mesmeric trance was induced, and sometimes used successfully, in overcoming pain in surgery by surgeons such as Esdaile, we realise that we are really concerned with substantially different although related phenomena. This matter has been discussed elsewhere (Gauld, 1988; Gibson, 1982, 1988a) and need not concern us here, although the confusion in connection with surgery is still perpetuated by modern writers such as Gravitz (1988). It is important only in relation to the public misconceptions about hypnosis, and to explain why clinical hypnosis has long been viewed with considerable although justified scepticism by more orthodox practitioners in medicine, psychology, and dentistry.

It has long been recognised that for purposes of surgery the attenuation of pain by hypnotic suggestion, although sometimes possible, is now largely a scientific curiosity as we have had perfectly satisfactory means of securing analgesia and anaesthesia by chemical agents for a long time. Applications of hypnosis to surgery are reviewed in Chapter 9. Nevertheless, hypnosis can be a useful adjunctive technique in certain conditions involving pain; even in some rare cases it is still used in modern surgery (Chertok, 1981, Ch. 1). Later in this chapter we will be concerned with conditions of pain in which hypnosis is the treatment of choice, either alone or integrated with other methods.

The public's belief in the analgesic potential of hypnosis causes some confusion and disquiet when it comes to considering conditions where pain is not incidental to the therapeutic process as in surgery and dentistry. Why, people wonder, have doctors not made widespread use of hypnosis in treating conditions of chronic pain such as migraine, neuralgia, low back pain, cancer, and a host of other painful conditions that are often resistant to pharmacological, surgical, and manipulative methods? Even in cases of acute pain attendant on, for instance, the treatment of burns (Margolis & DeClement, 1980), the aspiration of bone marrow from children with cancer (Hilgard & LeBaron 1984), and in general casualty departments (Goldie, 1956), hypnosis has been shown to have its uses as a means of inducing analgesia. Why then, people wonder, have the medical and allied professions shown comparatively little interest in it?

The reason for such neglect is partly to be found in the whole negative image surrounding hypnosis. Up until comparatively recently few scientific journals would publish papers concerned with clinical hypnosis, and the few specialist journals dealing with hypnosis had small circulations and were sometimes of ephemeral existence. Scepticism about the claims of therapists using hypnosis has often been justified by the lack of scientific rigour of those reporting their results, and sometimes by the exaggerated though vague claims they have made. The neurologists, oncologists, and surgeons of various specialisms have traditionally regarded themselves as dealing with "real" pain, and shown little interest in hypnosis. Where pain was deemed to be "imaginary" (or "hysterical") the patients could be referred to psychiatrists and clinical psychologists who deal with that ambiguous entity "the mind", and they could use hypnosis or other dubious procedures that were sometimes reported to be beneficial. Comparatively recently Merskey and Spear (1967, p.19) made a distinction between "organic" and "psychogenic" pain. They defined the former as:

> pain which is largely dependent on irritation of nerve endings or nerves, or else due to a lesion of the central nervous system, including some possibly patho-physiological disturbances like causalgia.

"Psychogenic" pain was seen as a category including all the other sorts of pain. Although they did not hold that "psychogenic" pain was imaginary, their definitions beg a number of questions about the nature of pain; the assumptions they embody go some way towards explaining why for so long there has been little attempt to inquire seriously into the therapeutic potentialities of hypnosis in the treatment of pain in controlled and integrated research programmes.

THE INCREASED ACCEPTANCE OF HYPNOSIS AS A MEANS OF ANALGESIA

At the First World Congress on Pain in 1975 (Bonica & Albe-Fessard, 1976) numerous papers were presented by a wide variety of specialists in pain research, but of the 148 published papers only two were concerned with the inhibition of pain in humans by means of hypnosis. At the Fourth World Congress on Pain in 1984 there was rather more time devoted to hypnosis in clinical pain control, one of the eight workshops being entirely devoted to hypnosis. There was also an extended video programme, and a presentation concerned with experimental pain and hypnosis (*Pain*, 1984). In 1987 the Fifth International Congress on pain had no less than seven presentations relating to the utilisation of hypnosis in various pain conditions: migraine pain (Berlin & Erdmann, 1987), the management of cancer pain (Brechner et al., 1987), self-hypnosis in the treatment of chronic pain (James & Large, 1987), the suppression of pain reflexes (Leonie, Willer, & Michaux, 1987), experimental analgesia for ischemic pain (Radke & Stam, 1987), tooth-pulp anaesthesia (Sharav & Tal, 1987) and, oral pain (Syrjala, Cummings, Donaldson, & Chapman, 1987).

Previously the attitude had been that hypnosis might be useful in certain cases, but only as a placebo calming the anxiety of patients in acute pain, or alleviating the depression and distress of those with chronic pain. The thinking of Ronald Melzack (1980) in the 1970s is expressed in the following passage:

> There is excellent research on the effects of hypnosis on experimental pain but virtually no reliable evidence from controlled clinical studies to show that it is effective for any form of chronic pain. That hypnosis has helped many individual patients is beyond dispute. But it remains to be shown that hypnotic suggestion is any better than a placebo pill or encouragement and moral support from the family physician or parish priest.

It is surprising that Melzack should publish this as late as 1980, for he had already participated in a well-controlled clinical study with chronic pain patients, in association with Campbell Perry, which gave most encouraging results. This study will be described later.

The publication of a later work by Melzack and Wall (1982) shows a development in their views about hypnosis. This book is largely an up-date of *The puzzle of pain* (Melzack, 1973) with some passages from earlier journal publications included. In assembling old and new text thus there are some rather contrary statements included. Later clinical studies appear to have convinced Melzack and Wall that hypnosis can be far more useful than was previously believed, even in the treatment of chronic pain. Referring to the study by Melzack and Perry (1975) concerning patients suffering from a variety of types of chronic pain, they acknowledged that training in hypnosis was remarkably effective in reducing the pain. EEG biofeedback alone was no more effective compared with the level of pain relief obtained through placebo treatment, but it enhanced the relief obtained by hypnosis still further. Melzack and Wall (1982, p.349) write:

> Melzack and Perry (1975) found that EEG biofeedback alone had no demonstrable effect on chronic pain compared to the level of pain relief obtained in 'placebo' baseline sessions. In contrast they found that hypnotic training instructions produced substantial relief of pain—significantly greater than the effect of biofeedback. The subjects reported an average of 22% pain reduction, and 50% achieved pain decreases of 33% or more. Despite the magnitude of the effect, it was not statistically greater than that of the 'placebo' baseline sessions. However, when the hypnotic training instructions were presented together with biofeedback the pain relief was significantly greater than that produced by baseline placebo sessions.

This study indicates a way forward for the future. Hypnosis is not to be regarded as the province of somewhat eccentric clinicians who take on cases of intractible pain when all other methods have failed, but as a useful technique that invites integration with the other techniques commonly in use in pain clinics, in doctors' surgeries, and elsewhere. Such integration is likely to teach us more about when and how hypnosis can be utilised.

Recognition in the 1980s of the usefulness of hypnosis in the treatment of both acute and chronic pain has resulted in the publication of a number of recent books and chapters in books dealing with hypnosis in relation to pain control. Among the more recent are Burrows and Dennerstein (1981), Elton, Stanley, and Burrows (1983), Gibson (1982), and Hilgard and LeBaron (1984). These books are of considerable scientific merit, and they contrast with the earlier and somewhat indifferent books on clinical hypnosis by therapists giving merely anecdotal accounts of how they treated pain patients with hypnosis. The recent rapid increase of interest in hypnosis as a means of pain control has had to wait upon significant progress in two field of research, in hypnosis and in pain. Integration of these two fields now promises much for the future.

Some authors of books concerning the treatment of pain are still chary of mentioning hypnosis. Thus a recent book by Philips (1981, Appendix X avoids mentioning "hypnosis" even when giving the wording of a fairly conventional hypnotic induction which uses both *relaxation* and *imagery* in the manner discussed in Chapter 1 of the present book. This induction even uses the metaphor of sleep in referring to the patient's subjective experience. Elsewhere in Philips's book (1988, p.181) there is one reference to hypnosis as such, but it is inaccurate. It is stated that "In certain types of people, pain can be affected, for short periods of time, by hypnosis—a mode of treatment that influences mental state only". In fact, as demonstrated in the study by Melzack and Perry (1975), and confirmed by others such as Elton, Burrows, and Stanley (Note 7), changes in the status of pain patients are not necessarily "for short periods". Also, as documented elsewhere in the present book, it is not just the mental state that is influenced by hypnosis, but considerable physiological changes can be achieved.

It matters very little that some writers are still reluctant to mention the word "hypnosis", even when using well-known hypnotic techniques, but it is unfortunate if they exclude from their bibliographies all the relevant modern studies on the treatment of pain in the extensive literature concerning the deliberate use of hypnosis in such therapy. Hughes (1986), in reviewing a rather indifferent book on the psychological treatment of pain, comments quite justly that "Regretfully hypnosis has never obtained widespread acceptance and this may, in part, be due to the unscientific manner in which it has been presented".

One important source of the increased attention that has been given to hypnotic techniques in the treatment of conditions of pain in the 1980s has been the International Association for the Study of Pain (IASP), which, with its prestigious journal *Pain*, has publicised the more scientific work in hypnosis in pain clinics and elsewhere. Ronald Melzack (1985), the President of the IASP, gave a most enthusiastic review of *Hypnotherapy of pain in children with cancer* (Hilgard & LeBaron, 1984), stating: "This is a marvellous book which should be read by everyone interested in pain." He went on to write: "In the hands of these writers, a lot of the mystery of hypnosis vanishes as we marvel at how well these procedures work". Increasingly, the journal *Pain* has included studies on hypnosis in pain therapy in its abstracts, and contributors have cited more studies from the hypnosis literature in their papers. Over the past three years we may note the following contributions to *Pain* as examples of those which have made reference to studies involving hypnosis as such: Cornwell and Donderi (1988), Hughes (1986), Large and James (1988), Lavigne, Schulein, and Hahn (1986), Merskey (1987), Schmidt (1987), Shaw and Erlich (1987), Womack, Smith, and Chen (1988).

INTEGRATING RESEARCH IN HYPNOSIS AND PAIN

Elsewhere in this book the somewhat differing theoretical frameworks relating to hypnosis are described, but at least these frameworks are stated with sufficient clarity for hypnosis to have become an accepted field of study, and one that can have a considerable practical pay-off when applied to the problems of the control of pain. Both hypnosis and pain have one common feature: it is difficult to define either of them adequately other than in ostensive terms (Chapter 1). Most modern authorities are agreed on this. The various concomitants of the two states are observable, but such concomitants are not unique, and people can simulate successfully states of both hypnosis and pain. In order to say that these states exist we rely basically on the subjective reports of those experiencing them, although neither is a "simple" experience. Christian Scientists can elaborate an argument that pain does not exist, and similarly there are also those who maintain that hypnosis does not exist (Hearne, 1982), but for the purpose of this discussion it will be assumed that both pain and hypnosis are meaningful entities.

One of the major factors responsible for the modern integration of research in the fields of hypnosis and pain, is the breakthrough in pain research that can conveniently be referred to the Gate Control theory of pain of Melzack and Wall (1965). Although there have been later modifications to the theory (Wall, 1978), the essence of the theory may be stated here in the simplest of terms.

Melzack and Wall postulated a facilitatory/inhibitory mechanism in the dorsal horn of the spinal cord. Neural impulses from the periphery travel along two types of nerve fibres, having large and small diameters. The afferent stimuli in the small fibres are those that can potentially be orchestrated into a percept of pain centrally after they have been conducted up to the brain via a series of synapses. Both types of fibre stimulate transmission cells in the dorsal horn of the spinal cord to initiate action, but such action is either inhibited or facilitated by the local tissue. Stimuli in the large fibres promote inhibition, and hence close the "gate", whereas the activity in the small fibres is facilitatory, so the "gate" swings open. A further mechanism is postulated. The large fibres project directly up to the brain which sends down feedback messages to the gate-control system. Thus not only is the state of the "gate" influenced by the stimuli arriving via the afferent fibres, both large and small, from the periphery, but the state of the brain is exerting a control. Thus in a condition of anxiety when a possible assault from the environment is anticipated, the efferent messages from the brain hold the "gate" wide open.

Although many other theorists have made distinguished contributions to pain theory since the mid-1960s, this Gate Control theory has been central to modern developments.

THE EFFECT OF HYPNOSIS ON PAIN

A General Statement

If we consider hypnosis in terms of the altered perception of the hypnotised subject, more than one change can be achieved in the pain-perceiving system by appropriate hypnotic suggestions. First, it must be emphasised that hypnosis *per se* does not have any effect on the perception of pain. As is well expressed by Hilgard and Hilgard (1983, p71).

> [We] can report that hypnosis alone, without analgesia suggestions does not reduce pain any more than it reduces other sensory functions. Through suggestions, the hypnotic subject can be made blind and deaf also, but without special suggestions he hears and sees as well within hypnosis as when not hypnotized. The same thing has repeatedly been found for the experience of pain.

The belief that a state of hypnosis confers a degree of analgesia automatically is widely held even by some medical men and other health practitioners who use hypnosis, and this belief partly relates to the old confusion between hypnotism and mesmerism. In "animal hypnosis" or tonic immobility, there is some evidence that a degree of analgesia is conferred on the immobile animal via the endorphin system (Carli, 1978), but this should not lead to confusion regarding hypnosis with humans. There is no unambiguous evidence that the endorphin system is implicated with hypnotically induced analgesia (De Benedittus, Panerai, & Villamira, 1984).

An obvious caveat must be made with regard to the above statements. As all treatments—pharmacological, surgical, manipulative, behavioural, and psychological—have a placebo component, hypnosis is no exception. If some trusted person goes through a procedure that is labelled "hypnotism", then the anxiety level of a person in pain will be reduced, and consequently the affective-motivational component of the pain experience will be reduced. It is this sort of procedure that is most often used in casualty departments, in dentistry, and indeed in the surgeries of GPs who occasionally make use of hypnosis.

However, although one of the components of the pain experience is enhanced by anxiety, the matter is more complex than this. It has been shown that it is in conditions where situational anxiety is high, placebos (whatever their form) are most effective in reducing pain. Where there is little anxiety, as in controlled laboratory experiments involving pain, then placebos are relatively less effective (Evans, 1974).

In summary, while it is important to realise that procedures labelled "hypnotism" may reduce pain in some circumstances via the placebo mechanism, it is a grave mistake to assume that this is all that can be done by hypnotic suggestion. In order that this matter may be further understood it is necessary to discuss what modern research has shown the experience of pain to consist of.

Different Ways of Attenuating Pain by Hypnotic Suggestion

It used to be assumed that pain was a single sensation like hearing, sight, and touch. From quite early on, however, it has been pointed out that the pain experience has more than one component. The recognition of two components, sometimes called a "sensory" and a "reaction" component, made certain pain phenomena more comprehensible (Beecher, 1959). Earlier in this chapter the Gate Control theory of Melzack and Wall that was published in 1965 has been recognised as a milestone in the progress of pain research. Although many other research workers have made distinguished contributions to our understanding of pain since the mid-1960s, it will be convenient to concentrate on the body of theory and research largely stemming from this breakthrough, much of it published in the journal *Pain*, which was founded in 1975 with Patrick Wall as Editor.

As pain is a subjective experience, much of what we know about it comes from how people describe the experience. Work on the semantics of pain produced a seminal paper by Melzack and Torgerson (1971). This work gave rise to the instrument, now very well known, the McGill Pain Questionnaire (Melzack, 1975). This questionnaire, which has now been given to thousands of pain patients as well as normal groups, shows that it is of practical value to conceptualise the complex experience of pain as having three components, "affective-motivational", "sensory", and "evaluative". It may be remarked in passing that many psychologists will be reminded of the tripartite "meaning of meaning" of Osgood and his associates who created the Semantic Differential (Osgood, Suci, & Tannenbaum, 1957). By the latter technique experience can be represented in three dimensions: "evaluation", "activity", and "potency". For reasons that are not entirely clear, there has really been no significant work relating the McGill Questionnaire to the Semantic Differential, although this might lead to some useful insights into pain experience and have practical implications for therapy.

It has been pointed out above the that the placebo element in any procedure labelled "hypnotism" will tend to lower the affective-motivational component of pain, just like any other procedure understood to be therapeutic in intent. But we can do a great deal more with hypnosis. As the perceptual processes of hypnotised subjects can be modified by suggestion, the verbal output of the hypnotist largely determining what is actually perceived, hallucinations both positive and negative can be created. Thus any dark object can be made to be seen as a black cat by the subject following the hypnotist's description of a cat, and any taste or odour may take on the qualities that are suggested. With some subjects who have the capacity to react very strongly to hypnosis, hallucinations can be created which are not simply distortions of what there is present in the room. Thus deeply hypnotised subjects can be induced to "see" a person sitting in a chair that is objectively empty, and believe in the reality of their hallucination. In such cases the false percept comes from their own memory of the appearance of that person.

Negative hallucinations involve the ablation from current experience of objects that are plainly there in the environment, and at the extreme it is possible to induce functional blindness, deafness, anosmia, and anaesthesia, such phenomena reminding us of the functional deficits met with in cases of conversion hysteria.

Hypnotically induced analgesia and anaesthesia are partly a modification of the sensory component of pain. Typically it is not an all-or-none phenomenon; the degree to which it is possible depends upon the talent for hypnosis possessed by the individual subject. With people of only average susceptibility to hypnosis, the pain sensation can be modified only to a limited degree, just as, for instance, although a bright light cannot be made to disappear from the vision of a moderately hypnotised person, it can be made to seem significantly dimmer.

It should be noted that the relationship between hypnotic susceptibility as measured by existing procedures, and the degree of analgesia that can be obtained by hypnotic suggestion is fairly strong. Most studies report correlations of between 0.5 and 0.6, but in the group of "high" susceptibles there are always a few individuals who benefit very little from suggested analgesia, and among the "low" susceptibles there are those who do benefit from the suggestive procedures.

We may usefully regard the lowering of the affective-motivational component of pain by hypnotic suggestion largely in terms of the closing of the spinal and thalamic "gates" of pain, because the sensorium is made less ready to receive the stimuli carried by the small-fibre efferents. Modifying in the sensory component is perhaps best viewed in terms of acting upon the higher perceptual processes whereby sense data are integrated within the brain systems. If we now turn to the evaluative component of pain, suggestions that the pain is "very slight", "hardly bothering you", "almost pleasant", etc. will affect judgemental processes. We are reminded of the fact that the operation of pre-frontal leucotomy does not typically remove the pain sensation, but patients report that it no longer bothers them (Freeman & Watts, 1950).

Too much should not be made of these postulated differences between the various routes whereby hypnosis may attenuate pain. Thinking along these lines, however, therapists will be aware of just what they are trying to do according to the individual needs of the patient. Suggestions have to be carefully worded in order that the intended modifications are effected.

THE THERAPIST'S TASK

Efficient utilisation of hypnosis in dealing with pain patients initially involves the therapist in two diagnostic tasks. First, the appropriate route to the induction of hypnosis must be determined; second, the exact nature of the individual patient's experience of pain must be explored and understood. Elsewhere in this book techniques for the induction of hypnosis are discussed, but it may be noted in passing that it is fairly useless to take a "cook book" approach to such induction. Many of the older books on clinical hypnosis (and some recent ones) publish standard "spiels" which are alleged to induce hypnosis if read to anyone. It is quite useless to repeat one of these "spiels" involving, say, relaxing in the sun, to a patient who is deficient in that sort of imagery and does not particularly like lying in the sun anyway. Similarly, some techniques involve motoric items such as induction based on hand levitation; but some people are rather lacking ideo-motor imagery, although they can quite easily employ other sorts of imagery. Many clinicians will have developed their own techniques for determining what sort of hypnotic suggestions an individual will respond to, but there are also standard scales, such as those discussed in Chapter 3, that give measures not only of the *degree* to which an individual responds to suggestions, but the *kind* of imagery he is most adept at using.

In the diagnostic task of trying to understand the exact nature of an individual's pain, use may be made of the McGill Questionnaire, which has been referred to already and with which a very great deal of research has been undertaken (Melzack, 1983). There is also the matter of the ongoing monitoring of the intensity of pain, or different components of it, hour by hour and day by day whilst the patient is in therapy, and this matter has given rise to standardised techniques such as that of Elton, Stanley, and Burrows (1983, Appendix). By carrying out this diagnostic task efficiently the therapist will come to *understand* the nature of the individual patient's pain experience, as far as it is possible for such an understanding to be established between two people Only by establishing a fairly adequate understanding will the therapist be able to manipulate the patient's perception of pain and offer more than just a bland and calming hypnotic reassurance that may do little good in some cases.

Illustrative Case Study 1

The following case illustrates some of the points that have been made above. A patient suffered from a form of neuralgia, which affected the region of the temples and ears and intensified when she was tired in the evenings. Her response to a standard hypnotic procedure involving hand levitation was poor. However, on the Creative Imagination Scale (see Chapter 3) she responded well to those items involving sensory fantasy. On the McGill Questionnaire her pain was shown to have a burning quality, but not to have many affective overtones.

Hypnotic suggestions were directed towards promoting a fantasy of lying on a beach in the warm sunshine and concentrating particularly on the pleasant heat of the sunshine on her bare abdomen. The object of this was to change the perception of pain to one of pure heat, to transfer the locus of experience from the face to the abdomen, and to evaluate the sensation as being pleasant. This involved daily practice on the patient's part, tape-recorded suggestions for the fantasied scene being supplied to her. After seven weeks the patient's assessment of the level of pain experience (assessed four times a day on a record sheet) showed a satisfactory drop, and she was taking fewer analgesics. Follow-up a year later showed that although the condition was still there, it often remitted and she seldom needed to take analgesic tablets.

PAIN AND THE HIDDEN OBSERVER

A matter that has come into prominence in recent years is the question of the "hidden observer" and the neo-dissociation theory that Ernest Hilgard (1986) has postulated as the result of his experimental work. In brief, it is proposed that even when complete analgesia has been obtained in hypnotised subjects according to their self-report, "some part of them" is experiencing the pain and can report on it by a technique of "automatic talking" similar to the "automatic writing" of which some people are capable. It need hardly be said that this remarkable phenomenon can be produced only in rather unusual people. A similar phenomenon is reported by Chertok and his associates (Chertok, Michaux, & Doin, 1977) working with two women undergoing surgery with hypnotically induced analgesia as the sole means of abolishing pain. In the Chertok experiments the report was obtained some time after the operation by re-hypnotising the patients and interrogating them. They reported that at the time of surgery, although they were not conscious of any pain, they felt that "some other person" was having a painful experience. Typically, in both the Hilgard and the Chertok experiments, the degree of pain experienced by the "hidden observer" was somewhere intermediate between the mild discomfort felt by the hypnotic consciousness, and the intense pain that would have been experienced in the waking state. In the Hilgard experiments the latter was determined by baseline testing before hypnosis.

These findings are not really so very surprising, and they attest to the fact that the absence of pain achieved by hypnotic suggestion is a true hallucination and is comparable to the functional deafness or blindness that can also be produced by hypnotic manipulations of perceptual processes. They are also comparable to the findings in the investigation of states of conversion hysteria.

Before hypnotic deafness is induced the subject may be told that when the hypnotist says "You can now hear again", hearing will be restored. Obviously, some part of the functionally deaf person is monitoring all that is being said all the time, so that the negative hallucination is removed by the spoken cue (Malmo, Boag, & Raginsky, 1954). One may choose to regard the hypnotically induced deafness as a piece of "play-acting", but such an explanation does not fit all the facts. In the clinical field we know that people prone to conversion hysteria tend to be rather histrionic personalities yet it is not useful to dismiss all their paralyses, local anaesthesias, and other functional disturbances as "play-acting". Successful therapy depends on a recognition that such disorders are, for them, perfectly real. In Sarbin and Coe's (1972) highly sceptical model of hypnosis, which conceptualises the hypnotic phenomena in terms of role enactment, there is room for so high a degree of involvement that the *role* and the *self* are undifferentiated and hypnotised people can become pain-free in their own current experience.

Illustrative Case Study 2

The relevance of the experimental findings of Hilgard and of Chertok to clinical work is illustrated by the following case. A patient had developed a general arthritic condition at the age of 30. She was not much incapacitated in her movements, but she suffered from periods of considerable pain. At first it seemed that hypnosis was as unsuccessful as the various other methods of pain control that had been tried, but after several sessions it was discovered that she had the capacity to dissociate her awareness to the extent that she could imagine very vividly getting "outside her body" and to view herself, as it were, form a detached standpoint. In this condition of autoscopy she was perfectly well aware that her body was suffering but it did not seem to be a matter that concerned her directly; it was somewhat as though the pain was being experienced by somebody else. Hypnotic training, which involved daily practice at home, was directed towards developing this dissociative capacity. It worked well at home, but less well when she was at work in an office, for it was accompanied by a certain drowsiness and relaxed inattention to detail.

HYPNOTIC ANALGESIA IN RELATION TO PHYSIOLOGICAL INDICES

It follows from the above that we should expect the physiological indices of pain, such as raised blood pressure, to be in accord with the assault on the tissues rather than with the conscious experience of the patient or the experimental subject after hypnotic analgesia has been induced. It is true that in the Hilgard experiments already referred to, when blood pressure was monitored during hypnotically induced analgesia, the stressor that was applied did not cause the blood pressure to rise as high as in baseline testing. Again, this is what we would expect, as rise in pressure responds to both physiological distress and to psychological disturbance. If the person remains calm then there is no *added* sympathetic arousal affecting the blood pressure.

An interesting study is reported by Bowers and Van der Meulen (Note 2) in which heart rate and GSR were monitored as physiological indices of pain experience in seven dental patients. Their teeth were being drilled, each patient having two dental caries repaired. One tooth was treated under chemical analgesia and the other with hypnotic analgesia. As chemical analgesics abolish the experience of pain it might have been expected that the autonomic indices would have remained unaltered. However, both heart rate and the number of GSRs increased dramatically during the drilling process whether the analgesia had been induced chemically or by hypnotic suggestion. According to Bowers (1983, p.27):

> Across all subjects, the type of analgesia utilized made no difference in the physiological responsiveness of subjects during this crucial period. In other words, *if* physiological reactivity is viewed as an index of pain, *then* chemical and hypnotic analgesias are equally ineffective in controlling dental pain.

The fact is that although physiological indices such as a raised heart rate and blood pressure are the ordinary concomitants of pain in normal waking experience, they are not good indicators when that experience is modified by drugs or hypnotic suggestion. An assault on body tissues will inevitably arouse the sympathetic nervous system even when the spinal and thalamic "gates" of pain are closed. It may also be remarked that such physiological indices also respond to much besides pain, such as anger and pleasurable excitement. The best indicator of the experience of pain is the subjective report, although the experiments of Hilgard and Chertok have shown that with exceptional people in exceptional circumstances there may be conflicting reports of subjective experience, perhaps given from different levels of consciousness.

CHRONIC PAIN: HYPNOSIS COMPARED WITH OTHER TREATMENTS

Earlier, in referring to the study of chronic pain patients by Melzack and Perry, it was noted that a combination of hypnotic suggestion and biofeedback technique was peculiarly effective. Looking to the future we may consider what techniques may be usefully integrated in programmes of treatment, particularly for chronic pain. As yet little has been accomplished in well controlled clinical studies, and laboratory studies using experimentally produced pain may not be wholly relevant.

Controlled clinical studies are not easy to carry out. There is abundant evidence that successful analgesia produced by hypnotic suggestion in cases of acute pain is highly relevant to what may be called the "hypnotic talent" of the individual patient (Wadden & Anderton, 1982). Degrees of such talent may be measured independently as discussed in Chapter 3. We know much less about this matter in relation to persistent and chronic pain. We are also much less well informed about what sort of personal talent makes for a good response to analgesic drugs, acupuncture, and biofeedback. Therefore, in controlled clinical studies where these techniques are used, and different methods are compared, there are a number of unknowns that make clear interpretation of the results difficult.

Elton and her colleagues (Elton, Burrows, & Stanley, Note 7) conducted a study with 50 patients suffering from various kinds of chronic pain in which the response of four groups treated severally with hypnosis, EMG biofeedback (using the frontalis muscle), psychotherapy, and placebo were compared. There was also a no-treatment group kept on the waiting list. On average, the patients had suffered from pain for 14 years, during which time all sorts of treatments had been tried without much success. They were therefore a very unpromising type of chronic patient.

All patients began the study with a baseline assessment of the degree of pain, and after 12 weeks their pain levels were again assessed. The groups treated with hypnosis and biofeedback showed considerable and statistically significant improvement, the former doing rather better than the latter, whereas there was much less improvement in the psychotherapy and placebo groups, and none at all in the no-treatment group. The latter three groups were then called for treatment by either hypnosis or biofeedback, and they too responded positively, showing that they were no different in potential. Follow-up three years later showed that the improvement was a permanent one for the majority of the patients.

It is apparent that the gains made by chronic pain patients when either hypnosis or biofeedback techniques are used can be maintained. The reason for this seems to be that these treatments teach a technique that the patients can use for ever after. In the hetero-hypnosis sessions it is usual to teach techniques of auto-hypnosis, and in this modern age cassettes of taped recordings can be made for each patient for home use (see also Chapter 5). Such recordings should, of course, be carefully prepared for each individual patient in accordance with their own special needs. The commercial recordings that give "blanket" suggestions are pretty useless, and for the same reason, so are the standard "spiels" that are given in many of the older books on clinical hypnosis.

That biofeedback is rather less successful than hypnosis, as was also demonstrated in the study by Melzack and Perry (1975), is quite understandable, as most of the re-training is done in the clinic where the apparatus is, whereas with hypnosis considerable gains must be due to the auto-hypnotic practice in the patients' own homes. However, if we consider biofeedback in terms of an operant conditioning process it is apparent that permanent gains are possible, especially where the two techniques are used together.

These studies have shown that even when pain conditions have persisted for many years, a well-designed programme of therapy can alter the patients' perceptual processes, and hence their experience of pain. Hypnosis is the ideal technique for effecting a permanent change, since it eventually puts the control of the condition entirely in the hands of the patient, in contrast to techniques that have a large placebo component which will eventually fade. It cannot be stressed too strongly that *hypnosis is something that patients learn to accomplish for themselves*: its success depends in large measure on the individual patient's own talents. The task of the therapist is to instruct patients in the complex and sometimes difficult techniques of altering their perception, and hence the experience of pain.

In 1933 Clark Hull wrote that "All sciences alike have descended from magic and superstition, but none has been so slow as hypnosis in shaking off the evil associations of its origins". This is particularly true of hypnosis in the clinical field, and we are just beginning to understand how it can best be used in the control of pain.

SUMMARY

In very recent year the techniques of the control of pain by hypnotic suggestion have been taken seriously by many of the most eminent clinicians and researchers in the pain field. This position contrasts with that which existed for many years when the reality of hypnotic analgesia was not denied, but was not considered to be of sufficient importance to warrant much attention. This recent interest has had to wait upon developments in the field of hypnosis research which have taken it further from the province of those clinical practitioners who would often give merely anecdotal reports of their work. On the other hand, there have been rapid developments in the field of pain research which have emphasised the importance of studying the psychological components of the experience of pain. Consequently, we are beginning to understand the mechanisms of hypnotic analgesia.

Until comparatively recently, hypnotically induced analgesia has generally been regarded simply in terms of allaying situational anxiety and hence as having some value as a placebo. Greater insight into the nature of pain has led to an understanding of how, in addition to the placebo effect inherent in all forms of treatment, when hypnotic suggestion is used properly it can modify the perception of pain in more than one of its components. Future progress is indicated to be in the direction of integrating hypnotic procedures with the other techniques whereby pain is controlled in clinical practice.

9 Hypnosis in Medical and Surgical Procedures

There are a number of medical and surgical interventions which cause varying degrees of discomfort and anxiety to patients. Sometimes the patient's distress is out of proportion to the actual level of pain or discomfort involved—as in the case of an injection or certain dental procedures discussed in Chapter 11—but occasionally the intervention may engender a significant degree of pain and suffering on the patient's part, such as in the chemotherapeutic treatment of cancer.

Hypnosis may be used to assist patients undergoing such interventions by alleviating the anxiety and pain involved. Of course there are effective and often necessary anxiolytic and analgesic medications. However, we shall see that hypnosis can be used as a complement to, and even as a substitute for, these medications in certain instances, in much the same way as in the medical conditions discussed in Chapter 7. Hypnosis may sometimes be preferable in order to avoid the side-effects or after-effects of, and the patient's dependency on, such medication, particularly if the medical procedure or treatment is to be undertaken regularly.

Another, slightly different, application of hypnosis is the use of hypnotic suggestions to improve the patient's response to, or recovery from, the medical or surgical intervention. This will be illustrated later in the case of the use of taped suggestions before and during surgery.

GENERAL PRINCIPLES

As with other applications of hypnosis the main ingredients are the alleviation of anxiety, discomfort, and pain by suggestions and imagery of relaxation and well-being, as well as distraction, and in some cases, dissociation. We emphasise again that much of this may be achieved quite naturally, without hypnosis, when treatment is conducted in a considerate and caring manner and the patient's special anxieties and apprehensions are handled with sensitivity. For example, one of the authors (M.Heap) has occasionally been treating patients with panic disorder who are suddenly faced with what for them is the terrifying prospect of being admitted to hospital for some surgical treatment. Often the main fear is panicking on the ward and even running home, thus appearing foolish in front of the ward staff and other patients. They have also the fear of the operation itself and sometimes of not coming round afterwards. Such patients are often reassured sufficiently to agree to admission when their therapist has explained to the ward team the nature of their panic disorder and their fears regarding hospitalisation.

This chapter considers some of the main areas of application of hypnosis in this field, though the list is not exhaustive.

EMBARRASSING PHYSICAL EXAMINATIONS

An example of the simple use of hypnotic suggestion and imagery in a routine physical intervention is the case of the highly anxious young lady undergoing gynaecological examination. Kohen (1980) illustrates such procedures with four cases. Typically, the patient is given the necessary reassurance and information concerning the examination and is then asked about her favourite activity (e.g. ice-skating or horse-riding). She is then asked to imagine engaging in this activity while the physician attends to the examination, keeping the patient informed of what he or she is doing. Suggestions of progressive relaxation and relaxed breathing are also offered. The imagery may be intensified by suitable commentary such as imagining the warmth of the sun on the face. Specific suggestions of muscular relaxation are given as appropriate—such as relaxation of the vaginal muscles during examination of the external genitalia. Post-hypnotic suggestions are given for using self-hypnosis for other purposes, including any future medical examinations.

INJECTIONS

Most people are able to endure an injection with at the most a tolerable degree of anxiety and require no special consideration. Injection phobia is not uncommon however, to the extent that some people will faint at the sight of the needle and avoid treatment which involves receiving an injection. Such a person was Mr N who had a life-long fear of injections and the sight of blood, particularly his own. At the age of 22 years he and several relatives were found to have haemochromatosis, an hereditary condition in which the patient has an excess of iron in the blood. The prescribed treatment simply consisted of blood-letting at regular intervals. This involved drawing off one pint of blood in the usual manner. Mr N was at that time without symptoms but was warned by the physician that, unless treated, by his mid-forties he was likely to develop severe life-threatening conditions such as diabetes and heart and liver-failure.

It is a measure of just how devastating phobic anxiety can be that Mr N stated that he was prepared to face these dire consequences rather than undertake the treatment being offered. He was referred to one of the authors (M. Heap) for help in overcoming this fear sufficiently to undertake his treatment. Initially he was desensitised *in vivo* to the sights and smells involved in this treatment (the treatment room and bed, syringes of various sizes, alcohol swabs, and so on). A video tape of an injection was shown, graded exposure being effected by progressively sharpening the focus. Hypnosis was practised using eye-fixation, progressive relaxation, imagining descending 20 steps to a beach, and further deepening by counting while imagining sleeping on the beach. Self-hypnosis was taught and practised with good effect. Using hypnosis, dummy-runs of the venepuncture procedure were performed by merely pressing a needle to the skin after swabbing. Next a small amount of blood was drawn by the physician while the therapist performed the hypnotic procedures. Thus Mr N was eventually able to have regular pints of blood drawn, though, at least until the author's departure from that particular hospital, he still required hetero- rather than self-hypnosis during the treatment. Nevertheless he was independently able to undergo some dental treatment which involved both injection of a local anaesthetic and suturing.

Some authors have adopted a psychodynamic interpretation of injection phobia. For example, Kraft (1984) presented a case illustration in which he combined both behavioural methods (systematic desensitisation in imagination) and analytical interpretations based on the patient–therapist transference. In Mr N's case the approach was purely behavioural but his history did reveal possible analytical avenues. He was outwardly a calm person who, except for his dread of blood and injections, seemed strangely indifferent to the facts of his illness. However, shortly after being informed that he had the illness he became temporarily sexually impotent. This may have arisen from the shock of hearing the news or the fact that he had just acquired a new girlfriend, although the latter would not normally have occasioned him undue anxiety. He confided to his mother what had happened and she told him that she knew the reason why, namely that at the age of two years he underwent a medical circumcision and initially he was inadequately anaesthetised. (His mother made the claim of hearing his screams from outside the operating room and actually running in to see what was happening.) Another interesting sideline was that his mother had always said there was "bad blood" in the family and that one day it would be discovered that there was some hereditary condition being transmitted. We need not infer some kind of paranormal insight to accept this possibility; perhaps over a number of generations, as a high proportion of family members met with early deaths, the vague notion evolved and was handed down that something was amiss in the family genes.

TREATMENT OF CANCER

There are a number of reports in the literature of the beneficial effect of hypnosis, not just in helping patients endure the suffering of cancer (Brechner et al., 1987; Hilgard & Hilgard, 1983; Meares, 1982/83; Sachs, 1987) but also in coping with pain and distress which can be side-effects of certain treatments. For example, Deyoub (1980) describes the case of a 30-year-old female cancer patient who was fearful about her impending radiotherapy. In preparation, she was hypnotised and age-progressed to the day of her first cobalt treatment. The procedures were described to her and reassurance given that she would come to no harm and that the cobalt machine "would deliver painless rays and would break up the tumour". She was also taught self-hypnosis and instructed to use this before cobalt treatment. The radiologist's report was satisfactory in terms of both the patient's tolerance of and her response to treatment.

Hypnosis also appears to have helped this patient cope with the pain, nausea, and anticipatory emesis associated with her 14-day chemotherapy cycle. Redd, Andreson, and Minagawa (1982) used hypnosis with six cancer patients experiencing nausea and vomiting in anticipation of chemotherapy. Hypnosis with suggestions of deep relaxation and pleasant imagery (rehearsed on tape) controlled these reactions which were unaffected by anti-emetic drugs. On occasions when hypnosis was suspended, the anticipatory reactions returned.

A report on this application in Britain has come from Walker et al. (1988). There were 14 patients with various cancers and each received between two and six sessions of training in hypnosis and cue-controlled relaxation ("one, two, three, relax!") reinforced with practice using a tape-recording. Suggestions were given of greater control over the symptoms, and "nausea management training" was instigated, which involves helping the patient experience nausea by means of appropriate stimuli and, using the hand-on-abdomen method with gentle massaging, to eliminate this nausea. Eleven of 13 patients with conditioned nausea and 9 of the 13 with conditioned vomiting improved; the numbers improving for pharmacological nausea and pharmacological vomiting were 8 out of 14 in each case. Similar procedures are described by Walker (1984) with patients having lymphoid tumours. Syrjala, Cummings, Donaldson, and Chapman (1987) examined ratings of oral pain by patients following chemotherapy and irradiation prior to bone marrow transplantation. Hypnosis treatment gave significantly lower pain ratings than training in cognitive strategies and therapist contact alone. Finally, Burish and Redd (1983) have reviewed five controlled studies on reducing conditioned aversive response to cancer chemotherapy which affirm the usefulness of hypnosis and related techniques.

HAEMODIALYSIS

Dimond (1981) provides an illustrative case of the use of hypnosis and psychological procedures (positive suggestion, self-hypnosis) and cognitive restructuring with appropriate imagery in patients undergoing haemodialysis who presented with problems of hyperemotionality during dialysis, inadequate blood-flow volume, injection phobia, and low pain tolerance. Surman and Tolkoff-Rubin (1984) have reported similar procedures in five dialysis patients.

SURGICAL PROCEDURES

Perhaps the application of hypnosis that creates the greatest impression in the mind of the lay reader is its use as a substitute for anaesthetic and analgesic medication in major surgical operations. Reports of this kind of painless surgery go back at least 150 years to the time of the mesmeric movement (Barber, Spanos, & Chaves, 1974), and two prominent names from this period are John Elliotson, who practised at University College Hospital, London, and James Esdaile who worked in India. The latter reputedly performed over 300 surgical operations (Esdaile, 1846) including the removal of massive scrotal tumours, with a mortality rate of 5% compared with the contemporary figure of 40%. Such reports appear to provide overwhelming evidence for a state theory of hypnosis, but strong counter-arguments have been put forward by non-state adherents such as Barber et al. (1974) and Wagstaff (1981). Gibson (1977) has also remarked on the implausibility of some of the earlier reports such as those of Elliotson and Esdaile. There is also the important point, stressed by Gauld (1988) and by Gibson (1988), that mesmerism is not quite the same thing as hypnosis (see Chapter 8). The procedures of Elliotson, Esdaile, and other mesmerists were quite different from the procedures that are used in hypnotism, and the "mesmeric state", which confers automatic anaesthesia, may be a special physiological state dissimilar to the state we call "hypnosis".

The reader is advised to be acquainted with these more restrained accounts of the anaesthetic possibilities of hypnosis and mesmerism. Here we are concerned with practice, and even as severe a critic as Wagstaff (1981, p.152) admits that "techniques labelled 'hypnosis' have achieved genuine success in the alleviation of pain in some cases", though he cogently challenges the utility of ascribing the apparent diminution or tolerance of pain to some altered state of consciousness termed "hypnosis". This controversy is also debated in Chapter 8.

For the practitioner or those curious about practices there are several texts (e.g. Marmer, 1959; Werbel, 1965), and Kroger (1977) does a very good overview of procedures, including the "dry run" method in which the patient is taken through the events of the operation in imagination, with suggestions of relaxation, comfort, diminution of pain sensations (including the transfer of glove anaesthesia), and suggestions of a good post-operative recovery. During the operation hypnosis is presumed to be maintained by appropriate suggestions of deepening relaxation and by reassurance. Nathan, Morris, Goebel, and Blass (1987) discuss the problem of the occurrence of unpredicted and therefore unrehearsed surgical maneouvres during the operation and suggest refinements for dealing with them.

Although hypnoanaesthesia can only be used as a total substitute for chemical anaesthesia in a minority of patients – Kroger (1977) suggests less than 10% are sufficiently hypnotisable – it may be more satisfactory in certain cases. Nathan et al. (1987) list the following: patients requiring repeated procedures; cases in which chemical anaesthesia would carry significant risks; those undergoing brain surgery with concurrent EEG monitoring, and emergencies in which chemical anaesthetics are unavailable or are refused. The same workers (Morris, Nathan, Goebel, & Blass, 1985) have described the use of hypnoanaesthesia in morbidly obese patients who cannot be safely managed with chemical anaesthesia.

Lewinstein (1978) and Lewinstein, Iwamoto, and Schwartz (1981) have described hypnotic rehearsal procedures in preparing anxious patients for ophthalmic surgery. As usual the patient is hypnotised and the entire operation is explained, reassurances and suggestions are administered of relaxation, comfort, reduction or elimination of premedication, relief from pain, "a smooth anaesthetic induction and recovery", and immobility. The patient may also be taught to enter hypnosis via the lifting of his or her wrist. Hypnoanaesthesia may in some cases replace chemical anaesthesia when the latter is considered risky.

John and Parrino (1983) assigned patients undergoing radical keratotomy to either a hypnotic relaxation group or a control group. The two groups did not differ in reported pain or awareness of the procedure, but the relaxation group reported feeling significantly better following surgery than the controls.

Hypnotic procedures for patients undergoing minor surgery such as suturing are also described by Kroger (1977). These involve the use of suggestions of relaxation and comfort, imagery, and distraction.

Do pre-operative suggestions influence outcome of surgery? Several reports in the literature indicate that they may (Benson, 1971; Field, 1974). Hart (1980) investigated the efficacy of tape-recorded hypnotic suggestion in patients preparing for cardiopulmonary bypass surgery. All 40 patients received information concerning their illness and operation, and were advised on post-discharge diet and activity. Twenty patients were also exposed on five occasions to a taped hypnotic induction on the two days prior to surgery. These patients required less units of blood following surgery; their post-operative anxiety levels were lower than those of the 20 controls and they had a more internal locus of control. Their diastolic blood pressure was also lower than the control patients during the first three days of admission. Greenleaf and Fisher (Note 10) have reported a similar study of self-hypnosis, again in preparation for open-heart surgery. There were two treatment conditions: one in which specific suggestions were given of minimal bleeding, clean wounds, and an alert defence system, and another in which more general suggestions and imagery of relaxation and safety were administered. The latter appeared to be the more effective and patients with a medium score on the Hypnotic Induction Profile (Spiegel & Spiegel, 1987) did better than high-scorers in terms of their recovery in intensive care (as measured by such parameters as medication required to stabilise blood pressure). Low-scorers were the least affected. It was speculated that medium-scorers might be better able than high-scorers to cope with unexpected intra-operative events.

Although clinical studies and individual case reports appear to affirm the benefits of hypnotic procedures in the preparation of patients for surgical operations, it is not altogether clear when, or if at all, they are more beneficial than non-hypnotic instructions for allaying anxiety, enhancing pain tolerance, and instilling confidence in the patient before and after the operation. The experienced surgeon, anaesthetist or nurse may need some persuading that they are anything more than what they themselves do naturally to prepare the patient by explaining simply and clearly what the operation entails, allaying any undue anxieties the patient may be harbouring, and inspiring hope for a speedy recovery. In fact there are several reports of such beneficial effects of simple non-hypnotic suggestions (Andrew, 1970; Egbert, Battit, Welsh, & Bartlett, 1964; Keifer & Hospodarsky, 1980). For example, Keifer and Hospodarsky (1980) found that patients undergoing abdominal hysterectomy who were informed on the eve of surgery that they would need lower-than-average dosages of post-operative analgesics did indeed require less medication than patients not so instructed; this result may merely demonstrate a compliance effect on pain tolerance, but it is an instructive study as it illustrates the potency of simple reassurance in influencing the kind of post-operative responses under discussion. This general theme will be taken up again in the conclusion of this chapter.

A rather more controversial use of suggestion in surgery, and one not so readily explicable in terms of compliance and expectation, is when the suggestions are delivered during the operation itself while the patient is under general anaesthesia. (These suggestions are not strictly hypnotic, although a case may be made for drawing a comparison—see Goldmann, 1988). A growing body of evidence supports the notion that anaesthetised patients on the operating table may be receptive to ongoing stimuli, even at a semantic level, particularly when the information is of emotional significance (Goldmann, 1988).[1] If this is so then it may be that pessimistic statements concerning the patient's condition made during an operation may have a deleterious effect on his or her recovery, whereas encouraging comments may be beneficial.

These speculations have been tested by a number of workers with promising

[1] These observations are clearly challenging for modern cognitive psychology which tends to the view that perceiving and recognising information such as verbal stimuli are active processes of construction (Neisser, 1967). However, there appears to be a notion in various quarters that a message acquires some peculiar effectiveness if the recipient is oblivious to it—for example, if it is masked by noise and rendered subliminal. Thus one may purchase from health shops and practitioners of "alternative medicine", "subliminal perception tapes" which are claimed to help the listener attain an extraordinary variety of accomplishments such as losing weight, enhancing memory, being a better lover, and improving his or her golf (see Heap, 1988d). The fact that the effects of such subliminal stimulation are marginal and difficult to measure (Dixon, 1971) suggests that the main beneficiaries of these tapes are likely to be the people who manufacture and sell them.

results (Bonke, Schmitz, Verhage, & Zwaveling, 1986; Pearson, 1961). For example, in a recent double-blind, placebo-controlled study at St. Thomas's Hospital (Evans & Richardson, 1988) patients presented, via earphones, with taped therapeutic suggestions while undergoing total abdominal hysterectomy were discharged from hospital on average 1.3 days before a control group who were presented with a blank tape. Suggestions included being relaxed and not feeling pain or being sick, and "third person" suggestions (e.g. "The operation seems to be going very well and the patient is fine"). The group who received these suggestions also experienced fewer half-days of pyrexia and reported fewer gastrointestinal problems than the controls, and, in contrast to the controls, in nearly all cases their recovery was rated by nursing staff as better than expected. However, no post-operative group differences were found in terms of reported nausea, vomiting, pain, and mood. Interestingly, while no patient was able to recall any intra-operative events, all but one of the suggestion group correctly guessed to which group they had been allocated, whereas the inferences of the controls were of chance accuracy. This finding may be explained by the experimental group's inferring from the quality of their recovery that they had indeed listened to the suggestion tape, although it may raise the suspicion that the double-blind precautions were not completely water-tight. In the control group there were no differences between the length of post-operative stages of patients who guessed they received the suggestion tape and those who received the blank tape (Evans & Richardson, personal communication). This implies that *believing* one has heard the suggestion tape does not influence post-operative outcome.

This was a well-controlled study and one which deserves to be replicated widely; though not the main advantage of these suggestion procedures, the earlier discharge of the treatment group has obvious economic benefits. As the authors suggest, refinements to their procedure may come from experimenting with the timing of the suggestions (which may also be administered during anaesthetisation and during recovery) and the type of suggestion employed. Indeed, a productive line of enquiry may be to compare standard suggestions with personalised ones—that is, suggestions tailored to the problems, needs, and anxieties of the individual patient. And, without the constraints of a research project, is it better to use a tape or to rely on the surgical team to make the appropriate suggestions spontaneously?

IN VITRO FERTILISATION

As was mentioned in Chapter 7, stress or anxiety may be an aggravating factor in some cases of unexplained infertility, and one source of anxiety may be failure to conceive. Infertility treatment programmes in themselves may be stressful for the couples involved (Hinton et al., 1988; Moghissi & Wallach, 1983). Indeed, Harrison, Callan, and Hennessey (1987) observed significant reductions in sperm density, sperm count, and sperm mobility in samples provided for *in vitro* fertilisation (IVF) which were correlated with an increase in total fertilisation failure.

Using an augmented version of the Hospital Anxiety and Distress Questionnaire (Snaith, 1983), Hinton and her colleagues (Hinton et al., 1988) have studied stress levels in three groups of couples undergoing an IVF programme namely:

1. A hypnotic treatment group who, as well as receiving fertility counselling and support, were trained in hypnosis (two half-hour sessions) which they practised at least twice daily using a tape. As well as standard induction and deepening procedures, the routine included the hand-on-abdomen technique with suggestion of increasing fertility and relaxation (e.g. "Deeper relaxation will allow your fertility level to rise, and increase your chances of conception").
2. A group who received counselling and support only.
3. A group identical to (1) but who had been offered and refused hypnotic treatment.

The results indicated that measured psychological stress was greater in women than in men (irrespective of the cause of infertility) and was greater with increased duration of infertility. (Interestingly, some couples were anxious that the cause of infertility should not reside in the husband.) Stress levels increased for all three groups at the time of their IVF attempt but, several weeks later, the hypnosis group showed the most marked recovery from stress. Interestingly, the only group who showed no recovery at all—that is, whose stress levels remained high post-IVF—were the refusers, suggesting they were a special group in terms of their way of coping with stress, either generally or with respect to their infertility and IVF treatment. At the time of the report, insufficient data were available on the outcome of the IVF treatment.

As in previous sections, we urge that reducing the stress incurred by these procedures should not be construed purely as a matter of finding the right set of "techniques". Harrison et al. (1987) outline some practical steps for rendering the IVF programme less of an ordeal for the couples concerned.

CONCLUSION

Our overview of the application of hypnotic procedures to patients undergoing medical procedures leads us to draw conclusions similar to those made in Chapter 7 concerning hypnosis with psychosomatic and other medical problems. The potential applications of hypnosis in this area are wide and appear to be concerned with beneficially altering the patients' perceptions of the various interventions and to thus alleviate pain and anxiety and promote relaxation, comfort, and a sense of mastery. Suggestions may also bring about physiological changes which alleviate the effects of these interventions and facilitate recovery. We again emphasise that we can only make these claims for hypnosis when it is administered in an environment where the patient is already benefiting from the support and reassurance which the medical and nursing staff are able to deliver in their normal daily interactions with those in their care. In many instances it may be that what is required is some encouraging and confidence-boosting words from the staff, and that putting these in the form of a standard hypnotic script is an unnecessary complication. Perhaps future researchers should consider this point when deciding what kind of control condition to adopt.

Finally, again we stress that if, as the studies do seem to indicate, hypnosis is of real value, then we must address the problem of its availability to the patient; the proper training of hospital staff in the use of hypnosis (as with any other skills they learn) within their day-to-day duties is a priority which professional rivalry and unwarranted restrictive practices should not be allowed to compromise.

10 Hypnosis in Obstetrics

THE HISTORICAL BACKGROUND

Hypnotic and mesmeric techniques were used with women in childbirth in the early nineteenth century. As reported by Foissac (1833), Husson showed that such techniques could help to eliminate or lessen the pain of labour. Towards the end of the century with the increasing interest in hypnotism following the work of Charcot (1887), Liébeault (1866), and Bernheim (1973) a good deal of obstetric hypnotism was practised, particularly in France (e.g. Dumontpallier, 1892; Mesnet, 1888; Luys,1890a,b; August Voisin, 1896). Interest in the possibilities of hypnotism in obstetrics was also manifest in other countries; in England there was Bramwell (1903) and Kingsbury (l891); in Germany, Schrenck-Notzing (1893); in Holland, de Jong (l889); in Austria, Pritzl, (1886); in Russia, Dobrovolski (1891); in America, Lichtschein (1898). Much of what we know about the use of hypnosis in childbirth today was discovered a century ago; the modern age has merely added the experimental method to clinical observations and anecdotal reports.

Interest in hypnotism suffered a general decline in the first decade of this century, but some attempt was made to revive hypnotic techniques in obstetrics after the First World War. Three main movements may be identified; the Natural Childbirth of Grantly Dick Read, the Russian psychoprophylactic methods of Velvovski, and the derivative methods of Lamaze and Vellay.

Natural Childbirth

Grantly Dick Read (1933) described his method and how he had come to develop it in his book *Natural childbirth*. He described how he had been called to deliver a child in a poor district of London, and when he had offered the woman chloroform she had refused it. After the confinement he asked the mother why she had not availed herself of the pain-killing drug and she replied that the whole process had not hurt at all, and added that, "It wasn't meant to was it doctor?" This question sent him wondering whether childbirth really should hurt and why it should, and eventually he decided that it should not hurt.

Read came to believe that civilisation had taught woman that they should regard childbirth as a very painful ordeal and hence they regarded the prospect of it with anxiety. This is a self-fulfilling prophecy, for anxiety will give rise to muscular tensions, which interfere with the natural operations of the womb and the associated muscles, thus giving rise to the considerable pain and preventing them from expelling the baby in the normal manner. The three evils of fear, pain, and tension are thus not normal to the natural process of childbirth, but have been engendered in the expectant mother by the assumptions current in our society.

It should be pointed out that Read did not deliberately choose to educate his patients in self-hypnosis, and in fact he specifically denied that he was using hypnotic methods, at least at the beginning of his career (Read, 1942). However, when experienced hypnotists such as Mandy, Farcus, Scher, and Mandy (1951) and Kroger (1952) came to examine his methods they were in no doubt that his technique depends largely on hypnotism. In fact, when Read described the behaviour of some of his best cases he gave a good description of the behaviour of someone in a somnabulistic state. In the later edition of his *Childbirth without fear* (Read, 1953) he partly retracted his repudiation of the fact that hypnosis was involved.

Read's method involved a prenatal training period which he regarded as serving three functions: education, physiotherapy, and psychotherapy. The "education" involved teaching the expectant mother the simple relevant facts of anatomy and physiology. In "physiotherapy" the mothers were given training in controlled muscular relaxation, a technique that takes some time to master and, as powerfully argued by Edmonston (1981), leads in the later stages to a hypnotic state in many people. "Psychotherapy" involved a good deal of direct suggestion to the effect that there would be no pain experienced in labour, only pressure, that anxiety was totally unnecessary and that the whole process would proceed smoothly and comfortably. Such powerful suggestions given repeatedly when the expectant mothers were in some degree of hypnosis could not fail to exert some influence when the time came for them to give birth. During labour, at the point when they were informed that they had reached the stage of two-finger dilation, mothers were instructed to employ the relaxation techniques that they had learnt, and in suitably constituted woman this would bring on a degree of hypnotic trance in which all the strong suggestion they had been given over the prenatal training period that there would be "no pain only pressure" would come to effect and they would experience a relatively pain-free labour.

Today there is surely no developed country in the world where general obstetric practice has not been influenced by Read's teaching. He probably had too exalted aspirations and claimed too much, for when controlled studies came to be done, often involving comparisons between thousands of mothers who had and who had not been given training for "natural childbirth" it was found, to the dissapointment of many, that the method neither shortened the labour nor reduced the incidence of lacerations and other obstetric complications of a physical kind. However, most of those who carried out the controlled studies agreed that those who had had the training showed less tension and anxiety, and as they asked for analgesics less frequently they obviously suffered from less pain. Good assessments of the results of Read's methods are given by Nixon (1951) and by Roberts, Wooten, McKane, and Hartnett (1953).

The Russian Psychoprophylactic Method

This method was derived quite deliberately from hypnotism, a branch of psychology that never suffered a partial eclipse in Russia in the twentieth century as it did in the West. At a Leningrad conference in 1951 it was stated that "the roots of the Psychophylactic Method are found in our previous hypnosuggestive method based on Pavlov's doctrines" (Nicoliaev, 1959). The Russians chief advocate was Velvovski and they claimed that their method was basically *physiological* and in harmony with the theories of Pavlov, which had official backing in the Communist ideology. Velvovski actually criticised Read for simply using hypnotism, whereas in his psychoprophylactic method the claim was that a considerable advance had been made in educating the expectant mother in correct thinking and hence reaching a proper physiological balance. We need not go into the somewhat complex arguments of the Pavlovian school in this matter. A good review of this Russian work is given by Chertok (1981).

The Lamaze Method

The version of psychoprophylactic method which is chiefly known in the West, is generally referred to as the Lamaze method because it was spread by the French doctor Ferdinand Lamaze who visited Russia in the 1950s and introduced similar methods into France whence it had spread all over the world (Lamaze & Vellay, 1956). It had tended to shed much of its Pavlovian overtones in the West, and though still depending basically on hypnotic techniques, it stresses the total education of mothers in relevant obstetric matters and has humanised the medical approach to childbirth in a desirable manner.

MODERN OBSTETRIC HYPNOSIS

In the 1950s and early 1960s there was considerable interest in and use of hypnotism in obstetric practice particularly in the U.S.A., but this suffered a partial eclipse for nearly 20 years for reasons that will be discussed later. In the 1980s, however, there has been a promising revival of interest in Europe, America, and Australia, as exemplified by such publications as Davidson, Garbett, and Tozer (1982), Fee and Reilley (1982), Fuchs (1980), Gibson (1982), Hilgard and Hilgard (1983), Moon and Moon (1984), Stone and Burrows (1980), Tarnowski and Smith (1986), and Tiba (1986).

OBJECTIONS TO HYPNOTISM IN OBSTETRICS

In view of the encouraging results obtained in various countries by the use of hypnotism in obstetric practice up to and during the 1950s we might have expected a wider use of it to have developed, whether it was called Natural Childbirth, the Psychoprophylactic Method of Velvovski, or the Lamaze Method. The report of the British Medical Association (1955, p.5) was generally favourable to the use of hypnotism in medicine, and it stated specifically that,

> there is a place for hypnotism in the production of anaesthesia or analgesia for surgical and dental operations, and in suitable subjects it is an effective method of relieving pain in childbirth without altering the normal course of labour.

In fact, the tide of medical opinion was to turn against hypnotism in obstetrics, and a current of hostility developed against it mainly in the U.S.A., for reasons that are not entirely clear. We will deal with the various objections to the use of hypnotic techniques that were raised under their different headings.

The Alleged Dangers of Hypnotism to Mental Health

A totally exaggerated view of the dangers to mental health was promoted by some psychiatrists, mainly of the "psychodynamic" persuasion, who influenced the American Medical Association to declare, as reported by Werner, Schauble, and Knudson (1982), that "only a psychiatrist (or psychiatrically trained physician) can use hypnosis without risking severe psychiatric damage to the obstetric patient". Such an opinion was not supported by any published facts, and in the light of modern knowledge it can be seen as being somewhat absurd. Nowadays, obstetric doctors, clinical psychologists, midwives, and obstetric nurses do in fact use hypnosis in the course of their work with perfect safety, and they have not had a specifically "psychiatric training", nor is it deemed that such a training is necessary, although their professional training naturally involves some relevant psychiatric knowledge.

The editor of *Obstetrics and Gynaecology* made a special point of warning against alleged dangers of employing hypnotism in obstetrics, making special reference to an article by Tom (1960, p.222), where he reported on "five cases in which psychiatric hospitalization was required following hypnosis". If we refer to the article in question, however, it is evident that none of the cases occurred in obstetric practice, and all the patients were psychiatrically disturbed anyway.

Later, the American Psychiatric Association (1961) strengthened the myth by placing hypnosis firmly within the province of *abnormal* psychology, a view that harked back to the discredited positions of Charcot at the Salpêtrière Hospital in the 1860s. They stated that "Hypnosis is a specialized psychiatric procedure", and made a discouraging recommendations that only those who had had at least 144 hours of training by qualified psychiatrists over a period from nine to twelve months should use hypnosis. Quite naturally medical and non-medical members of obstetric teams were deterred from using hypnosis by the prospect of so extensive a training. In the same year a conference on psychophysical methods in obstetrics stoutly opposed the use of hypnotism.

This current of opposition produced two effects. First, the beneficial tide of interest and research in the applications of hypnotism to obstetric practice, which characterised the 1950s was halted; second, those who continued to use hypnotism tended to cover it up by the use of such "euphemisms" as Natural Childbirth, psychoprophylaxis, and the Lamaze method, and did not frankly investigate what role actual hypnotic induction played in the benefits they conferred on pregnant and parturant women.

It is obvious that any technique or medication used in the obstetric practice will have its limitations and it is to the credit of the safety of hypnotism that the hostile lobby could find very few cases to publicise involving mishaps with hypnosis. The ordinary GP with no specialised knowledge of psychological medicine can be trusted to have the intelligence to recognise the very occasional woman patient with whom it is advisable to avoid using any such technique as hypnotism in obstetrics, and midwives and experienced nurses acquire a similar common sense approach. The position is well expressed by Perchard (1962, p.164) who writes:

> except in a psychiatrically ill patient and in the patient who gives a history of psychiatric illness or behaves in a way which suggests an abnormal personality, there seems to be no absolute contraindication to the use of hypnosis in either obstetrics or gynecology.

Werner (1959) reports that even women with a past history of post-partum neurosis can benefit from hypnotic training in the prenatal period. Two woman had been excluded from such training groups because of their previous post-partum neurotic episodes, but when they petitioned against such exclusion both were admitted to the hypnotic training group, and both were later delivered satisfactorily without medication, and without neurotic sequelae.

There were plenty of positive and reassuring studies involving large numbers of women where hypnosis was used in obstetrics, published in the early 1960s, e.g. August (1961), Beaudet (1963), Coulton (1960), Davidson (1962), Gross and Posner (1963), Guéguen (1962), Roig-Garcia (1961), and Zuspan (1960), but these failed to turn the tide of prejudice. Further progress in this field had to await considerable developments in hypnosis research, much of it carried out in non-clinical settings. The extent of the use of hypnosis by midwives in modern times is discussed in Chapter 13.

Is Obstetric Hypnosis too Time-consuming?

The idea that obstetric hypnosis requires a great deal of staff time is based upon a misunderstanding. Entering a hypnotic state is essentially a skill that a mother learns for herself. Some woman learn it quickly and easily, some are slower learners and show less aptitude, and a few woman can never fully utilise hypnosis. The idea that physicians have to devote a lot of time to hypnotising women in the period of prenatal preparation and in labour is mistaken. As there is nothing specifically "medical" about hypnosis an expectant mother can learn the skill from any member of the obstetric team. Again, although practice in the prenatal period, starting from about the sixth month, is desirable, it should be realised that even when there has been no prenatal hypnosis at all many women can benefit from hypnosis in labour even when it is the first time they have been hypnotised. Over half of August's (1961) 850 cases had never been hypnotised before, yet most of them derived considerable benefits from it in labour. Rock, Shipley, and Campbell (1969) used hypnotism on 22 mothers in labour who were entirely naïve to the hypnotic experience, with excellent results. They first applied a rather simple scale of hypnotic susceptibility, and they used the same technique of hypnotism with all of them when labour set in. The mothers who were most susceptible on the scale tended to experience less pain, and the group as a whole, even though no time at all had been spent on them for prenatal training, suffered less pain than those in a control group who were not hypnotised.

Some obstetricians who have used hypnosis successfully nevertheless regret the time they have spent on their patients. Thus Winkelstein (1958) states: "The special pre-labour training and the constant attendance on the patient during labour involve more time than the average obstetrician or general practitioner can afford or is able to devote". This implies that he employed a general programme that was unnecessary elaborate and time-consuming. Others such as Davidson (1962) have found that all the time necessary to train a group of six women in hypnosis was one and a half hours, and that this was highly cost efficient considering the benefits accruing. Her hypnotic group used less anaesthetics than control patients, and found the experience more rewarding. As hypnotised women have easier labours, the doctor saves time in the labour ward. There is some evidence that hypnosis actually shortens the duration of the first stage of labour (e.g. Davidson, 1962; Guéguen,

1978) but this claim has not been clearly established, and it us of no great importance. Charles, Norr, Block, Meyering, and Meyers (1978) claim that hypnosis does not in fact shorten the first stage; the decreased perception of pain in hypnosis may shorten subjectively the time of experienced labour, but not the actual duration of the physiological process. If there is a real saving of time it is in the lessening of complications that take up staff time.

Assuming that an ideal programme of prenatal training is carried out, we may refer to the model of Werner. He and his colleagues (Werner, Schauble, & Knudson, 1982) described the method thus:

> [The] format is for approximately 12 patients to meet in eight two-hour sessions, an average of 80 minutes per patient. With two two-hour sessions a week, 180 patients could be trained in one year. Since patients employing this modality with subsequent pregnancies usually need an average of only four sessions, training becomes even more economical in terms of time.
>
> This time expenditure appears highly economical in light of the time the physician saves in the labour and delivery periods, because these patients are controlled. Thus, in comparing the potential benefits of hypnosis with the actual demands placed on staff dealing with the obstetric patient, it would seem that the argument against hypnosis for this reason is unfounded.

As we have now moved forward from the era in which hypnotism was generally regarded as the prerogative of medically trained people, there is no reason at all why training in hypnosis should not be in the hands of midwives, nurses, and other non-medical personnel.

Does Hypnosis Rob the Mother of the Birth Experience?

If the birth experience does not cause too much pain, most women would prefer to get through it in a conscious rather than an unconscious state, and this has been argued against the use of hypnosis in labour. Thus Jacobson (1954) argued that his own method of conscious relaxation was to be preferred to hypnosis in labour because the mother remained fully aware of what was going on. This argument rests on the misunderstanding of the nature of hypnosis, because the hypnotic state need not cloud consciousness. It alters the perception of events in that anxiety is allayed and stimuli are not perceived as painful if the suggestions are properly presented in cases of first hypnosis with naïve patients. Where the mother has learned hypnosis over a period of time prenatally her perception of the whole event is altered. Labour is experienced as exciting, rewarding, and even as acutely pleasurable (Newton, 1975). Again, there is the mistaken idea that hypnosis necessarily imposes a complete blackout on the memory so that the mother cannot remember afterwards what the birth experience was like, but when post-hypnotic amnesia occurs it is ordinarily the product of very definite suggestions for amnesia that may be given in hypnosis.

Objections on Grounds of Personal Autonomy

Some women who have heard of obstetric hypnosis and admit that it may have many advantages for some people, feel nevertheless that it is not for them because they would find it impossible to give up any part of their personal autonomy. This objection against rests upon a misunderstanding about the nature of hypnosis. In Chapter 1 it was pointed out that hypnosis does not involve any extra compliance, nor does the hypnotised person show any increased compliance. This is one of the hardiest myths about hypnosis that still persists in face of all the contrary evidence, and still forms the basis of some theories of hypnosis (e.g. Wagstaff, 1981). In the first chapter we compared the experience of the hypnotised person with that of a spectator of a very good play or film in which the audience are "carried away" by the action, and experience the appropriate emotions. No one would maintain that their autonomy was being invaded by the actress playing Ophelia in her pathetic madness, though they might be deeply moved by empathy with the character's distress. Similarly, we can be carried away by great music if we are able to open ourselves to its influence without feeling that the musicians are invading our autonomy. The hypnotic experience is of this kind, and the dominance of one personality over another does not enter into it.

The parturant woman who employs hypnosis is far more in control of her body, of her emotions, of the whole situation, than the unhypnotised woman who feels that she is at the mercy of the doctor, the midwife, and the terrible pain that is invading her whole body like an alien force. The parturant woman wants her therapist to be an ally in enabling her to take control of the situation which otherwise might get out of hand.

Werner and his colleagues (Werner, Schauble, & Knudson, 1982, p.167) call their technique for the management of labour the "hypnoreflexogenous" technique and they urge that:

> the idea that hypnosis limits the patient's independence is a misconception. We feel that hypnosis offers that utmost in relaxation and build-up of self-confidence leading to a greater experience of control and free will. The hypnoreflexogenous technique is permissive, leading to enhanced perception and understanding. Hypnosis offers the patient the opportunity to learn how better to control her experience in the way that will be most productive to her.

Are Women Being Denied Analgesic Drugs?

We have now a range of excellent pharmacological techniques for controlling pain in labour, so it may be argued that we should concentrate on improving these techniques rather than seeking to substitute hypnotism for them. It should be clearly understood, however, that in all cases where labour has been under hypnosis the full range of pharmacological agents has been available if required. The use of one method does not preclude the other. In practice it has been found that comparing groups of women in labour using hypnosis with groups not using hypnosis, the former group use far fewer analgesic and anaesthetic drugs even for such post-partum measures as repairing episiotomy.

Those who have kept careful records of the percentages of women having labour under hypnosis who have needed no drugs at all report pain-free labour in from 35% to 90% of the populations studied (Cheek & LeCron, 1968; Coulton, 1960; Gross & Posner, 1973; Kline & Guze, 1963; Malyska & Christenson, 1967; Mellgren, 1960; Oystragh, 1970; Pascatto & Mead, 1967; Perchard, 1962; Tom, 1960). The fact that the drugs are freely available, *if required*, for women in hypnosis may make them more able to enter a satisfactory state of hypnosis and find, perhaps to their surprise, that as no pain is experienced they do not have to ask for analgesics.

There is no conflict, therefore, between hypnotic and pharmacological techniques applied to obstetrics; they complement one another. There is no reason at all why continued research and development in anaesthesiology should not be encouraged so that we shall have better agents available when needed, and the increasing use of hypnotic techniques in obstetrics can only aid such research. We do not need to stress the fact that the ideal should be no drugs at all for the sake of the mother's experience and the health of her baby. That there is some potential harm to infants through the use of drugs is obvious. Standley, Soule, Copan, & Duchowny (1974) studied the effects of local and regional maternal anaesthesia on 60 firstborn infants three days after birth, and their paper reviews other relevant studies. Pharmacological techniques have improved, but they are still not without their side-effects.

METHODS OF HYPNOTIC TRAINING AND APPLICATION

We cannot hope to do more in this chapter than to outline the general principles of programmes of training for obstetric hypnosis that are discussed in detail in various modern textbooks and substantial review articles (Beck & Hall, 1978; Burrows, 1978; Charles et al., 1978; Davenport-Slack, 1975; Fee & Reilly, 1982; Hilgard & Hilgard, 1983; Stone & Burrows, 1980; Werner, Schauble, & Knudson, 1982). In general, programmes of training begin between the fourth and seventh month, unless complications in pregnancy such as marked anxiety indicate earlier hypnotic treatment. There are generally about six or eight sessions, the initial ones being devoted to explaining the nature of hypnosis and assessing how the individual patient can best develop what skills she has relevant to hypnotic experience. After one or two individual sessions, group training may begin, and the patients are instructed to practise auto-hypnosis at home. There is a growing use of tape-recorded instructions for home use to assist the learning of the requisite skills. Stone and Burrows (1980, p. 320) record the following:

> Dr: "How do you like the classes?" Patient: "They're good, but I keep falling asleep." This almost invariably indicates a highly hypnotizable subject. The women are usually best seen monthly for the first few months, and perhaps weekly for the few weeks just

prior to the expected date of birth. If a mother has used hypnosis in an earlier pregnancy, two brief sessions of about 20 minutes, are often adequate preparation for later confinements.

Therapists generally advise against concentrating too much on the training being designed to overcome pain; the general tenor of the programme should be towards the more positive aim of helping the woman to enjoy having her baby. A lot of the initial training is simply teaching deep relaxation, but hypnosis permits far more than that, such as altering sensory perceptions and exploring how altered experience can be induced in the abdomen and pelvic region. The more adept the patient becomes in the employment of autohypnosis the less dependent she will be on the obstetric team when she comes to labour.

It should be explained to the patients that there is no one correct way of utilising hypnosis in labour, but each individual must use whatever talents she possesses in her own way. Some women can easily induce a relaxed state in which they can go through the stages of labour with little discomfort, using only as much muscular effort as is strictly relevant and necessary. With others, if discomfort mounts up to the level of real pain they can retreat, as it were, into a more profound trance state and distance themselves from the unpleasant events by techniques of dissociation, even imagining that it is really happening to somebody else, while still co-operating according to the instructions of the midwife.

By practising auto-hypnosis both in training groups and at home, the individual woman will learn just what techniques of management are within her repertoire. Hilgard and Hilgard (1983) discuss eight characteristics of hypnotic techniques that may be applied in labour:

1. *Training Rehearsal.* Rehearsal of the actual process of labour can give mothers the confidence they need and change their perception of the future event from that dreaded ordeal to a challenging and fulfilling event to be anticipated with pleasure. Some therapists such as Cheek and LeCron (1968) use hypnosis to project the pregnant woman forward in time to hallucinate the actual process of labour, and to indicate when the fantasy terminates in hearing the baby give its first cry. This exercise may also reveal any ambivalences and emotional hang-ups the woman has with regard to her future acceptance of the baby, so that they can be dealt with in advance.

2. *Relaxation.* That muscular relaxation is one of the basic components of hypnosis has been stressed by many authorities, although as discussed in Chapter 1, mental relaxation is equally important in the control of anxiety and pain. Grantley Dick Read's thesis was that much of the pain and distress sometimes experienced in labour is simply due to the woman tensing up her musculature in a totally unnecessary manner and producing ischemia and exhaustion. As the early stages of prenatal training normally concentrate on learning the techniques of relaxation, those women who can develop only a moderate degree of hypnotic skill are catered for by approaching some way along the road to complete comfort in labour.

3. *Symptom Substitution.* In dealing with labour pains, as with other forms of pain, it is possible to substitute one feeling for another. For instance, as reported by Lenox (1970), a young woman practised the modification of sensations in her body in experimental work at the Stanford laboratory. She was later to have two rather difficult births with large babies and without the benefit of an obstetrician practising hypnotism. However, she was able to use her previous experience of auto-hypnosis to convert the perception of pain to "a light tingling", and she also used this technique post-partum, when recovering from considerable surgical repair, as reported by Hilgard and Hilgard (1983).

4. *Symptom Displacement.* Another technique is to displace a symptom from one part of the body to another. If the rhythmic contractions in the abdomen become too uncomfortable the patient can clasp and unclasp her hands rhythmically utilising hypnosis to displace her attention from her abdomen to her hands.

5. *Direct Suggestion.* Direct suggestion by another person can assist in symptom removal. Thus Cheek and LeCron (1968) would suggest to patients that they were "numb from the waist down". This is practised in antenatal training sessions and individually in auto-hypnosis at home. Some people can acquire a considerable proficiency in self-induced analgesia. Direct suggestions from another person can, of course, be of considerable assistance in controlling menacing forces alone, the words of the hypnotist structuring a reality in which she is calm. The contractions are interpreted as pressure and not pain, and the patient is reassured that she is in control.

6. *Transfer of Location of Analgesia.* Dentists sometimes use an interesting technique for inducing analgesia in the gums. They get the patient to concentrate not on the gums, an area about which they are naturally apprehensive, but on the fingers. Numbness and analgesia of the fingers is then induced by direct suggestion, and when this is obtained the patients are instructed to massage the gums with their numb fingers with the assurance that the analgesia will spread from the fingers to the gums (Bernick, 1972). For some reason this technique is often successful when direct suggestion concerning the part of the body about which the patient is feeling anxious is less effective. In obstetrics the patient's own hands can be the vehicle through which a calming analgesia can be spread throughout the abdomen.

7. *Techniques of Dissociation.* Dissociative techniques can be practised successfully much more readily by some people than by others. In antenatal training patients are encouraged to choose their own "scene" and to visit it and daydream vividly in hypnosis. Some people have such a marked capacity for this that they may actually come to believe that they float out of their body and observe themselves from a detached viewpoint. This "out of the body experience" is characteristic of somewhat unusual people, as discussed by Gibson (1986), and the whole question has been well discussed in relation to hypnosis by Hilgard (1986). Dissociative ability can provide a welcome relief from pain, the patient who would otherwise suffer viewing the situation calmly as though the traumatic events were happening to somebody else.

8. *Post-hypnotic Suggestion.* Post-hypnotic suggestions can be given that will reduce the post-operative pain following surgery and ensure the comfort of the mother in the post-partum period. Difficulties in accepting the baby and in lactation are often due to maternal anxiety and physical shock, and these can be countered by strong suggestions for a confident and happy sense of well-being following the birth.

A CASE REPORT

Women's experience of labour conducted under hypnosis can be very varied indeed but the following report (Crasilneck & Hall, 1973, p.158) is by a mother who had had intense pain with her first two confinements and who chose to have the third under hypnosis. While the experience was not ideal, it represents a fairly above-average account of what usually happens in labour with the use of hypnosis where there has been adequate prenatal preparation.

> A 32-year-old physician who had had two previous pregnancies asked if we would use hypnosis during her third pregnancy. Her obstetrician was in agreement, as her first two pregnancies were marked by prolonged labor of about eighteen hours accompanied by much distress and pain. She responded well to hypnosis and was seen once a week during her pregnancy. Her labor started at 9.00 am and hypnosis was induced immediately. Three hours later she delivered a normal $7^1/_2$-pound male child. Some of her recorded comments were "I feel relaxed— no tensions, no fears, no anxieties ... I know the pain perception should be pretty rough at this point ... but I am comfortable ... very comfortable ... just a dull pain ... like having a period and yet I normally have a low pain tolerance ... I should be perceiving pain but I'm not ... I almost feel like a 3+ drunk, relaxed, lethargic, but my brain is functioning so clearly, only a tight band about my abdomen occasionally ... I just don't give a damn!"

This patient did not require any chemical anaesthesia during the labour or for the repair of the episiotomy, and her final comment was "No one could ask for an experience in which the pain was so intense during my first two deliveries and yet so completely blocked this time". It should be noted that the extremely short period of labour in this case is not typical of all deliveries under hypnosis.

CONCLUSION

The history of the use of hypnotic techniques in childbirth during and since the nineteenth century has been briefly described, and mention has been made of the fluctuation of interest in it by the medical profession. Because of the less than adequate knowledge about the nature of hypnosis that has persisted until comparatively recently, the practice of hypnotism has always been under suspicion and for that reason some useful hypnotic programmes applied to obstetrics have sometimes been presented as though they did not really involve hypnosis, as in the case of the Natural Childbirth of Grantley Dick Read. A definite prejudice against the use of hypnosis in obstetrics arose in the 1960s for reasons that have been discussed, but the decade of the 1970s was characterised by a greatly increased knowledge about hypnosis and hence in the 1980s we were witnessing more widespread use of obstetric hypnosis, as evidenced by a number of influential publications.

This chapter has examined various of the objections to obstetric hypnosis, and it is shown how these have been fairly answered by various authoritative clinicians who have made a wide use of hypnotic techniques. It seems likely that hypnotic techniques in childbirth will cease to be regarded as something "special", and perhaps competing with pharamacological techniques, but will become incorporated into general obstetric practice.

11 Hypnosis in Dentistry

INTRODUCTION

Hypnosis in dentistry has been used since very early in the scientific era. It was the dentists rather than the medical profession who paid what now seems to us a proper attention to the problem of pain in treatment, and the early introduction of anaesthesia by nitrous oxide and by ether was a dental innovation and only later introduced to general surgery (see Gibson, 1982, chapter 2). At the Assembly of the French Royal Academy of Medicine in 1837 a case was presented by Cloquet in which several dental extractions had been performed painlessly under "magnetic anaesthesia" by Oudet (1837). The Assembly would not accept the fact that painless extractions could be performed thus, and maintained that Cloquet must have been "tricked".

It is worth nothing that an interest in hypnotism among dentists was generated in the Second World War because battle casualties often produced injuries to the mouth that had to be repaired at the front, where the normal dental facilities and range of chemical analgesics were not always readily available. Obtaining analgesia by means of hypnotic suggestion was therefore a very useful technique. A paper by Sampimon and Woodruff (1946) describes such usage.

It may well be asked why we should now bother about producing analgesia in dentistry by hypnotic techniques as we have so many effective chemical anaesthetics in this modern age. But hypnosis is not used primarily in dentistry as a means of abolishing pain. Its major use is, as Moss (1963) points out, "to 'normalize' the patient so that we can manage him as we do other patients". Hypnotism has its place in modern dentistry, therefore, especially in the treatment of a minority of patients who have special problems in relation to treatment, problems that also exist to some degree in all medical practice but which are specially acute in relation to dentistry and deserve special study.

THE PATIENT FRIGHTENED OF DENTAL TREATMENT

For various reasons people are specially afraid of interference with the oral cavity which has a very special significance in our protective reactions. Janis (1958) found that patients' fear of treatment of dental operations was generally more acute than their fear of minor or even major surgery. Various studies have shown that what can be termed an actual dental phobia exists in from 6% to 16% of the general population (Gale & Ayer, 1969; Kegeles, 1963; Kleinknecht, Klepac, & Alexander, 1973; Marks, 1969). According to Gerschman, Burrows, and Reade (1979), about 16% of the population are avoiding having dental treatment because of general fears of treatment. We shall therefore first examine what can be termed general dental phobia and then more specific problems, and discuss how hypnotic techniques can assist in overcoming these problems. As noted above, the object of such techniques is to "normalise" the patient.

Fairfull Smith (1985) studied 20 patients with dental phobia referred to the Glasgow Dental Hospital and treated with a combination of behaviour therapy and hypnotic techniques. They were given half-hour sessions at weekly intervals, and received from two to eight sessions at weekly intervals, and were all taught a technique of self-hypnosis and instructed to practise it at home daily at least once, but preferably three times, employing sessions of from five to ten minutes. It was therefore a fairly intensive course of treatment. About 85% of the patients overcame their phobia to a degree that permitted normal dental treatment, and after two years they were symptom-free and attending for dental treatment regularly. Fairfull Smith remarked that the general mental health of these patients improved in that "other neuroses also disappeared". Whether this was entirely the case does not matter, but at least this accords with the general finding that if one phobic condition is eradicated or improved, the general status of the patient is improved. The idea originally proposed by such psychoanalytically oriented therapists as Bookbinder (1962) that there would be "symptom substitution" has received no support in practice. It is not clear from Fairfull Smith's paper what staff at the Glasgow Dental Hospital carried out the psychological therapy, for he himself was qualified as a dentist only.

Gall (1985) has classified dental patients into four categories: (1) those who accept whatever dental treatment is necessary without qualms. Many patients in this category do not require any local anaesthetic for drilling or filling procedures; (2) those who experience some anxiety about dental treatment but nevertheless overcome their fears and accept the treatment; (3) those who have a very acute fear of dental procedures, but are willing to attend although their anxieties create special problems during treatment; (4) those who are generally unable to attend for treatment, and when they do come it is only because of the severe pain of the neglected teeth drives them to overcome their fear. The patients in category (4) have often suffered a very traumatic experience at a dental surgery in the past, and even though the treatment they have now forced themselves to undergo on a special occasion has been painless and not involved any special trauma, they still retain their phobic attitude to dentistry.

Fear of dentistry is often acquired in childhood, and this is most unfortunate as it may lead to a neglect of oral hygiene in later years. As children are particularly susceptible to hypnosis there is a good case to be made for introducing dental techniques to them using some degree of hypnosis to allay any possible fears, even if this necessitates no actual dental treatment on the child's first visit. Writers such as Carpenter (1941), Harland (1960), and Morgan (1940) have studied the onset of children's fear of dentistry, and proposed measures for its avoidance.

The techniques of the late Fairfull Smith for inducing hypnosis in children in the dental chair and preventing the development of anxiety in the situation are becoming well known, and one such session with a little girl was filmed and presented on BBC television in September 1982. The following is an account, given by Hilgard and LeBaron (1984, pp. 179–180), of some of the late Fairfull Smith's methods with children:

> Dr G. W. Fairfull Smith . . . makes wide use of laughter in his practice with children. He explains his successful method for keeping child patients happy and pain-free while they are undergoing various dental procedures . . . The method employs liberal doses of laughter, magic games, and sometimes hypnosis. "I always try to create a 'laughter-happy' mind-set before starting to work." Dr Smith, who possesses a very hearty laugh, says that the more he laughs, the more the child laughs, because laughter is infectious. He inquires of the child, "Can you laugh with me?" After both laugh, he continues, "Come on, you can do better." So both laugh again more enthusiastically. And again if need be.
>
> If the procedure is a tooth extraction, the magic game begins with this question: "Do you know any magic words?. . . I've got one . . . Abracadabra. . . I'm going to rub your gums with my *magic finger* and we will both say it." Dr Smith rubs the gum with 2 percent Xylotox while he and the child repeat together "Abracadabra". Just before he injects Xylocaine, he announces, "I'm going to touch your teeth with my *magic wand* and we'll both say the magic word." They do, the child is intrigued, and he injects. The actual extraction is next. "Now you'll notice that your lip feels cotton-wooly and your tooth has gone to sleep . . . Sleep!"

It may be noted that Fairfull Smith is employing the ancient method of inducing hypnosis pioneered by the Abbé de Faria (1819/1906), as described in Chapter 2 of the present book, that of establishing proper rapport with the patient and then giving the suggestion to "Sleep!" Further details of Fairfull Smith's methods are given by Hilgard and LeBaron (1984, pp. 180–181):

> Describing how he goes about filling a tooth in a school-age child using hypnosis as the sole anaesthetic, Dr Smith told us about his patient Jane, who had a deeply decayed tooth to be drilled and filled. In front of Jane is a long cord belt . . . that rolls around and around on small pulleys to activate the drill. After he has established a lighthearted mood, Dr Smith places two bits of white cotton on the belt as it moves in its course, and then introduces an imaginative story: "Watch the two bunnies going round and round. Do you see them?" Jane's eyes fixate on the rabbits. "Pretty soon you will see a naughty fox chasing them (this is entirely hallucinated, with no cotton as a prop)... When you see a naughty fox chasing them, your hand and arm will get very light like a feather and your mouth will open." After a few complete runs of the belt, the hand and the arm rise, the mouth opens. "Now I'm going to use the vacuum on the tooth. It's a tickly machine. I'm going to tickle your tooth... It will make your nose very itchy and you'll laugh." By this time, Dr Smith is drilling and he says the children never notice, even though a nerve has been touched. Once the tooth was sufficiently drilled, the hole in the tooth was incorporated in the story as the hiding place for the bunnies after they had escaped from the fox—a hiding place whose entrance Dr Smith then closed with the filling. The procedure ended, Jane hopped out of the chair still smiling.

Some readers, familiar to some extent with the formal inductions of hypnosis that are described in many books, may not recognise the above description as being hypnotism, although of a kind that would only be effective with a child at an age when the borderline between fantasy and reality is not very firmly established. Because of this possible misunderstanding, Hilgard and LeBaron (1984, pp. 181) comment on Fairfull Smith's account very insightfully:

> The hypnotic procedures are introduced so subtly and informally that the reader may miss the extent to which some of the familiar features of hypnosis have been used. First,a compatible relationship with the hypnotist was established as a shared jovial mood. The attentive focus on bits of cotton moving with the belt serves to accomplish eye fixation which is followed by suggestions of arm levitation and mouth opening. The bunnies are hallucinated by using cotton as a prop, and the fox is hallucinated without props. Jane's eyes fixated but never closed, a familiar feature of hypnosis in young children. With mood always pleasant and attention focused outward, any pain Jane might have felt was dissociated or converted by suggestion to tickling in the tooth or itching in the nose.

Having dealt with the general question of the use of hypnosis in the treatment of generalised anxieties and fear of dental treatment and how the development of such fear may be avoided in the early dental experiences of children, we shall proceed to examine some common conditions that present to dentists, and which are often monosymptomatic, and how hypnosis can usefully be employed in their treatment.

WHO GIVES WHAT TREATMENT?

We generally take it for granted that all dental problems should be treated by professionals who are dentally qualified, just as medical problems should be diagnosed and treated by those who are medically qualified. There is, however, a certain "grey area" concerned with those problems that are predominantly psychological rather than somatic. All good dentists and GPs have to be good "psychologists" in the ordinary sense of the word, and the above description of Fairfull Smith's methods show him to have had a profound psychological insight into the problems of children coming to the dental surgery for their early experiences of dentistry and the place that hypnotism could have in dental practice. Dentists are not mere technicians. Professor Cawson of Guy's Dental Hospital in London criticised the training of dental undergraduates in that it did not lay sufficient stress on the skills of patient management. He considered that, "the first essential of the young graduate when he starts practice is to be an expert in patient management and that advanced technical skills are of secondary importance" (Cawson, 1969). Yet in all professional work the competent practitioner has to recognise just when the patient should be referred for additional treatment to a colleague in another professional discipline. Many GPs now recognise cases in which a patient is best referred to a psychiatrist or a clinical psychologist for the treatment of emotional problems that often present at the surgery in a psychosomatic form. Within the area of what is sometimes termed "psychological medicine" there has been over the past 30 years and longer considerable changes as psychiatrists and clinical psychologists have worked out between them just who treats what. Generally, a happy compromise has been reached, and patients get the best treatment under the care of multidisciplinary teams.

Now dentists have learned to make a wider use of hypnotism in their practice there has been a tendency for some practitioners who have dental qualifications only to set up in a practice as "hypnotherapists", treating all manner of psychological problems by hypnotism with less than adequate knowledge of the complexity of the work they are trying to do. Some dentists who have been practising "hypnotherapy" with cases quite unrelated to dentistry have applied to the prestigious British Society of Experimental and Clinical Hypnosis but have been refused membership on the grounds that they were acting outside their proper professional competence. Bernard Oliver, deals with the matter in general terms in an Editorial (Oliver, pp. 2–3, 1977) in which he quotes the advice given in the 1977 Annual Report of the Medical Defence Union:

> A dental surgeon reported that he and a number of colleagues, skilled in the practice of hypnosis, were finding that their skills were sought, not only in the course of dental practice, but also in the course of psychotherapy. He asked whether his membership of the Union covered him for such practice and whether the Union had views on the subject, it being known that members had been warned in the past about the possibility of 'abnormal and unusual results (including unfounded allegations of improper

behaviour by the dental surgeon when no chaperon is present)'. The member was advised that Section 33 (1) of the Dentists' Act 1957, which defines the practice of dentistry, does not include using hypnosis for non-dental problems. Accordingly, the cover given by the Union to a dental surgeon can only extend to his use of hypnosis in the course of dental treatment.

It should be noted that the case of Fairfull Smith's treatment of children with hypnosis described above was entirely proper and within his professional competence because he was preventing the development of any sort of dental phobia or antipathy to treatment. Once such phobias have developed, however, the matter is more complex and may, in some cases, be so bound up with the patient's general psychopathology that it calls for treatment on a broader basis by professional colleagues skilled in the general area of psychopathology rather than in dentistry. The matter is discussed by David Rowley (Rowley, 1986, p.121) who writes:

> It is a mistake to think that a dental phobia is actually a dental problem; it is a psychological problem in which the phobic object is the dentist, the drill, etc. Although the chances of harming the patient are remote, professional ethics should demand that the treatment of psychological problems should be left to the right professional agency.

This is not just a matter of interdisciplinary rivalry between professions. Two eminent members of the staff at the School of Dentistry in Tel Aviv (Kleinhauz & Eli, 1986) examine the question very thoroughly, citing four case reports of dental patients who had distressing psychological side-effects after dental hypnosis and requiring treatment from non-dental specialists. They make a strong case urging that "The professional using hypnosis should not stray from his area of expertise". In the treatment offered at a famous school of dentistry there is the advantage of immediate referral to appropriate professionals if necessary, but dentists working on their own are less favoured in the matter of interdisciplinary support with little delay. It is a matter for their careful consideration.

The question of dentists using hypnosis in therapy that lies outside the professional realm of dentistry has been debated elsewhere (Gibson, 1988; Nicolaou, 1988). The whole question of professional ethics and the demarcation between different professional skills is discussed in Chapter 13.

SPECIAL DENTAL PROBLEMS

Gagging

Gagging is an automatic reflex to the threat of some foreign body obstructing the airway. Normally it is no problem because dental procedures do not pose any threat to the breathing, and the patient trusts the dentist not to do anything that would constitute such a threat. However, in a small number of patients there is an abnormal degree of gagging, which may become so severe that ordinary dental treatment becomes impossible and the sufferer allows oral hygiene to deteriorate over a long period through fear of going to the dentist.

The abnormal gagging response may occur not only in the dental chair but even in such a matter as wearing and retaining necessary dentures, and people who suffer from this abnormal gagging response are not necessarily neurotic in any general sense. Wright (1980) investigated the matter with 53 people prone to abnormal gagging and could find no evidence of any personality abnormality in them. Other writers such as Levine (1960) and Savage and McGregor (1970) tend to see the problem in terms of more deep-seated personality disorders. Possibly, there are two main types of gagger as suggested by Eli and Kleinhauz (1985). The first are people who have had some severe and traumatic experience at some time when they were in a specially vulnerable state and this has produced an abnormal conditioned reaction, as it would with many of us. The second type are people who have suffered no specially severe experience but their general unstable personality has led to the build up of this particular phobic reaction. Therapists of a generally psychodynamic orientation tend to look for symbolic and complex causation of the abnormal gagging response in the latter type of person. In either case hypnosis combined with the ordinary principles of behaviour therapy is an ideal vehicle for treating the disorder, for as noted in Chapter 3 of this book, those with a special disposition to phobic responses often make excellent hypnotic subjects and respond very readily. The following is a case study of a man who had reacted badly to a previous dental procedure.

Case Study. A 32-year-old male exhibiting an extreme gagging reflex was referred to the Clinic. The reflex not only prevented dental treatment, but was sometimes provoked by the ingestion of food. The gagging had begun four years previously during an impression procedure, which produced a "horrible feeling of choking", although the patient insisted that fear of pain was "not a problem". Assuming that this experience had acted as a conditioning stimulus, the treatment of choice was hypnorelaxation combined with *in vivo* desensitisation. Eli and Kleinhauz (1985, p.102) go on to say:

> At the first session the patient achieved a good state of relaxation during which oral hygiene, scaling, and simple root extraction were completed. At the next session examination revealed extreme destruction of the lower first molar, caused by repeated postponement of treatment, making surgery unavoidable. Extraction was performed under good hypnorelaxation level in conjunction with local anaesthesia. There were no gagging problems. Additional dental treatment was carried out in other sessions under hypnorelaxation with good co-operation. Although the need for hypnorelaxation during dental treatment remains, the patient is now able to undergo routine treatment.

Eli and Kleinhauz also cite more complex cases in which there is some evidence of a generalised neurotic disposition,which is manifested in the presenting symptom of the abnormal gagging response. In such cases it is more doubtful whether dentists should attempt the treatment themselves as it is not a simple dental problem. This is well recognised by many dentists, who prefer to refer such cases in the first place to therapists such as clinical psychologists and psychiatrists who are specially trained to deal with generalised emotional problems. This point is noted by Rowley (1986, p.121) who writes:

> There are a number of potential problems in the use of hypnosis by dentists. One is that the patient may have some psychological problem which being hypnotized gives them the freedom to reveal. Since they are not qualified to deal with this, and it is really not possible effectively to screen patients for this, dentists must be aware that this is a possibility, albeit remote,and know what course of action to take. Such action would generally be advising the patient to seek help from another professional.

Reviews of the problem of gagging in dentistry and the various methods used to treat it have been published by Conny and Tedesco (1983a,b). Traditionally the problem has been dealt with by various sorts of pre-medication as described by Kramer and Braham (1977) and by Rothschild (1959), but although pre-medication may enable treatment to be carried out on a specific occasion, patients do not overcome the difficulty for the future and may still tend to avoid dental treatment because of their fear. The long-term object should be to enable patients to overcome the habit, and this is the purpose of hypnotherapy. Weyandt (1972) cites the case of a man who was unable to tolerate dental treatment without an anaesthetic because of his extreme gagging, but found that he could permit X-rays to be taken when hyponotised, and in later years he was able to undergo various dental treatments quite comfortably when in hypnosis and hence lost his fear of going to the dentist. In this context hypnotism would seem to be the ideal solution to a problem that prevents some people making visits to the dentist on a regular basis.

Excessive Bleeding

Excessive bleeding after tooth extraction or other such work on the gums is of course a special problem for patients suffering from haemophilia and demands very special measures for control. There are other patients, however, who are not haemophiliacs yet suffer from excessive bleeding from the gums after dental operations, and hypnotism offers a means by which such bleeding may be controlled. Hilgard and Hilgard (1983, p.158) comment:

> How the control of bleeding is achieved as a consequence of suggestion is by no means clear. It may be a secondary consequence of the general relaxation achieved under hypnosis; or it may be related to the specific control of vasomotor responses that can be developed through hypnosis and biofeedback, as in the selective control of hand temperature.

Newman (1971) cites the case of a woman who had bled for eight hours after the extraction of a tooth. On a later occasion she was hypnotised and after a tooth was removed she was given strong suggestions that she would not bleed and that her mouth would feel perfectly comfortable. The bleeding stopped after about one minute, and she felt so normal that she returned to work. This entire procedure involving hypnotism and extraction of a tooth took about 15 minutes only.

Hypnosis has also been used in the case of haemophiliacs despite the very special physiological problem they present. The following case study is reported by Dubin and Shapiro (1974) as summarised by Bowers (1983, p.145):

> A patient suffering a particularly severe form of haemophilia needed a left upper molar removed. There was particular concern about postoperative haemorrhaging, and, as a consequence, a decision was made to employ hypnosis as a way of minimizing the patient's blood loss. Training and preparation before surgery included repeated hypnotizing of the patient, suggestions for pain anaesthesia, and suggestions that he would not hemorrhage before or after surgery. The patient was told to accomplish this last suggestion by visualizing blood as water coming from a faucet that he could turn off, willfully constricting the blood vessels, or mentally suturing the sides of his wounds. According to the authors, 'the extractions was accomplished without incident and with minimal bleeding' (p.82). The 'patient was discharged on the eighth postoperative day, having required no blood or plasma replacement' (p.82).

It may be surprising that so physiological a condition as haemophilia, depending as it does on an abnormal constitution of the blood, should be modifiable as to its manifestations by hypnotic suggestion, but there is good evidence that this is the case. This matter is examined in detail in Chapter 7.

Bruxism and Myofascial Pain

Bruxism is the forceful grinding or clenching of the teeth when food is not being chewed. There are two main varieties, diurnal, which generally consists of a mere clenching of the teeth in periods of stress and is largely involuntary, and nocturnal, which is often a grinding motion that is frequently audible. This habit may result in the development of flat areas on the teeth, with facets, excessive wear and even fractures. The teeth are not the only site of injury in some cases. The powerful exercise of the related muscles may cause breakdown of the bone supporting the teeth and peridontal disease may result, with a loosening and loss of teeth (see Glaros & Rao, 1977).

A further result of bruxism may be that the masticatory muscles and those around the temporomandibulary joints are injured by the excessive strain, giving rise to the myofascial pain-dysfunction syndrome, a chronically painful condition of the face (Cannistraci, 1977). This pain is often one-sided, and once established it is very difficult to treat successfully.

The causes of bruxism have not been clearly established. It seems reasonable to suppose that the diurnal variety arises in people who are subject to a good deal of anxiety, and indeed to suppressed rage in which they "grind" or "gnash" their teeth. Lewis (1961) suggests that it is an expression of repressed oral aggression. The nocturnal variety does not appear to be associated with any special abnormality of personality; Hartman et al. (1987) made a quite detailed study of 16 people who suffered from nocturnal bruxism, but could find nothing unusual about their personality or way of life. It is likely that nocturnal bruxism is one of these habits characterised by Broughton (1968) as disorders of arousal, that is, an unusual and occasional result of the depth of sleep lightening and causing spasms of muscular movement.

Dental treatment of bruxism may take several forms, such as endeavouring to obtain optimal occlusion by selective grinding or restoration of the teeth. In addition, acrylic shields may be made to protect the teeth and thus to cure the habit (Greenwald, 1968). If the habit is cured by such appliances which are normally worn at night, it is probably due to an interruption of the feedback mechanism, as suggested by Scandrett and Ervin (1973). Several types of psychological treatment have also been used in the treatment of bruxism, including psychoanalysis (Goldberg, 1973), massed practice (Ayer & Levin, 1975), biofeedback (Piccione, Contes, George, Rosenthal, & Kargmark, 1982), and hypnotism (Graham, 1974). Naturally the latter type of treatment will appeal to the many dentists who now use hypnotism for various purposes in their surgeries. Hypnotism has been shown to be useful in the treatment of other nocturnal disorders of arousal such as enuresis, and it is appropriate to use it in the present context, although very little has been published concerning its effectiveness. When bruxism has led to the myofascial pain-dysfunction syndrome, hypnosis can also be effective, as reported by Golan (1971).

Dentists may feel fairly confident in the treatment of bruxism with hypnotism by themselves and have no need in most cases to refer patients to a professional colleague. In complex cases of myofascial pain, however, there may be additional complications involving the psychopathology of patients which is really outside the dental sphere. This matter has been discussed above with reference to the problem of gagging and the observation of Rowley (1986) on the matter. In severe cases of myofascial pain it may be necessary to supplement whatever dental work is necessary by referring patients to a pain clinic where they will get the benefit of therapy from an interdisciplinary team.

HYPNOSIS IN THE RELIEF OF OPERATIVE PAIN

We began this chapter with a reference to Oudet who extracted a tooth in 1837 with hypnosis as the sole analgesic and aroused much scepticism among his professional colleagues. We then went on to point out that, as there are now many suitable pain-killing drugs, relying on hypnosis as the sole means of analgesia is most unusual today and that hypnosis is used in the treatment of many problems in dentistry other than in the direct relief of pain. It is of interest, however, to note that hypnosis may be of used in pain-killing by enabling the anxious or phobic patient to accept the injection of a drug, and also in the mitigation of post-operative pain. Just occasionally, in rather special circumstances, hypnosis is used as the sole analgesic, and it is instructive to look at some of the cases.

Hypnosis as the Sole Analgesic

Crasilneck, McCranie, and Jenkins (1956) report the case of a woman who had a special allergy and who had reacted to the injection of procaine with nausea and various other unpleasant symptoms, and so she later neglected to seek further dental treatment until her teeth were in a very bad state and needing various complex and lengthy dental procedures. Because of her allergy and her past unhappy experience, she was persuaded to try such treatment with hypnosis as the sole analgesic. She reacted to hypnotism very favourably and achieved a satisfactory trance state, and with the aid of hypnosis she was able to dispense with analgesic drugs throughout five lengthy sessions of dental treatment.

Another recognised although uncommon use of hypnosis as the sole analgesic is with people who have a special attitude to health that involves the total rejection of the use of drugs. Such a case is reported by Weyandt (1972), concerning a man who needed to have seven upper maxilliary teeth extracted in order that he could be fitted with an upper denture, but was not prepared to accept the use of the drug injections that would normally be deemed necessary. He was willing to attend the surgery on a number of occasions on which the whole question of hypnotism was explained to him and there were practice sessions of hypnotic induction of a conventional kind. Preliminary non-painful procedures such as the taking of impressions for dentures were initiated in these early sessions and his capacity to produce analgesia in hypnosis was assessed. Fortunately he proved to be a very susceptible subject and the seven teeth were eventually extracted painlessly. Hypnosis also helped in the post-operative work of removing sutures, and in inducing tolerance of the newly fitted dentures. Such a long-continued series of sessions was quite time-consuming, but it did enable the patient to have the necessary work done without infringing what was for him an important matter of principle.

Another unusual case is reported by Radin (1972) who treated a man who suffered from a rheumatic heart and various associated symptoms that made a general anaesthetic inadvisable. The poor condition of his teeth was such that he needed a long course of treatment, and this he underwent over several months with the aid of hypnosis and without any chemical anaesthesia.

In the three cases just cited the patients were excellent hypnotic subjects, and it was only because they had such a good aptitude for hypnosis that drug-free treatment proceeded so successfully.

Hypnotic Analgesia in Normal Practice

Wadden and Anderton (1982) report a large number of studies by various therapists who used hypnosis in the alleviation of pain, and they make the point that the success of the analgesic suggestions is largely related to the degree of susceptibility to hypnosis of the individual patient. Their list of studies includes one by Gottfredson (1973) with dental patients in which the effectiveness of a chemical analgesic is compared with that of hypnotic suggestion. The relative degrees of susceptibility to hypnosis were formally assessed and it was found that patients who were highly susceptible to hypnosis were about twice as successful in benefiting from hypnotic analgesia as those who were assessed as being poorly susceptible.

There are also in this list of studies two dental studies by Joseph Barber (Note 1, 1977) which are very surprising in that they appear to go against the general trend of all the other studies reporting the use of hypnosis in the alleviation of pain. In the first of these there was no relationship between measured hypnotic susceptibility and the alleviation of pain. In the second study, although hypnotic susceptibility was not measured, it is reported that "99% completed the dental treatment without chemical anesthetic" (Wadden & Anderton, 1982, p. 232). The reasons for this surprising anomaly and astonishingly high rate of claimed success would seem to lie partly in the particular procedure used by Barber, and in the nature of the "hypnotic induction". Barber called this "Rapid Induction Analgesia" (RIA), but the form of words in it seems designed to calm and reassure patients rather than to produce any actual alterations in their perception of pain such as is usual in hypnotic suggestions for analgesia.

The nature of pain is discussed in detail in Chapter 8. Pain is a complex experience made up partly of an *emotional-motivational* component that is affected very much by the degree of anxiety that the patient is experiencing, and partly of a *sensory* component which is a matter of the perception of aversive stimuli that can be greatly modified by hypnotic suggestion. As already pointed out, the form of words of the RIA would appear designed to calm the *emotional-motivational* factor, but not to address the *sensory* factor at all.

Gillett and Coe (Note 9) tried to replicate Barber's study using 60 dental patients and, using Barber's criteria, they claimed a 52% success rate, but they add significantly: "It is one thing to claim 52% success overall, it is another to recognize that most of the success was shown on dental procedures *that may not require chemical anaesthesia in the first place*" (emphasis added). It seems likely that in Barber's study, as long as the patients were kept calm and reassured, they could endure dental procedures that were not particularly painful without demanding the chemical analgesics that were to hand if required. Barber's study and the "spiel" known as the RIA has come in for a good deal of comment and criticism. Van Gorp and Meyer (Note 17) found that the RIA was no more effective in reducing pain than a no-treatment control procedure. The latter study was experimental, and in the clinical study of Crowley (1980), using the RIA with podiatric surgery, it was found that only a "small percentage" of patients responded successfully in terms of real analgesia. Similarly, in a clinical study by Snow (1979) the success rate was rather low. Important criticisms of the RIA have also been made by Gibson (1985), Hilgard (1978), and Orne (1980b). Finally it should be noted that although the RIA by its title is alleged to be "Rapid", it takes all of 23 minutes to administer.

CONCLUSION

A good deal of space has been devoted to discussing and criticising the study of Barber (1977) with its astonishing claim of "99% success", and the RIA, because there is always the danger that this or that method of hypnotism can become oversold and the continuing scepticism that all hypnotism is something of a marginally respectable "con trick" will be reinforced. It is safe to say that while dental procedures that are not particularly painful anyway are tolerated much better when patients are calm and reassured, one has to obtain a considerable degree of hypnotic responsiveness before analgesia can be induced in really painful operations, and this is only possible when patients have a good aptitude for hypnosis.

It is useful for dentists who practise hypnotism to have an adequate knowledge of the wide possibilities and limitations of hypnotic procedures in the induction of analgesia and their applications to other dental problems. Above we quoted three examples of the use of hypnosis as the sole analgesic measure in some quite severe dental operations; these are unusual cases but they are illustrative in their own right. Hilgard and Hilgard (1983, p. 150) present a table reporting nine separate published studies in which, for one reason or another, hypnotic suggestion was the sole means of securing analgesia in quite major operations, and it is clear that this is a possibility when drugs are contra-indicated. As most people tolerate drugs well, hypnotism must be regarded as a useful adjuctive technique, first, for calming anxiety, and, second, for producing in most people a degree of relative analgesia, which enhances the traditional drug-based methods that are already in use, and facilitates their application in some difficult cases. This chapter has endeavoured to give an overview of the relevant evidence and to make a case for the expanding use of hypnotism in dentistry.

12 Hypnosis with Children

HYPNOSIS AS A NATURAL SKILL

How should one approach the use of hypnosis with children? Certainly not in the same way that one approaches hypnosis with adults! With adults we tend to work along the lines that they come to us with a specific problem (not the only one they have but certainly the most pressing one of the the moment) and we teach them a procedure termed "hypnosis" which they may use to help themselves overcome or alleviate in some way that particular problem. In reality, however, we are not teaching them anything which they can't already do, and as was argued in Chapter 3, their capacity to experience hypnosis is something which resides within themselves and only to a limited extent is dependent on the aptitudes of the hypnotist. Most people seem to discover fairly quickly their ability to experience hypnosis to the limits of their susceptibility. This contrasts with many skills and knowledge, which we acquire through life; often, as in the case of learning to read and write, we lack almost totally the relevant skills and information at the outset, and we require much teaching and practice to acquire them.

Hypnosis is not just a method by which the patient overcomes a particular problem—say anxiety, insomnia or headache. It is a procedure which can be adapted to meet the requirements of a wide range of circumstances in the person's life. Usually, however, in clinical practice we only show patients how to harness their hypnotic capabilities to help them cope with the particular situation or set of circumstances identified as the "problem".

The same reasoning applies with children and adolescents. Hypnosis in large part involves the ability to become absorbed in imaginal processes to the exclusion of other external stimulation and to attenuate critical and analytical thinking. Children are very good at this and to some degree it is an ability which diminishes as we age. In fact hypnotic susceptibility has been shown to peak some time during childhood, around 9 to 12 years (see Chapter 3). It is also believed (Lynn & Rhue, 1988) that those individuals who in childhood had a rich fantasy world tend to be good hypnotic subjects. These include individuals who created an imaginary companion or companions, and, sadly, those who were horribly abused by their parents. It seems that children thus treated may develop a defensive dissociation as a protection against the harsh realities of their lives, and it has been suggested that a few may develop multiple personalities in adulthood (Kluft, 1984; Kirsch & Barton, 1988). However, dissociation may not necessarily be a defensive reaction and may be a resource developed by many children who are well cared for and leading happy lives.

We may therefore argue that since children have the greatest natural aptitude for hypnosis, and since hypnosis can be helpful in coping with many situations and problems in everyday life, then children should be encouraged to practise self-hypnosis and be guided by adults in how to bring this resource to bear in different circumstances. In fact, if we take a wide-angled view of hypnosis, this idea is not far removed from what occurs naturally in the child's life: absorption in a bed-time story helps the child get off to sleep; similarly, attending to a video of a favourite cartoon may help distract from the discomfort of illness; and daydreaming may prove very productive for the purpose of writing a story. However, the formal teaching of this process to all children, involving as it would the regular practice of hetero- and self-hypnosis, may be too ambitious a goal. The child who is striving to overcome some personal difficulty, or one who knows constant pain, will be well-motivated to practise and apply hypnotic procedures, but where the pay-offs are not so immediately obvious then the necessary diligence may be unforthcoming. We also have the problem that although children and young people do appreciate discipline and prompting from authority figures, too often the process of learning, which should in some significant measure be a stimulating and challenging enterprise, is reduced to an interminable series of chores to be undertaken reluctantly and avoided when possible. Regrettably, this is a large part of the unofficial story of formal education. One has only to ask people of their experience of being "taught" sport or physical recreation, not to mention art, music, and literature, to realise the havoc sometimes wrought by those professionally designated as teachers of such pursuits.

HYPNOSIS IN EDUCATION

Notwithstanding these pitfalls, attempts have been made in some progressive quarters to introduce relaxation and fantasy procedures into the classroom, and the children involved, if motivated, may well be able to bring these skills and techniques to bear outside their school activities. For example, Galyean (1986) has outlined relaxation and guided imagery procedures both in the preparation for lessons and in facilitating learning new material. She reports that empirical investigations have demonstrated improvements in self-esteem and classroom behaviour in remedial students and significant gains in scholastic attainments. In this country Macmillan (1988) has presented encouraging results from his investigations of "suggestopaedia", a procedure developed by Lozanov (1978). Macmillan's method involves the preparation for learning using relaxation and rhythmic breathing followed by the presentation of the material to be learned (spelling rules in Macmillan's case) in bursts of 4–6 seconds with a 2–4 second pause between each statement. Children are seen in groups or individually. The best results have been obtained for able under-achievers. Macmillan believes that relaxation is the most important ingredient in this approach and rejects quasi-scientific notions of right- and left-brain differences put forward by some authors.

There is no doubt that the procedures described by Galyean and Macmillan have much in common with hypnotic techniques but there is no reason why schoolteachers should not be trained in their use. We wish to emphasise however that the use of formal methods of hypnosis with children should not be undertaken lightly. Some time ago, one of the authors (M.Heap) was involved, albeit in a mercifully peripheral capacity, in the case of a child who had participated in an after-school session of group hypnosis conducted by one of his teachers. During some kind of guided fantasy, the child experienced frightening visual distortions and returned home in great distress. The parents naturally took up the matter with the headmaster, and the local press carried the story. The teacher concerned was quite rightly dismissed, since he or she had no business to be engaged in such activities, but as a result of this the child was victimised by his classmates and left the school. The boy's distress continued at his new school and eventually the whole family moved to a new locality. Still traumatised by the experience and its sequelae, the boy again failed to settle and was referred to an adolescent unit.

A feature of this very sorry sequence of events was the never-ending procession of all manner of experts in child welfare—doctors, psychiatrists, psychologists, social workers, teachers, and educationalists, not to mention solicitors and barristers. All this was fuelled by the family's difficulty in coping independently with external stresses, and the interminable legal proceedings which held out the promise of financial compensation at some indeterminate date in the future. All, of course, with the best interests of the child at heart!

For further discussions of the use of hypnosis in educational settings the reader may consult Houghton (1988). Johnson, Johnson, Olson, and Newman (1981) have also reported improvements in self-esteem (but not academic performance) in "learning disabled" children who practised daily self-hypnosis over a period of six weeks.

HYPNOTIC INDUCTION PROCEDURES WITH CHILDREN

General Considerations

It is quite possible to employ the same standard induction and deepening methods with children as for adults, but the practitioner who invariably does so will soon encounter difficulties and disappointments, especially with younger children. This is because these methods, unless suitably modified, are often insufficiently stimulating to solicit the required degree of co-operation from children, who will easily be distracted by the search for more interesting forms of activity. The therapist must therefore make an all-out effort to establish a close rapport and a relationship of trust and acceptance. His or her role must be flexible, at various times representing a parent figure, friend, teacher, comforter, rival, authority-figure-to-rebel-against, and so on. In this relationship the child's interests, talents, and natural inclinations must be fully engaged and exploited. Moreover, the therapist must not assume the role of trying to do something *to* the child to *make* him or her better. It is vital that the child is actively engaged both in the experience of hypnosis and in the resolution of his or her problem. We hope our presentation will make this very clear.

Most children have a facility for vivid imagination and, as we shall see, this may be harnessed to good effect in the induction of hypnosis. The therapist must therefore ascertain and utilise the child's interests and fascinations; good material includes favourite sports, games, TV programmes, and holiday places, as well as fantasies such as riding on a magic carpet and space travel.

Other relevant characteristics of child subjects are a sense of adventure and curiosity, rebelliousness, and appreciation of challenge and suspense. "I wonder how Dr Who manages to take a nap with all those Daleks around?" may be a good introduction to a guided fantasy for an anxious child with sleep disturbances. Similar challenges, which may be liberally interspersed by the therapist during play or fantasy, may be introduced by expressions such as "I bet you don't know....", "Can you imagine how...?", "I'm very curious to know..", "I bet you can't tell me...", "I really don't know how...", and "Let's find out...".

With young children especially, fantasy methods, including the telling of stories by the therapist, may constitute the entire hypnotic sequence, and the child's response may be variable, sometimes being one of rapt attention while at other times he or she may be fidgety and easily distractible. The eyes may be closed all or some of the time, or they may remain open. For example, with the "magic television" technique described later, older children may be asked to close their eyes to imagine the television, whereas with younger children it may be easier to suggest that they imagine the television in the room itself. Some techniques involve the use of toys or puppets which, of course, require that the child's eyes be kept open, at least in the initial stages. In the case of older children, say those entering adolescence and beyond, and more compliant youngsters, the response to hypnotic methods more closely resembles that of adults—i.e. physically relaxed, quiescent, immobile, and with eyes closed the whole time. Whatever the case, however, the essential ingredient is that the subject's attention and fascination are held while therapeutic suggestions, ideas and imagery are offered either in a direct manner or often indirectly in the form of story and metaphor.

Formal Relaxation and Hypnotic Induction Procedures

While the stages of pre-induction, deepening, therapy, and alerting may not always be clearly differentiated with adult subjects, such is even more the case with children, and it is often quite inappropriate to structure a session of therapy around this framework. Some fantasy procedures, described later, may comprise the sum total of the interaction we refer to as "hypnosis", although there is no obvious "induction" or "deepening" component.

Notwithstanding this, it is quite possible for the purposes of therapy, especially with older children, to adapt the formal induction procedures used with adult subjects. We suggest, however, that methods involving sustained eye fixation with suggestions of eye heaviness be avoided; they are tedious, and children are not as responsive as adults to this suggestion (London & Cooper, 1969). Arm levitation may be used, although again this should not be unduly prolonged (it may be useful to help the child create the floating feeling by lightly lifting his or her hand) and the child's interest should be maintained by, say, the creation of suspense using the kinds of phraseology described earlier, and the use of imagery (e.g. "a big balloon tugging at your wrist").

Challenges in the form of suggestions of catalepsy of the eyelids ("you cannot open your eyes") and fingers ("you cannot unlock your fingers") may occasion some anxiety and should be used with discretion. Progressive relaxation and breathing techniques are useful if they can be rendered interesting to the subject. One way of doing this is for the therapist to assume an educative role, informing the child of how his or her body can become tensed up unnecessarily (the therapist and child can do some tensing-up exercises together by way of illustration and instances of tense situations in the child's life may be elicited). A rationale can then be provided to the child for learning how to relax and not be tense. For instance, it may be explained that the bad feelings of tension are often caused by the brain sending messages to the muscles in different parts of the body (hands, shoulders, stomach, face, etc.) telling them to tense up. "Now Mary", the therapist may continue, "I bet you'd like to learn how your brain can send messages to those muscles, telling them to relax again and that there's no reason to get all tensed up. Yes? This is a special way of relaxing—most grown-ups don't even know how to do this. Shall we find out how it works?" Then a progressive relaxation procedure may be instigated; it should not be an unnecessarily protracted affair and the child's attention needs to be engaged throughout if he or she is going to make use of this procedure—for example by regularly referring to the idea of the brain sending messages to the muscles. Thus, it is *the child* who is actively bringing about the desired changes for himself or herself, and not the therapist who is doing something *to* the child. To emphasise this, Aronson (1985) describes how the therapist can work with the child (in this case on a residential adolescent unit) to produce his or her own "personalised" hypnotic script which is then recorded on tape and practised twice weekly.

The reader may consider how other procedures, such as relaxed breathing, the hand-on-abdomen method, retrieval of resources, anchoring, and the variations of the clenched fist technique, all presented in Chapters 5 and 7, may be adapted for children. These methods are extremely useful in helping youngsters suffering from anxiety or pain.

Specific Induction Procedures for Children

There are a number of formal induction methods which tend to be more appropriate for children than adults. We shall briefly discuss three common ones here. The first does involve some eye fixation but this is not prolonged and is rendered more interesting for the child than adult methods. The child is instructed to hold a coin between thumb and forefinger, elevated and at arm's length. The coin may be chosen for some interesting quality—say brightness or unfamiliarity—and we prefer that it is held very loosely at the side by the rim. The child then fixates the coin while suggestions of arm and eye heaviness along with comfort and relaxation are given, plus the instruction that at some stage the coin will slip out of the hand and fall to the floor, and that as soon as that happens the eyes will close. A similar method is to draw a face on one of the child's thumbs; the child fixates the thumb at arm's length and suggestions of arm and eye heaviness, arm-lowering and eye-closure are administered, again with suggestions of general comfort and relaxation. Lots of ploys to maintain the child's interest can be invented by the therapist—e.g. "Look at Freddy" (the face on the thumb), "He's getting really tired too".

A third method is to ask the child to imagine sitting by the side of a pool in which is floating a large beach ball. The child then reaches out sideways to let his or her arm rest on the ball, which floats up and down, lifting and lowering the arm in a gentle rhythm as the child becomes more and more relaxed, tired, and sleepy, and that when he or she is very deeply relaxed the arm will gradually come to rest (or return to his or her lap).

Readers seeking other induction procedures for children are advised to consult texts such as Gardner and Olness (1981) and are reassured, too, that they should feel at liberty to draw on their own intuition and inventiveness, aided by the above guidelines.

IMAGINATION TECHNIQUES

Many of the methods appropriate for children involve the extensive use of imagery. Not only may these be considered as "induction" procedures, they may also constitute a significant part of the therapy. We will describe a number of the more commonly used techniques.

The Secret Place

The "secret (safe or happy) place" technique may also be employed with adults, and the main modification for children involves the use of appropriate language. For example: "Now, I wonder if you would like to close your eyes and imagine being somewhere really nice? Maybe somewhere where you've been on holiday or some place you've been with your friends... I bet you can imagine it so well it feels as if you're really there! ...Yes?...That's nice! And you know what it's like when you think of something really pleasant and exciting... You can feel really good right now! ... This is your *special* place—your *secret* place. It can be a *magic* place, where anything you *want* to happen, *can* happen. You can give it a name if you want—a special, secret name. You don't even have to tell me where your special place is, nor what the secret name is, but any time you want to feel better, you can always go in your imagination to your safe, secret place. Just say the name to yourself—like a secret password! Then imagine being there, feeling really safe, really good!" There may then follow further suggestions of relaxation, perhaps by counting 1 to 20 while the child continues to be absorbed in his or her imagery.

The above patter may well suit a younger child but, say with an intellectual adolescent, a more suitable wording may be required. Note, also, that the suggestions contain instructions for the practice of self-hypnosis and anxiety control, which may of course be elaborated upon as required.

The Secret or Magic Television

Here children are asked to imagine a secret television set which can show any programme they wish (or as indicated by the therapist). Nowadays the idea may be introduced that there are lots of videotapes to choose from. (The therapist need not be too concerned if a child's family does not possess a television or video-recorder since the child will most likely enjoy imagining owning one.) As with adults, it may be suggested in due course that material of relevance to the child's problem is appearing on the screen. This is illustrated in the case of Philip, described later.

Once again, this imagery may be employed as a trigger for self-hypnosis or anxiety control. This method may also be combined with the "secret place" technique. For example, nine-year-old David was first asked to imagine being in a safe place, and then having a special television with him. "Up a tree?" he exclaimed in astonishment. "Oh yes!" continued his therapist. "Why not?" This is a MAGIC television set!"

As was earlier stated, with some children this method may be more appropriately conducted with the eyes open. "I bet you can't see my magic television" the therapist may say, pointing to the wall opposite. "I wonder what's on now. Why not go and switch it on—it might be your favourite programme!"

Other Fantasy Techniques

There is an infinite number of fantasy procedures, and the therapist should be adept at constructing his or her own according to the needs and interests of the child. Apart from those already mentioned, regular favourites include flying on a magic carpet and travelling in a space ship. The therapist uses the fantasy to deliver suggestions, direct or indirect, of well-being, confidence, and ways of handling, or finding a solution to, the presenting problems.

Benson (1984, 1988), has detailed some useful fantasy procedures which she employs in her hypnotherapeutic work with disturbed children and adolescents. One, described as "ego-strengthening" invites the child to imagine making some magic biscuits: into the mixing bowl are poured all the good ingredients of the child's life, the happy memories, his or her good qualities, all the people who have been kind and caring, and so on. These are mixed together to make a supply of magic biscuits which the child can imagine eating whenever he or she needs to feel better. When the supply runs out, some more may be made in imagination.

Another example of symbolic fantasy used by Benson is the image of a journey to the centre of a maze (either a pencil-and-paper type or a life-size one with tall hedges). The centre of the maze, the child is informed, represents where he or she wants to be in the future. (This may first be elicited by imagining the scene, say when the child has reached the age of 20 years, appearing in a crystal ball.) The child is then asked to find a path through the maze, working round any obstacles and boundaries. He or she may signal (say with a finger) if unable to get past a barrier and is then invited to talk about what this barrier may symbolise and how it may be surmounted. (A similar fantasy is that of climbing to the top of a mountain, meeting all kinds of obstacles and hazards *en route*, then, on arriving at the summit, feeling strength and achievement, and the confidence to face other real-life problems and challenges which life may be presenting.)

Yet another fantasy is that of sorting out an untidy desk containing everything to do with the child's life, with different drawers for different aspects of his or her life. The child is instructed to clear out all the rubbish, to dust and tidy the drawers, keeping everything he or she needs in a safe place and putting aside any problems so that these may be dealt with later. When the child signals that all this has been done, he or she may then be encouraged to examine those problems set aside, imagining them all wrapped up in a paper parcel, each layer of the parcel being a different problem, there being one label on one side stating what the problem is, and another label on the reverse side giving some ideas of how the problem may be handled. The child is invited to say what the problems are, if he or she so wishes, and counselling is given concerning how they may be overcome. Once the child signals that he or she is ready to let go of the problem, it is thrown away in imagination.

STORY-TELLING METHODS

Several of the above fantasy procedures involve the use of symbolic imagery. For example, there is nothing inherently therapeutic about imagining eating some biscuits, unless the therapist explicitly creates a symbolic association between this activity and the desired feelings of comfort, confidence, and well-being.

It has been mentioned in previous chapters that some writers, especially those of the Ericksonian persuasion, have set great store by the use of metaphorical and anecdotal methods, whereby possible understandings and resolutions of the patient's problems are implicitly contained within the therapist's communications in allegorical form. It is not clear whether such methods should be termed "hypnotic", although they may be combined with hypnotic procedures. If such interventions have therapeutic value, then it seems likely that they may be especially useful with children, who easily become absorbed in a good narrative. Mills and Crowley (1986) have developed such procedures in their work with children. For example, they report the successful treatment of an eight-year-old enuretic boy, who amongst other things is told the story of Sammy, a baby circus elephant who helps carry buckets of water to the Big Top but keeps dropping them on the way. A wise old camel helps Sammy learn to carry the water to the right place. Another story involves two cartoon characters who come across some vegetables complaining that the gardener has been hurting them, but they musn't tell anyone about it as it's a secret. The vegetables are reassured that they can be helped and that there is a place where the gardener can go to learn how to take better care of his vegetables. The reader is left to guess what sort of problem this story addresses.

The latter story, in particular, is not dissimilar from the ploy of telling a child, in some instructive way, the history of a fictional child with a similar problem who succeeds in getting better. Benson (1988) gives a good case illustration of this method.

Levine (1980) has described how "personalised" audio-recording of stories may be constructed for children with insomnia. A story is put together for the child incorporating his or her interests and favourite activities, colours, foods, and so on. The narrative also contains themes relevant to the child's problems such as feelings of calmness, comfort, and relaxation. The tape is played at bedtime and, if necessary, when the child is awake during the night. A similar approach, using a sequence of bedtime stories on tape, was reported by Callow (Note 3) in his treatment of Katy, a nine-year-old girl with severe eczema. The central characters of the story are Kathy, who suffers from sore and itchy skin, and a boy who plays magic music on a flute. As Kathy listens to the music (which is heard on the tape) her skin starts to heal and her sleep improves.

FURTHER APPLICATIONS TO PSYCHOSOMATIC PROBLEMS

As with adults, hypnosis may be used either to facilitate the uncovering and resolution of underlying fears and conflicts, or as part of a more direct symptom–alleviation approach. When considering a parental request for hypnosis, however, the therapist should be alert to the possibility that this is a defensive manoeuvre to alleviate the family from any responsibility in resolving the problem. This applies of course to any individual therapy one might be asked to undertake with a child, when family therapy may be a more appropriate choice. We have the impression that the demand for hypnosis should be treated with special caution in this respect. There *are*, incidentally, reports of hypnosis being used in family therapy (Ritterman, 1983; Ross, 1988) and the interested reader is referred to these sources.

Numerous reports are to be found in the literature (single cases and clinical trials) of the use of hypnosis in alleviating relatively uncomplicated anxiety problems and psychosomatic disorders. The methods outlined in Chapters 5 to 8 may be appropriately adapted according to the recommendations outlined earlier. We stress the importance of exploiting the child's capacity for imagination and his or her gaining a sense of *mastery* over the particular problem or set of problems encountered. One way of facilitating this is to present the child with a valid explanation of the problem in a manner which he or she can comprehend and utilise. This was earlier illustrated at a simple level in the administration of suggestions for progressive relaxation. Another example is in the treatment of enuresis: it may be explained to the child, perhaps with the aid of diagrams, that when the bladder becomes full of urine the muscles send a message to the brain that he or she needs to go to the toilet to empty the bladder; or the brain can tell these muscles, which are very strong, to hold on to the urine until the child is ready to empty it in the right place.

For more detailed discussions of the treatment of enuresis the reader is advised to consult Gardner and Olness (1981). Olness (1975) reported a cure rate of 78% within the first month of treatment for 40 children, a figure similar to that of Stanton (1979b) who describes additional therapeutic ploys such as the use of background music, references to previous learning experiences and mesmeric passes. Edwards and van der Spuy (1985) have demonstrated the effectiveness of six weekly standardised sessions of hypnotherapy for enuretic children compared to no-treatment controls.

Olness and Conroy (1985) have remarked that children appear to have a more well-developed facility for control of their autonomic functions than adults. These authors reported that 8 out of 11 children were able to increase significantly levels of tissue oxygen when they listened to a tape-recording describing how the body cells obtain oxygen in exchange for carbon dioxide, and instructions to increase oxygen uptake. The children underwent a hypnotic induction procedure but there is no evidence as to whether or not this was necessary. Voluntary control of peripheral temperature (usually of the hands) using imagery and/or thermal biofeedback has also been reported (Dikel & Olness, 1980; Smith, 1985). Olness, Culbert, and Uden (1989) have reported that children may even by able to increase their salivary concentrations of immunoglobulin A using imagery and specific suggestions.

It was noted in Chapter 7 that measures of therapeutic outcome do not necessarily correlate with the observed degree of autonomic change (such as alteration in blood flow). Nevertheless, hypnosis does appear to be an effective adjuvant in the treatment of common psychosomatic complaints. Olness, MacDonald, and Uden,

(1987) in a study of juvenile migraine found that twice-daily, 10-minute sessions of self-hypnosis using imagery depicting symptom-relief (as invented by the child) was superior to both placebo and medication (Propanalol) after three months. Similarly Kohen (Note 13) found hypnotherapy (the "favourite place" technique, progressive relaxation, and controlled breathing) more effective than control procedures, such as waking suggestions and conversation, in children with asthma.

Case Illustration

The following very straightforward case illustrates the application of hypnosis in the alleviation of migraine and tension in an otherwise normal nine-year-old boy. The hypnotic induction includes a useful technique not presented earlier, namely covert modelling using the child's hero. Tilton (1984) describes a similar procedure in which the child imagines that his or her hero figure is actually delivering the therapeutic suggestions and instructions.

Philip was referred by his GP because of his tendency to become over-excited and ill whenever some out-of-the-ordinary event was about to take place. The usual triggers were school examinations, holidays, and sports events—Philip was a member of both the football and the cross-country team. Prior to such occasions he would become tense, nauseous, and at times physically ill, as a result of which he would sometimes have to miss the event.

When Philip was seen initially, his mother defined his main problem as migraine, and, indeed, in addition to the aforementioned problems, Philip suffered from migraine headaches (of the classical type), which were occasioned by the same circumstances described above but which also occurred without any obvious stress. These migraines were occurring at a rate of around two per week. On interview, it was ascertained that there appeared to be no obvious tensions at home or school, and a symptom-oriented approach was adopted. Philip revealed that he was a keen supporter of Liverpool United Football Club and his hero was Kevin Keegan. The rationale of the therapy was explained to him and he was asked to close his eyes and the magicTV fantasy was suggested. He reported that he was watching his favourite football team in action. The therapist then said "You know, Philip, I just wonder how Kevin Keegan manages to calm himself down before playing a match. Let's run the video back and see what he does while he's waiting in the changing room... OK? Now, can you see him sitting there? ... First of all he closes his eyes and breathes nice and easy..." The therapist then described Philip's hero going through a progressive relaxation procedure, followed by counting from 1 to 10, relaxing more deeply with each count; then the image was described of the footballer getting up and going out into the field feeling calm and full of confidence. Following this, Philip was invited to try out this method of relaxation for himself with prompting from the therapist. Finally his mother was invited back into the room to observe her son demonstrating his relaxation method. He was then instructed to practise this once a day as appropriate and whenever he felt himself getting tensed up.

Philip was seen for three more sessions at fortnightly intervals, then on two occasions at two-monthly intervals, the relaxation method being practised each time. Initially, the occurrence of migraines declined to once a fortnight, tailing off completely at follow-up; likewise his anticipatory nausea and sickness. Moreover, to the delight and surprise of his mother, Philip was selected for grammar school; she attributed his success to the therapy (there was no obvious evidence to support this) and requested that the sessions continue, but no more appointments followed when the therapist suggested that these should be made by ringing the surgery rather than fixing them in advance.

CHILDREN IN PAIN AND UNDERGOING UNCOMFORTABLE MEDICAL PROCEDURES

There is a growing literature on the application of the hypnotic procedures presented in this and previous chapters to the alleviation of pain and discomfort in children suffering from illnesses such as cancer, and children undergoing stressful medical procedures. We are indebted in this field to American authors such as Olness (1981), Zeltzer, LeBaron, and Zeltzer (1984) and Josephine Hilgard (Hilgard & LeBaron, 1984). In Britain the work of Fairfull Smith has been mentioned in Chapter 11, and we see growing interest, as evidenced by the activities of Lansdown and his colleagues (Lansdown, 1985), and Ioannou (1990). We hope that such work will flourish.

CONCLUSIONS

Hypnotherapy with children is challenging and rewarding. Hypnotic procedures may be fairly easily adapted so that they engage the natural talents, interests, and strivings of the child subject. Gardner and Olness (1982) list some themes of child development which hypnosis may exploit, namely the urge for experience, for mastery, for social interaction, for the inner world of imagination and for wellness. However, it is not easy to define what constitutes a hypnotic technique, because much of what is of importance to the therapy may take place in the natural interaction between the child and therapist. This makes research into the effectiveness of hypnotic interventions with children a difficult enterprise. Cohen, Olness, Colwell, and Heimel (1984) surveyed the use of hypnosis in 505 paediatric cases of problems such as enuresis and encopresis, acute and chronic pain, asthma, habit disorders, obesity, and anxiety, and concluded that in 51% there was complete resolution of the problem and in only 7% was no change observed. Moreover, it was possible to predict success after the first four visits or less.

In this country those using hypnotic procedures in child psychiatry and paediatric medicine are a small minority. In the last 10 years, however, we have witnessed a surge of interest amongst educational and child psychologists. We hope this will continue and flourish.

13 The Use of Hypnosis by Various Professions

In Chapter 2 the history of hypnosis was outlined, a history revealing that much of the investigation and use of hypnosis was carried out by medical men and by dentists. Clark Hull (1933, p.18) was later to point out that "The dominant motive throughout the history of hypnotism has been clinical, that of curing human ills. A worse method for the establishment of scientific principles among highly elusive phenomena can hardly be devised."

Although the establishment of scientific principles in the general topic of hypnotism has not yet proceeded very far, some progress has been made in the latter part of the twentieth century, and this has largely been the result of academic research in university departments, principally through the work of experimental psychologists, which has paid off in the clinicial field.

HYPNOSIS AS A MEDICAL SPECIALISM

Because of its historical origins, hypnosis has generally been regarded as an essentially *medical* specialism, although there is nothing specifically "medical" about it. It is a psychological phenomenon and is properly within the domain of psychologists. However, it is entirely understandable that the medical profession should have come to regard it as "belonging" to them, although granting that dentists have an equal right to practise it since the dental profession is closely allied to theirs.

We may note that the Report of the Sub-committee appointed by the British Medical Association (1955, pp.5–6) to consider the matter of the clinical use of hypnosis stated that:

> the use of hypnotism in the treatment of physical and psychological disorders should be confined to persons subscribing to a recognized ethical code which governs the relations between doctor and patient. This would not preclude its use by a suitably trained psychologist or medical auxiliary of whose competence the medical practitioner was personally satisfied, and who would carry out, under medical direction, the treatment of patients selected by the physician.

Several features of this statement should be noted; the competence of the non-medical therapist would have to be assessed by a medical doctor; the therapy would be carried out under medical supervision; the patient to be treated would need to be selected by the medical doctor. This was written before the professions of clinical and educational psychologists were not as firmly established as they are today, when it is well recognised that psychologists are not medical auxiliaries but independent professionals in their own right. Medical thinking concerning the practice of hypnotism was slow in recognising the realities of the situation. As late as 1978 a medical writer (Waxman, 1978a) wrote to the *British Medical Journal* as follows (emphasis added):

> Sir, with the increased use of hypnotism may I, through the courtesy of your columns, make some points concerning its use by unqualified persons for the purposes of entertainment *or by lay therapists*... Doctors and dentists are bound by a code of ethics which safeguard the public and patients against abuses in the use of hypnotism. *It is they alone* who can assume full clinical and legal responsibility for their patients; *unqualified persons are not so bound.*

Dr Waxman goes on to quote from the BMA's 1955 Report which has been mentioned earlier, and the tenor of his whole letter is that, with the exception of "doctors and dentists", all other persons using hypnotism are "unqualified" and "lay". This assumption is incorrect. The substance of this letter was repeated in the *Proceedings of the British Society of Medical and Dental Hypnosis* (BSMDH) (Waxman, 1978b), and provoked a letter from a reader which is worth reproducing in part:

> I was deeply distressed by the editorial and letter by Dr David Waxman concerning 'lay' hypnotists in the Society's Proceedings dated November 1978. Apparently clinical psychologists such as myself are to be categorized as 'lay' hypnotists as we are neither medical doctors nor dentists. Our minimum qualifications include an honours degree in psychology and postgraduate training in clinical psychology at least.
>
> Members of the Society will appreciate the important historical and contemporary contributions made by psychologists to our understanding of the nature of hypnosis and its clinical applications. They will be aware also that relative to clinical psychologists many doctors and dentists have had considerably less training in and experience of the assessment and treatment of mental illness. (Walker, 1979, p.63)

The writer of this letter also pointed out that in practice the Society in question, the BSMDH, had admitted clinical psychologists, himself included, to some of its training workshops.

The original letter in the *British Medical Journal* had been answered by Gibson (1978) who pointed out that the term "lay" was ambiguous, and that from originally meaning "non-clerical" it had now come to mean "non-medical" in the understanding of some people, but that such a meaning was unwarranted. Gibson also pointed out that in the National Health Service (NHS) much behaviour modification was being carried out by clinical psychologists, some of whom used hypnosis at their discretion, and that hypnosis was also being used by specially trained nurses and by physiotherapists within the NHS.

It may be said, therefore, that during the 1970s the medical profession in the U.K. as a whole had accepted the fact that they and the dentists did not have a prerogative of the use and control of hypnotism, as had been envisaged by the 1955 BMA Report. In most other countries this had long been acknowledged, although here and abroad there are always individuals who take a contrary view. It was noted in Chapter 10 that a group of American psychiatrists made an effort to obtain a monopoly of the practice of hypnotism (American Psychiatric Association, 1961) but such endeavour had little lasting effect. The International Society of Hypnosis (ISH), the prestigious world-wide learned and professional society, had already been founded in 1959, and it comprised psychologists, medical doctors, and dentists. The ISH Directory reveals that members of certain other professions have been admitted in special cases, principally qualified medical social workers.

THE BRITISH SOCIETY OF EXPERIMENTAL AND CLINICAL HYPNOSIS

In the U.K. the 1970s saw a considerable increase in the use of hypnotism by clinical and educational psychologists, and this resulted in the founding of the British Society of Experimental and Clinical Hypnosis (BSECH) in 1977, which covered the three professions recognised by the International Society. That its Constitution did not permit members of other professions to join was due to the fact that a great number of people, with no training in any recognised therapeutic profession, were using hypnotism in private practice and were anxious to gain some status by joining a society such as this. A very conservative policy was therefore necessary to get the new Society on its feet, and to ensure that it gained proper prestige both nationally and internationally. After it had been established some years, the policy of the BSECH was relaxed somewhat to permit the granting of membership to properly qualified people in other professions who had a legitimate use for hypnosis, each case being considered on its merits. At this point we wish to emphasise a cardinal rule for membership of the BSECH (which is also explicit in the bye-laws of the ISH to which the BSECH is affiliated), namely that all members must undertake to use hypnosis strictly within the scope of their professional work and qualifications. We find it necessary to highlight this, because there is much about the popular conception of hypnosis which leads unqualified practitioners to believe that acquiring the skills of hypnosis endows them with the competence to a multitude of problems which previously lay outside their range of expertise. This is a complete misconception; by acquiring the techniques of hypnosis practitioners are able to expand their repertoire of therapeutic procedures but not to extend their practice into areas for which they have no professional qualifications or training. For example, if a practitioner wishes to use hypnosis in the context of psychodynamic therapy, he or she must already have undertaken proper training in this field and be qualified in the understanding of psychological disorders.

A number of conclusions flow from this. First, the BSECH insists that those of its members at universities or polytechnics who have academic qualifications in psychology (a Bachelor's degree or perhaps a PhD) but no qualifications in applied psychology (say, a postgraduate degree or diploma in clinical or educational psychology) must restrict their use of hypnosis to teaching and experimental investigations and not attempt to treat psychological problems, since this is not within the terms of reference of their work.

In the case of dentists, it follows that they should restrict their use of hypnosis to problems encountered in dentistry. Their attendance at training workshops on hypnotic procedures does not qualify them to extend their range of interventions to the treatment of their patients' emotional problems unrelated to dentistry, such as depression and sexual troubles (see Gibson, 1988b; Nicolaou, 1988). The other professional hypnosis society in the U.K., the BSMDH, does not appear to adhere to such stipulations with its members, and it is not uncommon nowadays to meet dentists with part-time psychotherapy practices, whose notions of human psychology scarcely differ from those of the fringe practitioners advertising in the local newsagent's window, and who, in many cases, have fallen prey to the cult of Milton Erickson and Neuro-linguistic Programming. The question of the limits to the practice of hypnosis by dentists has been more fully explored in Chapter 11.

The use of hypnosis by medical practitioners also needs to come under the same logical scrutiny. As Walker intimates in his previously quoted letter, training in medicine does not necessarily include the formal psychotherapeutic treatment of patients with psychological problems. Is it the case that attendance at a few training workshops in hypnosis is sufficient for the GP or other medical specialist to undertake psychotherapy with those patients whom they would previously have referred for treatment by a psychiatrist or a psychologist?

Two anecdotes may be relevant to this question. The first involves an inquiry to the BSECH from a social worker about a young woman who was in great distress following private hypnotherapy with a general practitioner. She had been age-regressed and recalled an incident when she was sexually assaulted by a member of her family. Following this revelation, the therapist announced that the cause of her problem had now been illuminated and that was the end of the therapy! The reader has only to recall the discussion of age-regression in Chapter 6 to understand why this patient was so distressed.

The second anecdote concerns a businessman who was admitted to an acute psychiatric ward with agitated depression and thoughts of suicide. For several months he had been treated by his GP with sessions of hypnosis, the main component of which appeared to be Hartland's ego-strengthening routine. It was noted in Chapter 4 that depressed patients require sensitive handling and are unlikely to respond to exhortations to get better, even when these are given during hypnosis. Not surprisingly, the patient's depression deepened and his financial affairs deteriorated to such a degree that he was compelled to sell his business, after which he was admitted to hospital and in time responded favourably to the ward regime and anti-depressant medication.

These anecdotes are not intended to convey the impression that it is typical for patients to suffer at the hands of medical practitioners using hypnosis outside their range of competence. They are mostly likely exceptional, but they challenge the assertion that sensitivity and expertise in the practice of hypnosis has something to do with the possession of a degree in medicine. If the two therapists concerned had been lay practitioners, no doubt these cases would have been used by some as evidence for the need to protect the public by legally restricting the use of hypnosis to professionally qualified people. This matter will be discussed more fully later.

Notwithstanding these caveats, the logic which urges restraint in the practice of hypnosis by one set of professionals, opens up possibilities for others who have been excluded by conventional wisdom. There are several professions whose members are engaged in work of a therapeutic nature and whose patients would benefit from the inclusion of hypnosis in their armamentum of skills. Let us now consider these professions.

HYPNOSIS IN MIDWIFERY

In Chapter 10 the usefulness of hypnotic techniques in obstetrics was described and discussed, and we might expect that the professional body that is concerned with the care of pregnant women and their delivery, the midwives, would have a special use for such techniques. When we examine the reality of the current use of hypnosis by midwives the position is summed up by Maureen Hickman (1978, p.55), who points out its usefulness in both delivery and in antenatal preparation but admits that "Antenatal preparation for childbirth by hypnosis is not widely practised".

Some textbooks on midwifery do not even mention hypnotic or psychoprophylactic techniques (e.g. Towler & Butler-Manuel, 1980; Gibbert, 1965), and some are definitely hostile (e.g. Browne & Dixon, 1978). Hostile books generally admit the theoretical advantages of hypnosis but dismiss it as a practical technique, and sometimes the statements made about it are not accurate.

In fact there is plenty of evidence from controlled studies showing that antenatal preparation can be very effective and that there is a good case for using hypnosis during labour (Enkin, Smith, Dermer, & Emmett, 1972; Hughey, McElin & Young, 1978; Klusman, 1975; Scott & Rose, 1976). More realistic objections are raised by Chamberlain (1984, p.143):

> *Psychoprophylaxis*. If taught individually, learned properly and applied in labour by sympathetically trained attendants, this can give good pain relief for a lot of early labour... Unfortunately this method is often group taught and badly learned. Further, many labour ward staffs are out of sympathy with the ideas and so may not be able to support the woman at the critical time.

It is doubtful whether individual rather than group tuition of pregnant mothers is really superior, and it is not only early labour that is improved. However, to the extent that Chamberlain's other criticisms may be justified, the remedy should obviously be that more effort should be put into the provision of efficient antenatal preparation of mothers by midwives, and that labour ward staffs should be educated in the matter of hypnotic techniques so that they will not be "out of sympathy". Such hostility can only be the result of ignorance.

In this book we can only point out the benefits of hypnotic techniques in antenatal preparation and in the conduct of labour by midwives. It is unnecessary here to repeat the material that was presented in Chapter 10. But in admitting the unsatisfactory state of midwifery in this respect, we should try to examine just what factors have led to the present position. It seems that the relations between the medical profession and that of midwifery are unsatisfactory for historical reasons, and that doctors are, on the whole, unwilling to let midwives exert the degree of independence that their skills justifies. This matter has been the subject of a good deal of research in recent years, and the work of Green, Kitzinger, and Coupland (1986), as detailed in their recent report, highlights many of the important issues. A full consideration of this matter is obviously outside the scope of this book, but it should be noted that midwives as such are not hostile to the use of hypnotic techniques, or would not be if they had a proper degree of autonomy, but many of their medical colleagues are reluctant to see them exercising such a degree of professional independence.

At the beginning of this chapter we examined the lingering reluctance of some doctors to admit that clinical psychologists were perfectly entitled to use hypnosis responsibly, and this is the present position with regard to midwifery. Margaret Myles (1981, p.744), herself an experienced midwife and tutor, advocates the use of hypnotic techniques by midwives, but strangely adds that "Midwives could use hypnosis without carrying it to the hypnotic state". She does not explain why she adds this caution, and it may indicate the belief common in an older generation that there was some special mystique about the hypnotic state and that only doctors could be expected to take responsibility for fully hypnotised patients.

In summary, we advocate that the education of midwives should include a proper course of psychological instruction in which the topic of hypnosis is adequately dealt with.If they are introduced to the realities of the subject, and are trained to use hypnotic techniques responsibly and efficiently, they will find a proper use for it in the exercise of their profession.

HYPNOSIS IN PHYSICAL MANIPULATION

Using the term "profession" in its widest sense, there are several related professions that use physical manipulation and have a legitimate use for hypnosis. Therapeutic systems involving physical manipulations are operated by practitioners variously called osteopaths, chiropractors, and physiotherapists, not to mention the "alternative therapists" who use some of the less well-known systems. Not all such practitioners are operating therapeutic systems alternative to that of orthodox medicine, and in fact the Chartered Physiotherapists are practising within the structure of the NHS. A brief but useful description of the various manipulative therapies is given by Chaitow (1982).

There is a great deal of controversy concerning the theoretical bases of the various "systems", and the practitioners have different forms of professional organisations. There is nothing to stop an individual from calling himself an osteopath, chiropractor or physiotherapist and operating without reference to any professional organisation at all and without any formal qualifications. We have not the space to discuss this matter here. What these operators have in common is that they try to restore health by various physical means: the laying on of hands, by massage, by manipulation of joints, and by instructing patients in remedial exercises. Hypnotic techniques can obviously be of help in such physical therapy. A suitable degree of muscular relaxation can be induced by suggestion, and unnecessary pain can likewise be avoided by suggestion. There is some potential danger in the inhibition of pain by suggestion, as an unskilful practitioner may carry out undesirable manipulations which the patient would normally resist if pain were fulfilling its usual protective function. Hypnotism is certainly a technique that can be abused by the unskilful.

In Chapter 7 we overviewed some published case reports on the use of hypnosis in the rehabilitation of patients with neurological and neuromuscular disorders. These reports indicate that hypnotic suggestions may be used to augment physiotherapeutic and other rehabilitative procedures designed to restore normal neuromuscular function (e.g. Kimura, 1975; Pajntar, Roskar, & Vodonick, 1985).

There is an obvious need for this work to be developed, but at present in the formal training given to the physiotherapists who work in NHS hospitals and in clinics, there is no education in and practice of hypnotic techniques. Very recently, the British Society of Experimental and Clinical Hypnosis has been accepting individual Chartered Physiotherapists at its training workshops, provided that they give an undertaking to use hypnosis only in the proper exercise of their professional skills. There is an understandable reluctance on the part of that Society to admit physiotherapists as a body to membership, as some of them are practising "hypnotherapy" with patients suffering from a variety of emotional disorders unrelated to the conditions that are the proper concern of physiotherapists. It is to be hoped that the Chartered Physiotherapists will remedy this unsatisfactory situation so that they co-operate fully with other professionals, and education in hypnotic skills may become part of their recognised training.

HYPNOSIS IN SPEECH THERAPY

Speech therapists constitute a distinct and independent professional group. Although they frequently work in close co-operation with psychologists, physicians, and other specialists, they have professional autonomy and are not, in the U.K. at any rate, to be considered as "medical auxiliaries". Their full training course takes four years of university-based study and practice. Their work covers a wide range of communication disorders, both acquired and congenital, in children and adults.

In recent years speech therapists have made increasing use of hypnotic techniques in their work and have formed their own hypnosis society, which is recognised by the College of Speech Therapists, the British Society for the Practice of Hypnosis in Speech Therapy (BSPHST). There are certain traditional methods of voice therapy that have been developed over the years, but some therapists such as Lucas and Levy (1984) consider that they are sometimes inappropriate and can even generate anxiety. More is needed than mechanical practice of correct speaking. Vocal production, which includes both speech and singing, is a very curious ability in that it depends very heavily on emotional attitudes and can easily be disrupted by strained interpersonal relations. Not only can the motor output to the speech organs be disrupted by anxiety, but the feedback mechanisms can likewise be disturbed. The fictional account of George du Maurier's Trilby, the girl who had fine vocal organs but who could not sing except under the hypnotic influence of Svengali, is much over-drawn, but it appeals to us all because we intuitively appreciate that it accords with our own experience of the association between emotional attitude and voice production.

The conditions that exemplify best the dependence of speech on emotional factors are acquired dysphonia (impaired voice resulting in a hoarse or breathy speech) and aphonia (total loss of voice). Here hypnosis may be of assistance, and Dunnet and Williams (1988) recommend its use employing the "affect bridge" technique described in Chapter 7 of this book.

In their section on "Applications of hypnosis to organic and functional disorders" (Dunnet & Williams, 1988, pp.247–250), an excellent account of the use of hypnotic techniques in modern speech therapy is given, and professionals in this discipline are to be congratulated on realising the potential of this technique in the very special problems that they deal with. A small questionnaire study of the use of hypnosis in speech therapy (McFarlane, 1987) revealed that although the technique was used with patients suffering from a wide variety of communications disorders, its use was most frequent with voice and fluency disorders. Hypnosis was used more frequently with adults than with children, although it did not appear to be more effective with any one particular age group.

In contrast to the Chartered Physiotherapists, the speech therapists appear to be sensitive to the necessity for restricting their use of hypnosis strictly within their own professional domain. Their society, the BSPHST, has a Constitution that states: "It shall be obligatory upon members to sign a declaration of undertaking to restrict their application of hypnosis to the management of referred speech therapy patients, and within the therapeutic constraints accepted by their professional body and to uphold this at all times in practice". It would appear that this professional discipline has taken the use of hypnotic techniques seriously, both in considering their manifest potential for enhancing professional skills and in guarding against the possible misuse of hypnosis, and it provides a suitable model which other professions might follow.

THE USE OF HYPNOSIS BY NURSES

In the opinion of the authors, and in the general consensus of members of the BSECH, nurses' training would not be usefully augmented by the blanket provision of training in hypnosis, and this applies even to registered mental nurses and community psychatric nurses. In fact, all too often an applicant for membership of the BSECH from a nurse appears to be motivated by his or her ambition to become a private "hypnotherapist", rather than to employ hypnosis within his or her everyday work. However, the rules of the BSECH, and indeed those of the ISH, provide for the training in hypnosis of those loosely described as "ancillary" or "para-medical" staff. We will not quibble over these labels but state that what these provisions have in mind is the training or staff to carry out hypnosis within a medical setting and under the supervision of a medical person or clinical psychologist.

There now exists within the mental illness services of the NHS "nurse behaviour therapists", who have trained extensively in behaviour therapy; similarly, there are nurse cognitive therapists. These nurses are released from routine nursing duties and are assigned to carry out their therapy within the hospital. Conceivably, then, we could have "nurse hypnotherapists", trained in hypnosis and taking referrals for "hypnotherapy". This is not, however, a satisfactory arrangement because, unlike behaviour therapy and cognitive therapy, hypnosis is not a therapy. As we shall argue later, there is no rational justification for having such professionals as "hynotherapists" whose task it is to treat a multitude of different problems and afflictions using hypnosis. One could justifiably train qualified nurse behaviour therapists and cognitive therapists to apply hypnosis to their work; a more useful project would be to train nurses in hypnotic skills appropriate to the speciality in which they work. A good example might be in an Accident and Emergency Department, in which the kind of procedures described by Ewin (1986a,b) (see Chapter 7) could be undertaken by nurses working on the unit. Other specialities include Obstetrics and Gynaecology, Cardiology, Dermatology, and Surgery. The interventions would be symptom-orientated; other psychiatric or psychotherapeutic interventions would, as is presently the case, be requisitioned by a referral to the appropriate department.

THE USE OF HYPNOSIS BY SOCIAL WORKERS

Whilst it is the business of social workers to help people who are troubled and in distress (and in many cases suffering from psychological and emotional problems) it is not immediately obvious that their interventions are likely to be assisted in any way by their possessing the skills of hypnosis. The kind of service they render to their clients is largely of a practical nature—sorting out welfare and housing entitlements, monitoring the well-being of individuals and families considered to be "at risk" in some way, intervening when crises do occur, giving supportive counseling and advice, and so on.

There are, however, social workers whose roles includes structured counselling and psychotherapy with individuals, groups and families presenting with psychological problems. For example, the multi disciplinary team at a child guidance unit usually includes a psychiatric social worker who, along with his or her colleagues, may be engaged in the above kinds of psychotherapeutic work. Clearly there is scope for employing hypnosis, and there are indeed social workers using hypnosis in this context. The problem we have found, however, is that there is often nothing of substance in the training of social workers to qualify them to engage in formal therapy. Our impression is that they have often acquired their knowledge and skills in piecemeal fashion by attending workshops here and there in the absence of any clear training curriculum. This seems to be a weakness of their professional training and one that needs remedying.

Nevertheless, there are social workers who have undertaken extensive training in the form of diplomas or Master's degrees in psychotherapy or counselling, organised by universities, polytechnics, and other recognised centres of learning. We believe that social workers with such credentials are well qualified to be trained to use hypnosis in their work.[1]

LAY PRACTITIONERS AND THE LEGAL RESTRICTION OF HYPNOSIS

The Status of "Hypnotherapists"

In Britain, there are no legal requirements pertaining to the use of hypnosis for therapeutic purposes, and anyone is at liberty to call himself or herself a "hypnotherapist" or, for that matter, a "psychotherapist". In some European countries, and in some states of Canada and Australia, the practice of hypnosis is restricted by law

[1] At the Annual General Meeting of the BSECH in 1988, members advised against admitting social workers without such training. Prior to this the policy of the BSECH Council had been less stringent.

to a number of professional groups, such as doctors, dentists, and psychologists.

Few people in this country who advertise their services as "hypnotherapists" are qualified to be employed to carry out formal psychological therapy within the Health Service. "Hypnotherapy" does not exist as a profession in the NHS; there are a number of doctors, dentists, psychologists, and so on, who use hypnosis to some degree in their NHS work. "Hypnotherapy" is not a registered profession.[2] Those who advertise themselves as "hypnotherapists" are often termed "lay" therapists, although there is no clear line of demarcation between lay and non-lay practitioners. Many lay therapists have trained on private courses, and there appear to be a growing number of such courses in this country. Some consist of one or two short workshops, some are merely correspondence courses, whereas others are part-time courses of one or more years' duration and aim to provide trainees with some knowledge of psychopathology and of different types of psychological therapy. Both the BSECH and the BSMDH offer short training courses to their members, both of an introductory and of a specialist nature. These workshops are designed to provide trainees with knowledge and experience of hypnotic procedures which they may apply strictly within their professional work. We find that when the last caveat is heeded, it is sufficient to provide members with short, intermittent workshops rather than an extensive course of training, since members already possess the necessary qualifications and expertise in the field in which they are working.

Because hypnosis is a set to augmentative procedures in therapy of one sort or another, the notion of having a profession of generic "hypnotherapists" trained to do hypnosis, and thus deemed competent to treat all manner of physical and psychological ailments, does not make good sense. It is better for the health service to train members of appropriate professions, as described above, to use hypnosis within their speciality. However, in our experience such ideas are resisted by those who regard hypnosis as their rightful property, such as some members of the medical and dental profession, and some private organisations that train people to be "hypnotherapists".

Arguments for the Legal Restriction of Hypnosis

Many non-lay practitioners would like to see laws restricting the use of hypnosis to certain qualified professional people, and the outlawing of hypnosis as a means of entertainment (The 1952 Hypnotism Act places some restrictions on the latter). We note that many lay practitioners of hypnosis and psychotherapy also support the idea of legalisations as long as their organisations and the qualifications they award are the ones that are granted legal authority.

[2] Some private practitioners use the title "Consultant Hypnotherapist", presumably for no other reason than it sounds better than just "Hypnotherapist". Recently a local newspaper carried an advertisement offering training in hypnotherapy by a "Senior Consultant Hypnotherapist". The grandeur of this title creates a paradox, for one might ask, what would a "Senior Consultant" be doing by offering to teach his trade in the "Classified Ads" alongside dateline services and massage parlours?

There are several recent papers (Haberman, 1987; Judd, Burrows, & Dennerstein, 1985; Kleinhauz & Eli, 1989) relating alleged instances of patients suffering distress at the hands of incompetent private "hypnotherapists", and actual assault (Hoencamp, 1989; Venn, 1988). The BSECH occasionally receives correspondence from members of the public complaining about their treatment by lay therapists, and most psychiatrists and psychologists are able to recount tales told by their patients of visits to self-styled "hypnotherapists". One lady we know of, on consulting such a person, was invited to lie on a bed that heaved up and down while its occupant listened to the sound of the sea through a pair of headphones. Not surprisingly, the lady felt rather ill after this experience. Undaunted she consulted another "hypnotherapist" who, as she was going out at the end of the session, pinched her on the bottom. A telephone call from her worried husband elicited the explanation that his wife needed "a jolt to her system".

Intimate advances by lay therapists may be more common than are reported. Heap (1984b) has described several instances which have come to light through the inquiries of the BSECH, and there have been others since. For example, several women have described how they have been persuaded to allow the therapist to have physical contact with them, say in the form of an embrace, on the pretext that this would help them to "release their inhibitions". More intimate involvement has been encouraged, ranging from kissing and fondling to, in the case of one correspondent, full sexual intercourse.

In none of the aforementioned cases was a hypnotic induction employed to elicit the co-operation of the patient. It was only necessary to persuade her that actions she would normally consider unseemly and contrary to her moral principles were acceptable within the context of the patient–therapist relationship. The rationale of this is reminiscent of the experiments of Milgram (1963, 1974) in which an attempt was made to get subjects to act out of character and administer seemingly painful electric shocks to another person, on the understanding that they were participating in an authentic programme of scientific research.

As well as reports of patients being sexually assaulted and raped during hypnosis (Hoencamp, 1989),[3] there have been reports of patients apparently being traumatised directly as a result of hypnotic interventions by an unqualified practitioner (see earlier references) and by stage hypnotists (Waxman, 1988). More frequently, however, we have observed that when patients complain about lay therapists it is not because of any adverse effects of hypnosis *per se*, but because they are treated unsympathetically and discourteously, or the therapy is banal or absurd and is an

---

[3] In 1988, Mr Michael Gill, a hypnotherapist from Angelsey, was jailed for two years for indecent assault on women who consulted him for therapy. Three rape charges were ordered to stay on the file (*Daily Express*, October 1988). Hypnotic procedures appeared to have been used, but it is not clear to what extent they were instrumental in eliciting compliance, since the victims were also persuaded that the assaults were part of the therapy. With hindsight they perceived the events of the session as unacceptable and the intentions of the therapist as malevolent.

obvious waste of money. Occasionally, as in the previously mentioned incidents of assault, the therapist exploits their vulnerability and readiness to give him the benefit of any doubt concerning his demands.

Finally, it may be argued that relying on treatment from a lay hypnotherapist may lead people to neglect the early signs of progressive disease which if undiagnosed and untreated can be life-threatening in the later stages. Unless therapists have had a thorough and relevant professional training, which normally involves many years of undergraduate and postgraduate work, they will not be competent to diagnose precisely what is wrong with patients, and to liaise with other professionals, nor will they be competent to monitor the progress of a disorder. This objection applies to many practitioners of so-called "fringe medicine".

Arguments against the Legal Restriction of Hypnosis

In defence of lay practitioners, we ought to say that the types of complaints mentioned above are probably very much the exception rather than the rule. It is more likely that these therapists include many sincere people whose sensitivity and insightfulness may compensate for their often odd or simplistic notions.[4] Moreover, an impressive string of professional and academic qualifications does not guarantee that the holder will be an effective therapist. Note also, that one reason given by the Government for not pursuing with legislation on the registration of hypnosis is the lack of any overt pressure from the public (Waxman, personal communication). Consider too, that the kind of complaints cited above concerning inconsiderate and unsympathetic treatment are all too often made by patients about their own doctors and consultants. No doubt lay therapists will hear some very sorry stories from their clients about their experiences at the hands of the professionals. Also, it is not unknown for professionals to misbehave themselves with their patients.

We are not satisfied that legal restraints on the use of hypnosis are really in the best public interest. For one thing, the experts are unable to agree what hypnosis is, how to define it, or whether it exists at all. Moreover, as we have frequently emphasised, hypnotic procedures resemble and overlap with other psychological methods such as progressive relaxation and autogenic training.

We believe that instead of investing our energies in trying to present hypnosis as a dangerous practice and the property of a qualified few, we should make hypnosis more widely available within the Health Service by recognising that many of our colleagues have a legitimate use for this procedure with their patients, and we should seek to provide them with proper training and standards of practice.

---

[4] Perhaps the best-known lay hypnotist in this country is Mr Joe Keeton from Hoylake. We cast no doubts on Mr Keeton's ability as a therapist, but we consider his claim to be able to modulate his voice to the frequency of his patients' brain waves (expressed in his book *Encounters with the past)* to be a typical example of the absurd ideas often professed by lay hypnotherapists. Let us add that having attended many professional symposia, meetings, and conferences, we observe that lay therapists do not have the monopoly of bizarre ideas concerning hypnosis and human psychology in general.

People have a right to choose how to solve their problems, and this includes the choice of consulting either an orthodox professional or a lay or "alternative" practitioner. However, freedom of choice can only exist when there is sufficient information on the choices available. A case can therefore be made for regulating the use of certain professional labels. For example, members of at least two lay organisations of hypnosis call themselves "doctors". This may cause considerable confusion among members of the public who assume that either the person so designated has a medical degree or holds a Doctor of Philosophy degree, signifying his or her attainment of excellence in some field of academic study or scientific research. Since in almost all instances it is the public who, through their taxes, pay to train these people, then it is reasonable that they demand that the use of the term "doctor" should be reserved only for persons who have successfully undertaken that training.

Finally, we suggest that the law acknowledges that anyone who is consulted by another person with the clear intention of benefiting from some form of treatment, should be liable to prosecution for any coercing of the patient for sexual, financial or other illegitimate gain.

References

Adams, H., Feuerstein, M., & Fowler, J. (1980). Migraine headache: Review of parameters, etiology and intervention. *Psychological Bulletin*, 217–237.

Agle, D.P. & Mattson, A. (1976). Psychological complications of hemophilia. In M.W. Hilgartner (Ed.), *Hemophilia in children* (pp. 137–150). Littleton, Mass. Publishing Sciences Group.

Ahsen, A. & Lazarus, A. (1972). *Clinical behavior therapy*. New York: Bruner/Mazel.

Alladin, A. (1984). Hypnosis in the treatment of head pain: In M. Heap (Ed.), *Proceedings of the First Annual Conference of the British Society for Experimental and Clinical Hypnosis* (pp. 12–33). BSECH publication.

Alladin, A. (1988). Hypnosis in the treatment of severe chronic migraine. In M. Heap (Ed.), *Hypnosis: Current clinical, experimental and forensic practices* (pp. 159–166). London: Croom Helm.

Alladin, A. (1989). Cognitive hypnotherapy for depression. In D. Waxman, D. Pedersen, I. Wilkie, & P. Mellett (Eds.), *Hypnosis: The Fourth European Congress at Oxford* (pp. 175–182). London: Whurr Publishers.

Alladin, A. & Heap, M. (in press). Hypnotherapy and depression. In M. Heap & W. Dryden (Eds.) *Handbook of hypnotherapy in Britain*. Milton Keynes: Open University Press.

Allen, K. (1982). An investigation of the effectiveness of neuro-linguistic programming procedures in treating snake phobics. *Dissertation Abstracts International, 43*, 861B.

Alpers, B.J. & Mancall, E.L (1971). *Clinical neurology*. Philadelphia: F.A. Davies & Co.

American Medical Association (1985). Scientific status of refreshing recollection by the use of hypnosis. *Journal of the American Medical Association, 253*, 1918–1923.

American Psychiatric Association (1961, 15 February). *Training in medical hypnosis: a statement of position by the APA*. Document available from the Central Office, Washington, D.C.

Anderson, J.A.D., Basker, M.A., & Dalton, E.R. (1975). Migraine and hypnotherapy. *International Journal of Clinical and Experimental Hypnosis*, *23*, 48–58.

Anderson, J.A.D., Dalton, E.R., & Basker, M.A. (1979). Insomnia and hypnotherapy. *Journal of the Royal Society of Medicine, 72*, 734–739.

Andrasik, F. & Holroyd, R.A. (1980). A test of specific and non-specific effects in the biofeedback treatment of tension headache. *Journal of Consulting and Clinical Psychology, 48*, 575–586.

Andrew, J.M . (1970). Recovery from surgery, with and without preparatory instruction, for three coping strategies. *Journal of Personality and Social Psychology, 15*, 223–226.

Andreychuk, T. & Skriver, C. (1975). Hypnosis and biofeedback in the treatment of migraine headache. *International Journal of Clinical and Experimental Hypnosis, 23*, 172–183.

Araoz, D.L. (1978). Clinical hypnosis in couple therapy. *Journal of the American Society of Psychosomatic Dentistry and Medicine, 25*, 58–67.

Aronson, D.M. (1985). The adolescent as hypnotist: Hypnosis and self-hypnosis with adolescent psychiatric inpatients. *American Journal of Clinical Hypnosis, 28*, 163–169.

Ås, A. (1962). Non-hypnotic experiences related to hypnotizability in male and female college students. *Scandinavian Journal of Psychology, 3*, 112–121.

Ås, A. (1963). Hypnotizability as a function of non-hypnotic experiences. *Journal of Abnormal and Social Psychology, 66*, 148–150.

August, R. (1961). *Hypnosis in obstetrics*. New York: McGraw Hill.

Ayer, W.A. & Levin, M.P. (1975). Theoretical basis and application of massed practice exercise for the elimination of tooth grinding habits. *Journal of Periodontology, 46*, 306–308.

Bakal, D.A. (1975). Headache: A biopsychological perspective. *Psychological Bulletin. 62*, 369–382.

Baker, E.L. (1981). A hypnotherapeutic approach to enhance object relatedness in psychotic patients. *International Journal of Clinical and Experimental Hypnosis, 29*, 136–147.

Bandler, R. & Grinder, J. (1979). *Frogs into princes*. Moab, Utah: Real People Press.

Bandura, A. (1971). *Principles of behaviour modification*. London: Holt.

Banyai, E.I. & Hilgard, E.R. (1976). A comparison of active-alert hypnotic induction with traditional relaxation induction. *Journal of Abnormal Psychology, 85*, 218–224.

Barabasz, A.F. & McGeorge, C.M. (1978). Biofeedback, mediated feedback and hypnosis in peripheral vasodilation training. *American Journal of Clinical Hypnosis, 21*, 28–37.

Barabasz, M. (1987). Trichotillamania: a new treatment. *International Journal of Clinical and Experimental Hypnosis, 35*, 146–154.

Barber, J. (1977). Rapid induction analgesia: A clinical report. *American Journal of Clinical Hypnosis, 19*, 138–147.

Barber, T.X. (1964). Hypnotizability, suggestibility, and personality: A critical review of research findings. *Psychological Reports, 14*, 299–320.

Barber, T.X. (1969). *Hypnosis: A scientific approach*. New York: Van Nostrand.

Barber, T.X. & Calverley, D.S. (1965). Hypnotizability, suggestibility and personality: II. Assessment of previous imaginative fantasy experiences by the Ås, Barber, Glass and Shor questionnaire. *Journal of Clinical Psychology, 21*, 57–58.

Barber, T.X., Spanos, N.P., & Chaves, J.F. (1974). *Hypnosis, imagination and human potentialities*. New York: Pergamon Press.

Barber, T.X. & Wilson, S.C. (1978). The Barber Suggestibility Scale and the Creative Imagination Scale: Experimental and clinical applications. *American Journal of Clinical Hypnosis, 21*, 84–108.

Barkovec, T.D. & Hennings, B.L. (1978). The role of physiological attention-focussing in the relaxation treatment of sleep disturbance, general tension and specific stress reaction. *Behaviour Research and Therapy, 16*, 7–19.

Barnett, E.A. (1981). *Analytical hypnotherapy: Principles and practice*. Kingston, Ontario: Junica.

Barrios, A.A. (1973). Posthypnotic suggestion as higher-order conditioning: A methodological and experimental analysis. *International Journal of Clinical and Experimental Hypnosis, 21*, 32–50.

Basker, M.A. (1970). Hypnosis in migraine. *British Journal of Clinical Hypnosis, 2*, 15–18.

Basker, M.A. (1979). A hypnobehavioural method of treating agoraphobia by the clenched fist method of Calvert Stein. *Australian Journal of Clinical and Experimental Hypnosis, 7*, 27–34.

Beaudet, S.C. (1963). Hypnosis in a schizophrenic obstetric patient. *American Journal of Clinical Hypnosis, 8*, 47.

Beck . A .T. (1976). *Cognitive therapy and emotional disorders*. New York: International University Press.

Beck, A.T., Rush, A.J., Shaw, B.F., & Emery, G. (1983). *Cognitive therapy of depression*. New York: Guilford Press.

Beck, N.C. & Hall, D. (1978). Natural childbirth—a review and analysis. *Obstetrics and Gynecology, 52*, 371–379 .

Beecher, H.K. (1959). *The measurement of subjective responses*. New York: Oxford University Press.

Benson, G. (1984). Short-term hypnotherapy with delinquent and acting-out adolescents. *British Journal of Experimental and Clinical Hypnosis, 1*, 19–28 .

Benson, G. (1988). Hypnosis with difficult adolescents and children. In M. Heap (Ed.), *Hypnosis: Current clinical, experimental and forensic practices* (pp. 314–324). London: Croom Helm.

Benson, H. (1975). *The relaxation response*. New York: William Morrow & Co.

Benson, H., Rosner, B.A., Marzetta, B.R., & Klemchuk, H.P. (1974). Decreased blood pressure in borderline hypertensive subjects who practice meditation. *Journal of Chronic Disease, 27*, 163–169.

Benson, V. (1971). One hundred cases of post-anesthetic suggestion in the recovery room. *American Journal of Clinical Hypnosis, 14*, 9.

Benton, A. (1985). *Left side, right side: A review of laterality research*. London: Batsford Academic and Educational.

Ben-Zvi, Z., Spohn, W.A., Young, S.H., & Kattan, M. (1982). Hypnosis for exercise-induced asthma. *American Review of Respiratory Disease, 125*, 392–395 .

Berlin, J. & Erdmann, W. (1987). Hypnosis in the treatment of classical migraine. *Pain*, Supplement 4, 580.

Berne. E. (1967). *Games people play: The psychology of human relationships*. Harmondsworth, Middx: Penguin Books.

Bernheim, H. (1886/1973). *Hypnosis and suggestion in psychotherapy*. New York: Jason Aronson (originally published in French, 1886) .

Bernick, S.M. (1972). Relaxation, suggestion and hypnosis in dentistry. *Pediatric Dentistry, 11*, 72–75 .

Bertrand, A. (1826). *Du magnétisme animal en France et des jugements qu'en ont parle les sociétés savantes*. Bossange Paris.

Binet, A. & Féré, C. (1888). *Animal magnetism* (English translation). New York: Appleton (originally published in French, 1886).

Birkett, P. (1979). Relationships among handedness, familial handedness, sex and ocular sighting dominance. *Neuropsychologia, l7*, 533–537 .

Bishay, E.G. & Lee, C. (1984). Studies of the effects of hypnoanaesthesia on regional blood flow by transcutaneous oxygen monitoring. *American Journal of Clinical Hypnosis, 27*, 64–69.

Bishay, E.G., Stevens, G., & Lee, C. (1984). Hypnotic control of upper gastro-intestinal hemorrhage: A case report. *American Journal of Clinical Hypnosis, 27*, 22–25 .

Blakeslee, T.R. (1980). *The right brain: A new understanding of the unconscious mind and its creative powers*. Basingstoke: Macmillan Education Ltd.

Blanchard, E.B. & Andrasik, F. (1982). Psychological assessment and treatment of headache: Recent developments and emerging issues. *Journal of Consulting and Clinical Psychology, 50*, 859–879.

Blanchard, E.B. & Andrasik, F. (1985). *Management of chronic headaches: A psychological approach*. New York: Pergamon Press.

Blanchard, E.B. & Young, L.D. (1974). Clinical applications of biofeedback training: A review of evidence. *Archives of General Psychiatry*, 30, 573–589.

Bonica, J.J. & Albe-Fessard, D. (Eds.)(1976). *Advances in pain research and therapy*. New York: Raven Press.

Bonke, B., Schmitz, P.I.M., Verhage, F., & Zwaveling, A. (1986). Clinical study of so-called unconscious perception during general anaesthesia. *British Journal of Anaesthetics, 58,* 957–994.

Bookbinder, L. (1962). Simple conditioning versus the dynamic approach to symptom substitution: A reply to Yates. *Psychological Review, 10,* 71–77.

Borkovec, T.D. & Fowles, D.C. (1973). Controlled investigation of the effects of progressive and hypnotic relaxation on insomnia. *Journal of Abnormal Psychology, 82,* 153–158

Bowers, K.S. (1971). Sex and susceptibility as moderator variables in the relationship of creativity and hypnotic susceptibility. *Journal of Abnormal Psychology, 78,* 93–100.

Bowers, K.S. (1983). *Hypnosis for the seriously curious.* New York: W.W. Norton & Co.

Bowers, K.S. & Kelly, P. (1979). Stress, disease, psychotherapy and hypnosis. *Journal of Abnormal Psychology, 88,* 490–505.

Braid, J. (1843). *Neurypnology: Or the rationale of nervous sleep considered in relation with animal magnetism.* London: Churchill.

Braid, J. (1846). *The power of the mind over the body.* London: Churchill.

Braid, J. (1855). *The physiology of fascination and the critics criticized.* Manchester: Grant.

Bramwell, J.M. (l903). *Hypnotism: Its history. practice and theory.* London: Alexander Moring.

Brattberg, G. (1983). An alternative method of treating tinnitus: relaxation hypnotherapy primarily through the home use of a recorded audio cassette. *International Journal of Clinical and Experimental Hypnosis, 31,* 90–97.

Braun, B.G. (1984a). Hypnosis and family therapy. *American Journal of Clinical Hypnosis, 26,* 182–186.

Braun, B.G. (1984b). Uses of hypnosis with multiple personality. *Psychiatric Annals, 14,* 34–40.

Brechner, T., Reeves, J.L., Giannini, J.A., Khoury, G.F., de Mayo, R., & Maslow, E.R. (1987). The comparative effectiveness of hypnosis combined with analgesic tailoring versus analgesic tailoring alone in the management of cancer pain. *Pain,* Supplement 4, 5341.

Brende, J.O. & Benedict, B.D. (1980). The Vietnam combat delayed stress response syndrome: hypnotherapy of 'dissociative symptoms'. *American Journal of Clinical Hypnosis, 23,* 34–40.

British Medical Association (BMA) (1955). Medical use of hypnotism. *British Medical Journal, 1,* 23 April, Supplement Appendix X.

Broughton, R.J. (1968). Sleep disorders: Disorders of arousal? *Science, 159,* 1070–1078.

Browne, J.C.McC. & Dixon, G. (1978). *Antenatal care.* Edinburgh: Churchill Livingstone.

Buranelli, V. (1975). *The wizard from Vienna.* London: Peter Owen.

Burish, T.G. & Redd, W.H. (1983). Behavioral approaches to reducing conditioned responses to chemotherapy in adult cancer patients. *Behavioural Medicine Update, 5,* 12–16.

Burrows, G.D. (1978). *Obstetrics. gynecology and psychiatry.* Melbourne: Hi Impact Press.

Burrows, G.D. (1980). Affective disorders and hypnosis. In G.D. Burrows & L. Dennerstein (Eds.), *Handbook of hypnosis and psychosomatic medicine* (pp. 149–170). New York: Elsevier Press.

Burrows, G.D. & Dennerstein, L. (Eds.)(1981). *Handbook of hypnosis and psychosomatic medicine.* New York: Elsevier Press.

Byrne, S. (1973). Hypnosis and the irritable bowel syndrome: Case histories, methods and speculations. *American Journal of Clinical Hypnosis, 15,* 263–265.

Cannistraci, A. (1977). Biofeedback—the treatment of stress-induced muscle activity. In H. Gelb (Ed.), *Clinical management of head, neck and TMJ pain and dysfunction. A multidisciplinary approach to diagnosis and treatment.* Philadelphia: W.B. Saunders.

Carasso, R.L., Kleinhauz, M., Peded, O., & Yehuda, S. (1985). Treatment of cervical headache with hypnosis, suggestive therapy and relaxation techniques. *American Journal of Clinical Hypnosis, 27,* 216–218.

Carli, G. (1978). Animal hypnosis and pain. In F.H. Frankel & H.S. Zamanski (Eds.), *Hypnosis at its bicentennial.* New York: Plenum Press.

Carpenter, C.H. (1941). What techniques may be used to secure relaxation in a child patient? *Journal of Dentistry in Children, 80,* 233–237.

Cautela, J.R. & McCullough, L. (1978). Covert conditioning: A learning-theory perspective on imagery. In J.L. Singer & K.S. Pope (Eds.), *The power of human imagination: New methods in psychotherapy*. New York: Plenum Press.

Cawson, R.A. (1969). Some shortcomings of dental education. *British Dental Journal, 127,* 556–561.

Cedercreutz, C. (1978). Hypnotic treatment of 100 cases of migraine. In F.H. Frankel & H.S. Zamansky (Eds.) *Hypnosis at its bicentennial*, New York: Plenum Press.

Cedercreutz, C., Lähteenmäki, R., & Tulikoura, J. (1976a). Hypnotic treatment of headache and vertigo in skull injured patients. *International Journal of Clinical and Experimental Hypnosis, 24,* 195–200.

Cedercreutz, C., Lähteenmäki, R., & Tulikoura, J. (1976b). Hypnotic treatment of post traumatic headache. In J.J. Bonica & D.A. Fessard (Eds.), *Advances in pain research and therapy* (pp. 887–889). New York: Raven Press.

Chaitow, L. (1982). *Osteopathy*. Wellingborough: Thorsons.

Chamberlain, G. (1984). *Lecture notes on obstetrics.* Oxford: Blackwell Scientific Publications.

Charcot, J.M. (1887). *Clinical lectures on diseases of the nervous svstem. Vol. III.* London: The New Sydenham Society.

Charles, A.G., Norr, K.L., Block, C.R., Meyering, S., & Meyers, P. (1978). Obstetric and psychological effects of psycho-prophylactic preparation for childbirth. *American Journal of Obstetrics and Gynecology , 131,* 44–52.

Cheek, D. & LeCron, L. (1968). *Clinical hypnotherapy*. New York: Grune & Stratton.

Chertok, L. (1981). *Sense and nonsense in psychotherapy*. Oxford: Pergamon Press.

Chertok, L., Michaux, D., & Doin, M.C. (1977). Dynamics of hypnotic analgesia: some new data. *Journal of Nervous and Mental Disease, 64,* 88–96.

Clarke, J.C. & Jackson, J.A. (1983). *Hypnosis and behavior therapy: The treatment of anxiety and phobias*. New York: Springer Publishing Co.

Clawson, T.A. & Swade, R.H. (1975). The hypnotic control of blood flow and pain: The cure of warts and the potential use of hypnosis in the treatment of cancer. *American Journal of Clinical Hypnosis, 8,* 275–280 .

Clemenow, L.P., King, A.R., & Brantley, P.J. (1984). Psychological factors in childhood illness. In H.E. Adams & P.B. Sutker (Eds.), *Comprehensive handbook of psychopathology*. New York: Plenum Press.

Coe, W.C. (1973). Experimental designs and the state-nonstate issue in hypnosis. *American Journal of Clinical Hypnosis, 6,* 118–128.

Cohen, D.P., Olness, K.N., Colwell, S.O., & Heimel, A. (1984). The use of relaxation-mental imagery (self-hypnosis) in the management of 505 pediatric behavioural encounters. *Journal of Developmental and Behavioural Pediatrics, 5,* 21–25 .

Colgan, S.M., Faragher, E.B., & Whorwell, P.J. (1988). Controlled trial of hypnotherapy in relapse prevention of duodenal ulceration. *Lancet, 2,* 1299–1300 .

Collison, D. R. (1975). Which asthmatic patients should be treated by hypnotherapy? *Medical Journal of Australia, 1,* 776–781.

Collison, D.R. (1978). Hypnotherapy in asthmatic patients and the importance of trance depth. In F.H. Frankel & H.S. Zamansky (Eds.), *Hypnosis at its bicentennial: selected papers*. New York: Plenum Press.

Conny, D.J. & Tedesco, L.A. (1983a). The gagging problem in prosthodontic treatment. Part I: Description and causes. *Journal of Prosthetic Dentistry, 49,* 601–606.

Conny, D.J. & Tedesco, L.A. (1983b). The gagging problem in prosthodontic treatment. Part II: Patient management. *Journal of Prosthetic Dentistry, 49,* 757–761.

Conrad, P.L. (1985). The hypnotic treatment of a case of intention tremor and muscle spasm. *Australian Journal of Clinical and Experimental Hypnosis, 13,* 121–128.

Copeland, D.R. (1986). The application of object relations theory to the hypnotherapy of developmental arrests: The borderline patient. *International Journal of Clinical and Experimental Hypnosis, 34,* 157–168.

Cornwell, A. & Donderi, D.C. (1988). The effect of experimentally induced anxiety on the experience of pressure pain. *Pain, 35,* 105–113.

Coulton, D. (1960). Hypnosis in obstetrical delivery. *American Journal of Clinical Hypnosis, 2,* 144.

Crasilneck, H.B. & Hall, J.A. (1973). Clinical hypnosis in problems of pain. *American Journal of Clinical Hypnosis, 15,* 153–161.

Crasilneck, H.B. & Hall, J.A. (1985). *Clinical hypnosis, principles and applications.* New York: Grune & Stratton.

Crasilneck, H.B., McCranie, E.J., & Jenkins, M.T. (1956). Special indications for hypnosis as a method of anesthesia. *Journal of the American Medical Association, 162,* 1606–1608.

Crasilneck, H.B., Stirman, J.A., Wilson, B.J., McCranie, E.J., & Fogelman, M.J. (1955). Use of hypnosis in the management of patients with burns. *Journal of the American Medical Association, 158,* 103–106.

Crowley, R. (1980). Effects of indirect hypnosis (Rapid Induction Analgesia) for relief of acute pain associated with minor podiatric surgery. *Dissertation Abstracts International, 40,* 4549.

Daniels, L.K. (1976). The effects of automated hypnosis and hand warming on migraine: A pilot study. *American Journal of Clinical Hypnosis, 19,* 91–94.

Daniels, L.K. (1977). Treatment of migraine headache by hypnosis and behaviour therapy: A case study. *American Journal of Clinical Hypnosis, 19,* 241–244.

Daniels, L.K. (1980). The use of multiple hypnotic behaviour therapy techniques: rationales and procedures. *Journal of the American Society of Psychosomatic Dentistry and Medicine, 27,* 124–132.

Darnton, R. (1968). *Mesmerism and the end of the enlightenment in France.* Cambridge, Massachusetts: Harvard University Press.

Davenport-Slack, B. (1975). A comparative evaluation of obstetrical hypnosis and antenatal childbirth training. *International Journal of Clinical and Experimental Hypnosis, 12,* 266.

Davidson, G.P., Garbett, N.D., & Tozer, S.G. (1982). An investigation into audiotaped self-hypnosis training in pregnancy and labor. In D.Waxman, P.C. Mesra, M.Gibson, & M.A. Basker (Eds.), *Modern trends in hypnosis.* New York: Plenum Press.

Davidson, J.A. (1962). Assessment of the value of hypnosis in pregnancy and labour. *British Medical Journal, 13,* 951.

Davidson, P. (1987). Hypnosis and migraine headache: reporting a clinical series. *Australian Journal of Clinical and Experimental Hypnosis, 15,* 111–118.

Deabler, H.L., Fidel, E., Dillenkoffer, R.L., & Elder, S. (1973). The use of relaxation and hypnosis in lowering high blood pressure. *American Journal of Clinical Hypnosis, 16,* 75–83.

De Benedittus, G., Panerai, A.E., & Villamira, M.A., (1984). Effects of hypnotic analgesia in high and low susceptible subjects during experimental visceral pain: A psychophysiological and neurochemical approach. *Pain,* Supplement 2, S365 .

Degun, G.S. & Degun, M.D. (1977). Hypnotic abreaction: A case of an agoraphobic and claustrophobic patient. *Bulletin of the British Society of Experimental and Clinical Hypnosis, 1,* 5–6.

Degun, M.D. & Degun, G.S. (1988). The use of hypnotic dream suggestion in psychotherapy. In M. Heap (Ed.), *Hypnosis: Current clinical, experimental and forensic practices* (pp. 221–233). London: Croom Helm.

Delprato, D.J. & Holmes, P.A. (1976). Facilitation of arm levitation responses to previous suggestions of a different type. *International Journal of Clinical and Experimental Hypnosis, 26,* 167–177.

Dengrove. E. (Ed.) (1976). *Hypnosis and behavior therapy.* Springfield, Illinois: Charles C. Thomas.

Deyoub, P.L. (1980). Hypnosis for the relief of hospital induced stress. *Journal of the American Society of Psychosomatic Dentistry and Medicine, 27,* 105–109 .

Dikel, W. & Olness, K. (1980). Self hypnosis, biofeedback and voluntary peripheral temperature control in children. *Pediatrics, 66,* 335–340 .

Dimond, R. E. (1981). Hypnotic treatment of a kidney dialysis patient. *American Journal of Clinical Hypnosis, 23*, 284–288.

Dixon, N.F. (1971). *Subliminal perception: The nature of a controversy*. London: McGraw-Hill.

Dobkin de Rios M. & Friedmann, J.K. (1987). Hypnotherapy with Hispanic burns. *International Journal of Clinical and Experimental Hypnosis, 35*, 87–94 .

Dobrovolsky, M. (1891). Huit observations d'accouchements sans douleur sous l'influence de l'hypnotisme. *Revue de l'Hypnotisme Expérimentale et Thérapeutique, 6*, 274–277, 310–312.

van der Does, A.J.W. & van Dyck, R. (1989). Does hypnosis contribute to the care of burn patients? *General Hospital Psychiatry, 11*, 119–124.

van der Does, A.J.W., Spijker, R.E., & van Dyck, R. (1988). Hypnosis and pain in patients with severe burns: A pilot study. *Burns, Including Thermal Injury, 14*, 399–404.

Drummond, F.E. (1981). Hypnosis in the treatment of headache: A review of the last 10 years. *Journal of the American Society of Psychosomatic Dentistry and Medicine, 28*, 87–101.

Dubin, L.L. & Shapiro, S.S. (1974). Use of hypnosis to facilitate dental extraction and hemostasis in a classic hemophiliac with high antibody titer to Factor VIII. *American Journal of Clinical Hypnosis, 17*, 79–83.

Duke, J.D. (1964). Intercorrelation of suggestibility tests and hypnotizability. *Psychological Record, 14*, 71–80.

Dumontpallier D. (1892). De l'action de la suggestion pendant le travail de l'accouchement. *Revue de l'Hypnotisme Expérimentale et Thérapeutique, 7*, 175–177.

Dunnet, C.P. & Williams, J.E. (1988). Hypnosis in speech therapy. In M. Heap (Ed.), *Hypnosis: Current clinical, experimental and forensic practices*. London: Croom Helm.

van Dyck, R. (1988). Future oriented hypnotic imagery: Description of a method. *Hypnos: Swedish Journal of Hypnosis in Psychotherapy and Psychosomatic Medicine, 15*, 60–67.

Edelmann, R.J. (1987). *The psychology of embarrassment*. Chichester, U.K.: John Wiley.

Edelmann, R.J. & Connolly, K.J. (1986). Psychological aspects of infertility. *British Journal of Medical Psychology, 59*, 209–219.

Edelmann, R.J. & Golombok, S. (1989). Stress and reproductive failure. *Journal of Reproductive and Infant Psychology, 7*, 79–86.

Edmonston, W.E. (1981). *Hypnosis and relaxation: Modern verification of an old equation*. New York: John Wiley and Sons.

Edwards, S.D. & van der Spuy, H.I. (1985). Hypnotherapy as a treatment for enuresis. *Journal of Child Psychology and Psychiatry, 26*, 161–170 .

Egbert, D.L., Battit, G.E., Welsh, C.E., & Bartlett, M.K. (1964). Reduction of postoperative pain by encouragement and instructions to patients. *New England Journal of Medicine, 270*, 825–827.

Eli, J. & Kleinhaus, M. (1985). Hypnosis: a tool for an integrative approach in the treatment of the gagging reflex. *International Journal of Clinical and Experimental Hypnosis, 33*, 99–108 .

Ellenberger, H.F. (1970). *The discovery of the unconscious: The history and evolution of dynamic psychiatry*. New York: Basic Books.

Elliotson, J. (1843). *Numerous cases of surgical operations without pain in the mesmeric state*. London: H. Baillière.

Ellis, A. (1962). *Reason and emotion in psychotherapy*. New York: Lyle Stuart.

Elton, D., Stanley, G., & Burrows, G. (1983). *Psychological control of pain*. Sydney: Grune & Stratton.

Enkin, M.W., Smith, M.L., Dermer, S.W., & Emmett, J.D. (1972). An adequately controlled study of the affectiveness of P.P.M. training. In N. Morris (Ed.), *Psychosomatic medicine in obstetrics and gynaecology*. Basel: Karger.

Epstein, L.A. & Abel, G.G. (1977). An analysis of biofeedback training effects for tension headache patients. *Behaviour Therapy, 8*, 37–47 .

Erickson, M.H. (1961). Historical note on the hand levitation and other ideomotor techniques. *American Journal of Clinical Hypnosis, 3*, 196–199 .

Erickson, M.H. & Rossi, E.L. (1979). *Hypnotherapy: An exploratory casebook.* New York: Irvington.

Erickson, M.H., Rossi, E.L., & Rossi, S.H. (1976). *Hypnotic realities: The induction of clinical hypnosis and the indirect forms of suggestion.* New York: Irvington.

Esdaile, J. (1846). *Mesmerism in India and its practical application in surgery and medicine.* London: Longmans, Brown, Green & Longmans.

Evans, C. & Richardson, P.H. (1988). Improved recovery and reduced postoperative stay after therapeutic suggestions during general anaesthesia. *Lancet, 2,* 491–493.

Evans, F.J. (1974). The placebo response in pain reduction. In J.J. Bonica (Ed.), *Advances in neurology, Vol. 4.* New York: Raven Press.

Evans, F.J. (1979). Hypnosis and sleep: Techniques for exploring cognitive activity during sleep. In E. Fromm & R.E. Shor (Eds.), *Hypnosis: Developments in research and new perspectives* (2nd edn) New York: Aldine Publishing Co.

Evans, F.J. & McGlashan, T.H. (1987). Specific and non-specific factors in hypnotic analgesia: A reply to Wagstaff. *British Journal of Experimental and Clinical Hypnosis, 4,* 141–147.

Ewer, T.C. & Stewart, D.E. (1986). Improvement in bronchial hyper-responsiveness in patients with moderate asthma after treatment with a hypnotic technique: A randomised controlled trial. *British Medical Journal, 293,* 1129–1132.

Ewin, D.M. (1974). Condyloma acuminatum: Successful treatment of four cases by hypnosis. *American Journal of Clinical Hypnosis, 17,* 73–78.

Ewin, D.M. (1979). Hypnosis in burn therapy. In G.D. Burrows, D.R. Collison, & L. Dennerstein (Eds.), *Handbook of hypnosis and psychosomatic medicine* (pp. 269–275). New York: Elsevier Press.

Ewin, D.M. (1986a). Emergency room hypnosis for the burned patient. *American Journal of Clinical Hypnosis, 29,* 7–12.

Ewin, D.M. (1986b). The effect of hypnosis and mental set on major surgery and burns. *Psychiatric Annals, 16,* 115–118.

Ewing, E. (1985). Hypnotherapy—A suitable case for treatment. *Bulletin of the College of Speech Therapists,* April, *396,* 1–21.

Eysenck, H.J. (1943). Suggestibility and hypnosis—an experimental analysis. *Proceedings of the Royal society of Medicine, 36,* 349–353.

Eysenck, H.J. (1952). The effects of psychotherapy: An evaluation. *Journal of Consulting Psychology, 16,* 319–324.

Eysenck, H.J. & Furneaux, W. D. (1945). Primary and secondary suggestibility: An experimental and statistical study. *Journal of Experimental Psychology, 35,* 485–523.

Fagan, J. & Shepherd, I.L. (Eds.) (1971). *Gestalt therapy now: Theory, techniques, applications.* New York: Harper Colophon.

Faria, J.C. de, Abbé (1906). *De la cause de sommeil lucide: ou étude sur la nature de l'homme.* 1819, 2nd edn, D.G. Delgado (Ed.). Paris: Henri Jouvet.

Fava, M & Guaraldi, A.P. (1987). Prolactin and stress. *Stress Medicine, 3,* 211–216.

Fee, A.F. & Reilly, R.R. (1982). Hypnosis in obstetrics: A review of techniques. *Journal of the American Society of Psychosomatic Dentistry and Medicine, 29,* 17–29.

Feinstein, A.D. & Morgan, R.M. (1986). Hypnosis in regulating bipolar affective disorders. *American Journal of Clinical Hypnosis, 29,* 29–37.

Fellows, B.J. (1988a). Editorial comment. *British Journal of Experimental and Clinical Hypnosis, 5,* 111–116.

Fellows, B.J. (1988b). The use of hypnotic susceptibility scales. In M. Heap (Ed.), *Hypnosis: Current clinical, experimental and forensic practices,* London: Croom Helm.

Field, P. (1974). Effects of tape-recorded hypnotic preparation for surgery. *International Journal of Clinical and Experimental Hypnosis, 22,* 54–61.

Finer, B. (1987). Hypnotherapy in burns rehabilitation. *Hypnos: Swedish Journal of Hypnosis in Psychotherapy and Psychosomatic Medicine, 14,* 110–112.

Finkelstein, S. (1982). Re-establishment of traumatically disrupted finger flexor: A brief communication. *International Journal of Clinical and Experimental Hypnosis, 30,* 1–3.

Foissac, P. (1833). *Rapports et discussions de l'Académie Royale de Médecine sur le magnétisme animal.* Paris: Baillière.

Forbes, J. (1845). *Mesmerism true—mesmerism false.* London: J. Churchill.

Frankel, F.H. (1975). Hypnosis as a treatment method in psychosomatic medicine. *International Journal of Psychiatry in Medicine, 6,* 75–85.

Frankel, F.H. (1982). Hypnosis and hypnotizability scales: A reply. *International Journal of Clinical and Experimental Hypnosis, 33,* 377–392.

Frankel, F.H. & Misch, R.C. (1973). Hypnosis in a case of long-standing psoriasis in a person with character problems. *International Journal of Clinical and Experimental Hypnosis, 21,* 121–130.

Frankel, F.H. & Orne, M.T. (1976). Hypnotizability and phobic behavior. *Archives of General Psychiatry, 33,* 1259–1261.

Freeman, R.M. & Baxby, K. (1982). Hypnotherapy for incontinence caused by the unstable detrusor. *British Medical Journal (Clinical Research), 284,* 1831–1834.

Freeman, W. & Watts, J .W. (1950). *Psychosurgery in the treatment of mental disorders and intractible pain.* Springfield, Ill.: C.C. Thomas.

Friedman, H. & Taub, H.A. (1977). The use of hypnosis and biofeedback procedures for essential hypertension. *International Journal of Clinical and Experimental Hypnosis, 25,* 335–347.

Friedman, H. & Taub, H.A. (1978). A six-month follow-up of the use of hypnosis and biofeedback procedures in essential hypertension. *American Journal of Clinical Hypnosis, 20,* 184–188.

Friedman, H. & Taub, H.A. (1984). Brief psychological training procedures in migraine treatment. *American Journal of Clinical Hypnosis, 26,* 187–200.

Friedman, H. & Taub, H.A. (1985). Extended follow-up study of the effects of brief psychological procedures in migraine therapy. *American Journal of Clinical Hypnosis . 28,* 27–33.

Fromm, E. (1968). Dissociative and integrative processes in hypnoanalysis. *American Journal of Clinical Hypnosis, 10,* 174–177.

Fromm, E. (1984). Hypnoanalysis—with particular emphasis on the boderline patient. *Psychoanalytic Psychology, 1,* 61–76.

Fromm, E. (1987). Significant developments in clinical hypnosis during the past 25 years. *International Journal of Clinical and Experimental Hypnosis, 35,* 215–230 .

Fuchs, K. (1980). *The use of hypnosis in obstetrics.* Second European Congress of Hypnosis, Dubrovnik.

Fuchs, K., Paldi, E., Abramovici, H., & Peretz, B.A. (1980). Treatment of hyperemesis gravidarum by hypnosis. *International Journal of Clinical and Experimental Hypnosis, 28,* 313–323.

Furneaux, W.D. & Gibson, H.B. (1961). The Maudsley Personality Inventory as a predictor of susceptibility to hypnosis. *International Journal of Clinical and Experimental Hypnosis, 9,* 167–176.

Gale, E.N. & Ayer, W.A. (1969). Treatment of dental phobias. *Journal of the American Dental Association, 78,* 130.

Galin, D. (1974). Implications for psychiatry of left and right cerebral specialization. *Archives of General Psychiatry, 31.* 572–583.

Gall, J. (1985). The difficult dental patient. In D. Waxman, P . Misra, M. Gibson, & M.A. Basker (Eds.), *Modern trends in hypnosis.* New York: Plenum Press.

Gallup, G.G. (1974). Factual status of a fictional concept. *Psychological Bulletin, 31,* 836–853.

Gallup, G.G., Nash, R.F., Potter, R.J., & Donnegan, N.H. (1970). Effects of varying conditions of fear on immobility reactions in domestic chickens. *Journal of Comparative and Physiological Psychology, 73,* 442–5.

Galyean, B.C. (1986). The use of guided imagery in elementary and secondary schools. *Hypnos: Swedish Journal of Hypnosis in Psychotherapy and Psychosomatic Medicine. 13,* 50–55.

Gardner, G.G. & Olness, K. (1981). *Hypnosis and hypnotherapy with children.* New York: Grune and Stratton.

Gauld, A. (1988). Reflections on mesmeric analgesia. *British Journal of Experimental and Clinical Hypnosis, 5,* 17–24.

Gazzaniga, M.S. (1970). *The bisected brain.* New York: Appleton-Century Crofts.

Gerschman, J.A., Burrows, G.D., & Reade, P.C. (1979). The role of hypnosis in dental phobic illness. *Australian Journal of Clinical and Experimental Hypnosis, 4,* 58–64.

Gibbert, G.F. (1965). *A short textbook of midwifery.* London: J. & A. Churchill.

Gibbons, D .E. (1979). *Applied hypnosis and hyperempiria.* New York: Plenum Press.

Giblin, P.T., Ager, J.W., Poland, M.L., Olson, J.M., & Moghissi, K.S. (1988). Effects of stress and characteristic adaptability on semen quality in healthy men. *Fertility and Sterility, 49,* 127–132.

Gibson, H.B. (1977). *Hypnosis: Its nature and therapeutic uses.* London: Peter Owen.

Gibson, H.B. (1978). Letter. *British Medical Journal,* 30 September.

Gibson, H.B. (1981). H.J. Eysenck's contribution to hypnosis research. In R. Lynn (Ed.), *Dimensions of personality.* Oxford: Pergamon Press.

Gibson. H.B. (1982). *Pain and its conquest.* London: Peter Owen.

Gibson, H.B. (1984). Book review of Ernest L. Rossi (Ed.), *The collected papers of Milton H. Erickson,* by Milton H. Erickson, Vols I and II. *International Journal of Clinical and Experimental Hypnosis, 32,* 254–256.

Gibson, H.B. (1985). A comment on Barry Hart's "Type of suggestion and hypnotizability in clinical work". *British Journal of Experimental and Clinical Hypnosis, 2,* 94–97.

Gibson, H.B. (1986). An experimental study of autoscopic phenomena in normal students. *Imagery, 2,* 115–119.

Gibson, H.B. (1987). Is hypnosis a placebo? *British Journal of Experimental and Clinical Hypnosis, 4,* 149–155.

Gibson, H.B. (1988a). Gauld's reflections on mesmeric analgesia. *British Journal of Experimental and Clinical Hypnosis, 4,* 149–155.

Gibson, H.B. (1988b). Should professionals stick to their own lasts? *British Journal of Experimental and Clinical Hypnosis, 5,* 153–157, 161–162.

Gilbert, P. (1984). *Depression: From psychology to brain state.* London: Lawrence Erlbaum Associates Ltd.

Glaros, A. & Rao, S. (1977). Effects of bruxism: A review of the literature. *Journal of Prosthetic Dentistry, 38,* 149–157.

Golan, H.P. (1971). Control of fear reaction in dental patients by hypnosis: Three case reports. *American Journal of Clinical Hypnosis, 13,* 279–284.

Golan, H.P. (1985). Using hypnotic phenomena for physiological change. *American Journal of Clinical Hypnosis, 28,* 157–162.

Goldberg, G. (1973). The psychological, physiological and hypnotic approach to bruxism in the treatment of peridontal disease. *Journal of the American Society of Psychosomatic Dentistry and Medicine, 20,* 75–91.

Goldie, L. (1956). Hypnotism in the casualty department. *British Medical Journal. 2,* 1340–1342.

Goldmann, L. (1988). Cognitive processing under general anaesthesia. In M. Heap (Ed.), *Hypnosis: Current clinical, experimental and forensic practices* (pp. 68–76). London: Croom Helm.

Goodman, H.P. (1962). Hypnosis in prolonged resistant eczema: A case report . *American Journal of Clinical Hypnosis, 5,* 144–147.

Gottfredson, D.K. (1973). *Hypnosis as an anesthetic in dentistry.* Unpublished doctoral dissertation. Brigham Young University.

Grabowska, M.J. (1971). The effect of hypnosis and hypnotic suggestion on the blood flow in the extremities. *Polish Medical Journal, 10,* 1044–1051.

Graham, G. (1974). Hypnoanalysis in dental practice. *American Journal of Clinical Hypnosis, 16,* 178–187.

Graham, G.W. (1975). Hypnotic treatment for migraine headaches. *International Journal of Clinical and Experimental Hypnosis, 23,* 165–171.

Graham, J.R. & Wolff, H.G. (1938). Mechanism of migraine headache and action of ergotamine. *Archives of Neurology and Psychiatry, 39,* 737–763.

Gravitz, M.A. (1988). Early uses of hypnosis as surgical anesthesia. *American Journal of Clinical Hypnosis, 30,* 201–208.

Gravitz, M.A. & Gerton, M. I. (1984). Origins of the term hypnotism prior to Braid. *American Journal of Clinical Hypnosis, 27,* 107-110.

Green, J., Kitzinger, J., & Coupland,V. (1986). *The division of labour: Implications of medical staffing structures for midwives and doctors in the labour ward.* Cambridge: Child Care and Development Group, University of Cambridge.

Greenleaf, M. & Natali, C. (1987). Hypnosis and Jenck's breathing exercises for the treatment of psychophysiological factors in Raynaud's disease: A case study. *Hypnos: Swedish Journal of Hypnosis in Psychotherapy and Psychosomatic Medicine, I4,* 127–133.

Greenwald, A.S. (1968). The bruxism appliance and its varied application: Outline of procedure. *New York Journal of Dentistry, 38,* 443.

Grinder, J. & Bandler, R. (1981). *Trance-Formations.* Moab, Utah: Real People Press.

Gross, H. & Posner, N. (1963). An evaluation of hypnosis for obstetric delivery. *American Journal of Obstetrics and Gynecology, 87,* 912–919.

Gruenewald, D. (1984). On the nature of multiple personality: comparisons with hypnosis. *International Journal of Clinical and Experimental Hypnosis, 32,* 170–190.

Gruzelier, J. (1988). The neuropsychology of hypnosis: In M. Heap (Ed.). *Hypnosis: Current clinical, experimental and forensic practices* (pp. 68–76). London: Croom Helm.

Guéguen, J. (1962). L'accouchement sous hypnose. *Gynécologie et Obstétrique, 61,* 92–111.

Gur, R.C. & Gur, R.E. (1974). Handedness, sex and eyedness as moderating variables in the relation between hypnotic susceptibility and functional brain asymmetry. *Journal of Abnormal Psychology, 83,* 635-643.

Haberman, M.A. (1987). Complications following hypnosis in a psychotic patient with sexual dysfunction treated by a lay hypnotist. *American Journal of Clinical Hypnosis, 29,* 166–170.

Haggard, H.W. (1932). *The lame, the halt and the blind.* London: Heinemann.

Hall, H.R. (1982/83). Hypnosis and the immune system: A review with implications for cancer and the psychology of healing. *American Journal of Clinical Hypnosis, 25,* 92–103.

Hammond, C.D. (1984). Myths about Erickson and Ericksonian hypnosis. *American Journal of Clinical Hypnosis, 26,* 231–245.

Hammond, C.D. (1988). Will the real Milton Erickson please stand up? *International Journal of Clinical and Experimental Hypnosis, 36,* 173–181.

Hand, I. & Lamontagne, Y. (1976). The exacerbation of interpersonal problems after rapid phobia removal. *Psychotherapy Theory, Research and Practice, 13,* 405–411.

Haralambous, G., Wilson, P.H., Platt-Hepworth, S., Tonkin, J.P., Hensley, V.R., & Kavanagh, D. (1987). EMG biofeedback in the treatment of tinnitus: An experimental evaluation. *Behaviour Research and Therapy, 25,* 49–55 .

Harland, R.W. (1960). Children's fears. *Australian Dental Journal, 5,* 18–22

Harper, R., Lenton, E.A., & Cooke, I.D. (1987). Prolactin and subjective reports on stress in women attending an infertility clinic. *Journal of Reproductive and Infant Psychology, 3,* 3–8 .

Harrison, K.L., Callan, V.J., & Hennessey, J.F. (1987). Stress and semen quality in an *in vitro* fertilization program. *Fertility and Sterility, 48,* 633–636 .

Harrison, R.F., O'Moore, A.M., O'Moore, R.R.,& McSweeney, J.A. (1981). Stress profiles in normal infertile couples: Pharmacological and psychological approaches to therapy. In V. Insler & G. Betterndorf, G. (Eds.), *Advances in diagnosis and treatment on infertility.* Amsterdam: Elsevier.

Harrison, R.F., O'Moore, A.M., O'Moore, R.R., & Robb, D. (1984). Stress in infertile couples. In R.F. Harrison, J. Bonnar, & W. Thompson. (Eds.). *Fertility and sterility.* Lancaster: MTP Press.

Hart, B.B. (1984). Hypnotic age regression of longstanding phobias: 2 case studies. In M. Heap (Ed.), *Proceedings of the First Conference of the British Society of Experimental and Clinical Hypnosis*. (pp. 54–61). BSECH publication.

Hart, B.B. (1988). Applications to psychological therapies: Overview. In M. Heap (Ed.), *Hypnosis: Current clinical, experimental and forensic practices* (pp. 201–207). London: Croom Helm.

van der Hart, 0. (1985). Metaphoric hypnotic imagery in the treatment of functional amenorrhea. *American Journal of Clinical Hypnosis, 27,* 159–165.

Hart, R.R. (1980). The influence of taped hypnotic induction treatment procedure on the recovery of surgery patients. *International Journal of Clinical and Experimental Hypnosis, 28,* 324–332.

Hartland, J. (1971). *Medical and dental hypnosis and its clinical applications.* (2nd edn) London: Ballière Tindall.

Hartmann, E. (1984). *The nightmare*. New York: Basic Books.

Hartmann, E., Mehta, N., Forgione, A., Brune, P., & LaBrie, R. (1987). Bruxism: personality traits and other characteristics. *Sleep Research, 16,* 350.

Harvey, R.F., Hinton, R.A., Gunary, R., & Barry, R.E. (1989). Individual and group hypnotherapy in the treatment of refractory irritable bowel syndrome. *Lancet, 1,* 424–425.

Heap, M. (1980). Book review of M.H. Erickson, E.L. Rossi, & S.I. Rossi: *Hypnotic realities. Bulletin of the British Society of Experimental and Clinical Hypnosis, 3,* 25–27.

Heap, M. (1984a). A comment on Fewtrell's "Psychological approaches to panic attack". *British Journal of Experimental and Clinical Hypnosis, 1,* 27–29.

Heap, M. (1984b). Four victims. *British Journal of Experimental and Clinical Hypnosis (Newsletter), 2,* 60–62.

Heap, M. (1984c). Comments on Wright and Humphreys' "The use of hypnosis to enhance covert sensitisation: Two case studies". *British Journal of Experimental and Clinical Hypnosis, 1,* 15–17.

Heap, M. (1985a). Ego-strengthening: Further considerations. In M. Heap (Ed.), *Proceedings of the Second Annual Conference of the British Society of Experimental and Clinical Hypnosis* (pp. 77–80). BSECH publication.

Heap, M. (1985b). Hypnosis and the client-centred approach. In M.Heap (Ed.), *Proceedings of the Second Annual Conference of the British Society of Experimental and Clinical Hypnosis* (pp. 66–69). BSECH publication.

Heap, M. (1987). Book review of Y.M. Dolan: *A path with a heart. British Journal of Experimental and Clinical Hypnosis, 4,* 41–44.

Heap, M. (1988a). Neuro-linguistic programming: a British perspective. *Hypnos: Swedish Journal of Hypnosis in Psychotherapy and Psychosomatic Medicine, 15,* 4–13.

Heap, M. (1988b). Born-again mesmerism? *The Psychologist, 1,* 261–262.

Heap, M. (1988c). Neurolinguistic programming: An interim verdict. In M. Heap (Ed.), *Hypnosis: Current clinical, experimental and forensic practices* (pp. 268–280). London: Croom Helm.

Heap, M. (1988d). In search of the 'alternative' in alternative medicine. *British and Irish Skeptic,* January/February, 30–31.

Heap, M. (1989). Neurolinguistic programming: What is the evidence? In D. Waxman, D. Pedersen, I. Wilkie, & P. Mellett (Eds.) *Hypnosis: The Fourth European Congress at Oxford* (pp. 118–124). London: Whurr Publishers.

Hearne, K. (1982). A cool look at nothing special. *Nursing Mirror,* 20 January.

Hickman, M.A. (1978). *Midwifery*. Oxford: Blackwell.

Hilgard, E.R. (1965). *Hypnotic susceptibility*. New York: Harcourt, Brace & World.

Hilgard, E.R. (1978). Hypnosis and pain. In R.A. Steinbach (Ed.), *The psychology of pain*. New York: Raven Press.

Hilgard, E.R. (1982). Hypnotic susceptibility and implications for measurement. *International Journal of Clinical and Experimental Hypnosis. 33,* 394–403.

Hilgard, E.R. (1984). A book review of Ernest L. Rossi (Ed.), *The collected papers of Milton H. Erickson*, by Milton H. Erickson, Vols I to IV. *International Journal of Clinical and Experimental Hypnosis, 32,* 257–265.

Hilgard, E.R. (1986). *Divided consciousness: Multiple controls in human thought and action.* New York: John Wiley and Sons.

Hilgard, E.R. & Bentler, P.M. (1963). Predicting hypnotizability from the Maudsley Personality Inventory. *British Journal of Psychology, 54,* 63–69.

Hilgard, E.R. & Hilgard, J.R. (1983). *Hypnosis in the relief of pain.* Los Altos, California: W. Kaufmann Inc.

Hilgard, E.R., Sheehan, P.W., Monteiro, K.P., & McDonald, H. (1981). Factorial structure of the Creative Imagination Scale as a measure of hypnotic responsiveness: An internal comparative study. *International Journal of Clinical and Experimental Hypnosis, 29,* 66–76 .

Hilgard, E.R. & Tart, C.T. (1966). Responsiveness to suggestions following waking and imagination instructions and following induction of hypnosis. *Journal of Abnormal Psychology, 71,* 196–208.

Hilgard, J.R. (1970). *Personality and hypnosis: A study in imaginative involvement.* Chicago: University of Chicago Press.

Hilgard, J.R. (1974). Imaginative involvement: Some characteristics of the highly hypnotizable and the non-hypnotizable. *International Journal of Clinical and Experimental Hypnosis, 22,* 138–56.

Hilgard, J.R. & LeBaron, S. (1984). *Hypnotherapy of pain in children with cancer.* Los Altos, California: W. Kaufmann Inc.

Hoencamp, E. (1989). Sexual coercion and the role of hypnosis in the abused therapeutic relationship. In D. Waxman, D Pedersen, I. Wilkie, & P. Mellett (Eds.) *Hypnosis: The Fourth European Congress at Oxford* (pp. 160–174). London: Whurr Publishers.

Höfle, K.H. (1980). Selbstubende Methoden beim primaren Raynaud-Syndrom. *Psychotherapy, Psychosomatik, Medizinische Psychologie, 30,* 174–179.

Holroyd, J. (1987). How hypnosis may potentiate psychotherapy. *American Journal of Clinical Hypnosis, 29,* 194–200.

Hoogduin, K. (1988). Hypnotizability in obsessive-compulsives. *Hypnos: Swedish Journal of Hypnosis in Psychotherapy and Psychosomatic Medicine, I5,* 14–19.

Houghton, D.M. (1988). Hypnosis with anxious schoolchildren. In M. Heap (Ed.), *Hypnosis: Current clinical, experimental and forensic practices* (pp. 288–300). London: Croom Helm.

Hughes, A.M. (1986). Book review of J. Barber & C. Adrian (Eds.), *Psychological approaches to the management of pain. Pain, 27,* 131.

Hughey, M.J., McElin, T.W., & Young, T. (1978). Maternal and fetal outcome of Lamaze-prepared patients. *Obstetrics and Gynecology, 51,* 643–647.

Hull, C.L. (1933). *Hypnosis and suggestibility: An experimental approach.* New York: Appleton Century Crofts.

Humphreys, A. (1984). Neutral hypnosis, progressive muscular relaxation and the relaxation response: A review. *British Journal of Experimental and Clinical Hypnosis. 1,* 19–27.

Humphreys, A. (1986). Review of the literature on the adjunctive use of hypnosis in behaviour therapy. *British Journal of Experimental and Clinical Hypnosis, 3,* 95–102.

Humphreys, A. (1988). Applications of hypnosis to anxiety control. In M. Heap (Ed.), *Hypnosis: Current clinical, experimental and forensic practices* (pp. 105–114). London: Croom Helm.

Inhelder, B. (1982). Some aspects of Piaget's genetic approach to cognition. *Society for Research in Child Development, Monograph 27,* 19–34.

IJCEH. (1972). *International Journal of Clinical and Experimental Hypnosis,* Vol. 20.

International Congress on Experimental Psychology: Second Session (1982). London: Williams & Norgate.

Ioannou, C. (1990). Behavioural management of acute pain following renal transplantation. *Journal of Child Psychology and Psychiatry.* (submitted).

Ireland, C.E., Wilson, P.H., Tonkin, J.P., & Platt–Hepworth, S. (1985). An evaluation of relaxation training in the treatment of tinnitus. *Behaviour Research and Therapy, 23,* 423–430.

Jacobson, E. (1954). Relaxation methods in labor. *American Journal of Obstetrics and Gynecology, 67,* 1035.

James, F.R. & Large, R.G. (1987). Evaluation of the efficacy of self hypnosis in the treatment of chronic pain. *Pain,* Supplement 4, S171.

Janet, P. (1925). *Psychological healing: A historical and clinical study* (English translation by E. and C. Paul). New York: Macmillan (originally published in French, 1919).

Janis, I.L. (1958). *Psychological stress,* New York: Wiley.

Jemmott, J.B., Borysenko, J.Z., Borysenko, M., McClelland, D.C., Chapman, R., Meyer, D., & Benson, H. (1983). Academic stress, power motivation and decrease in secretion rate of salivary secretory immunoglobulin A. *Lancet, 2,* 1400–1402.

Jemmott, J.B. & Locke, S.E. (1984). Psychosocial factors, immunologic mediation, and human susceptibility to infectious diseases: How much do we know? *Psychological Bulletin, 95,* 78–108.

John, M.E. & Parrino, J.P. (1983). Practical hypnotic suggestion in opthalmic surgery. *American Journal of Opthalmology, 96,* 540–542.

Johnson, G.M. (1987). Hypnotic imagery and suggestion as an adjunctive treatment in a case of coma. *American Journal of Clinical Hypnosis, 29,* 255–259.

Johnson, K. & Korn, E.R. (1980). Hypnosis and imagery in the rehabilitation of a brain-damaged patient. *Journal of Mental Imagery, 4,* 35–39.

Johnson, L.S., Johnson, D.L., Olson, M.R., & Newman, J.P. (1981). The uses of hypnotherapy with learning disabled children. *Journal of Clinical Psychology, 37,* 291–299.

Johnson, R.F.Q. & Barber, T.X. (1978). Hypnosis, suggestions, and warts: An experimental investigation implicating the importance of "believed-in efficacy". *American Journal of Clinical Hypnosis, 20,* 165–74.

de Jong (1889). Cited by E. Benbillon (Ed.). *Premier Congrès International de l'hypnotisme experimentale et thérapeutique tenu à l'Hôtel Dieu de Paris du 8–12 Août 1889.* Paris: Doin.

Judd, F.K., Burrows, G.D., & Dennerstein, L. (1985). The dangers of hypnosis: A review. *Australian Journal of Clinical and Experimental Hypnosis, 13,* 1–15.

Karle, H.W.A. (1988a). Hypnosis in analytic psychotherapy. In M. Heap (Ed.), *Hypnosis: Current clinical, experimental and forensic practices* (pp.208–220). London: Croom Helm.

Karle, H.W.A. (1988b). Hypnosis in the management of tinnitus. In M. Heap (Ed.), *Hypnosis: Current clinical, experimental and forensic practices* (pp. 178–185). London: Croom Helm.

Karle, H.W.A. & Boys, J.H. (1987). *Hypnotherapy: A practical handbook.* London: Free Association Books.

Kegeles, S.S. (1963). Some motives for seeking preventive dental treatment. *Journal of the American Dental Association, 7,* 90–8.

Keifer, R.C. & Hospodarsky, J. (1980). The use of hypnotic technique in anesthesia to decrease post-operative meperidine requirements. *Journal of the American Obstetrics Association, 79,* 693–695.

Kihlstrom. J.F. (1985). Hypnosis. *Annual Review of Psychology, 36,* 385–418.

Kimura, S. (1975). Behaviour therapy for cerebral palsy by hypnotic methods. *Bulletin of the British Psychological Society, 28,* 240.

King, M.G. & Stanley, G.V. (1986). The treatment of hyperhidrosis: A case report. *Australian Journal of Clinical and Experimental Hypnosis. 14,* 61–64.

Kingsbury, J.O. (1891). Accouchement pendant le sommeil hypnotique. *Revue Hypnotique, 5,* 298–300.

Kirmayer, L.J. (1988). Word magic and the rhetoric of common sense: Erickson's metaphors for mind. *International Journal of Clinical and Experimental Hypnosis, 36,* 157–172.

Kirsch, I. & Barton, R.D. (1988). Hypnosis in the treatment of multiple personality: A cognitive-behavioural approach. *British Journal of Experimental and Clinical Hypnosis, 5,* 131–137.

Kleinhauz, M. & Eli, S. (1986). Potential deleterious effects of hypnosis in the clinical setting. *American Journal of Clinical Hypnosis, 29,* 155–159.

Kleinknecht, R.A., Klepoc, R.K., & Alexander, L.D. (1973). Origins and characteristics of fear of dentistry. *Journal of the American Dental Association, 86,* 842.

Kline, M.V. (1984). Multiple personality: Facts and artifacts in relation to hypnotherapy. *International Journal of Clinical and Experimental Hypnosis, 32,* 198–209.

Kline, M.V. & Guze, H. (1963). Self–hypnosis in childbirth: A clinical evaluation of a patient conditioning program. *Journal of Clinical and Experimental Hypnosis, 3,* 142.

Kluft, R.P. (1984), Aspects of the treatment of multiple personality disorder. *Psychiatric Annals, 14,* 51–55.

Klusman, L.E. (1975). Reduction of pain in childbirth by the alleviation of anxiety during pregnancy. *Journal of Consulting and Clinical Psychology, 43,* 162–165.

Kohen, D.P. (1980). Relaxation/mental imagery (self-hypnosis) and pelvic examinations in adolescents. *Developmental and Behavioral Pediatrics, 1,* 180–186.

Kraft, T. (1983). Injection phobia: A case study. *British Journal of Experimental and Clinical Hypnosis. 1,* 13–18.

Kramer, R.B. & Braham, R.L. (1977). The management of the chronic or hysterical gagger. *Journal of Dentistry with Children, 44,* 111–116.

Kroger, W.S. (1952). Natural childbirth: Is the Read method of "Natural Childbirth" waking hypnosis? *Medical Times, 80,* 152.

Kroger, W.S. (1977). *Clinical and experimental hypnosis in medicine, dentistry and psychology.* Philadelphia: J.B. Lippincott.

Kroger, W.S. & Fezler, W.D. (1976). *Hypnosis and behavior modification: Imagery conditioning.* Philadelphia: J.B. Lippincott.

Krugman, M., Kirsch, I., Wickless, C., Milling, L., Golicz, H., & Toth, A. (1985). Neuro-linguistic programming treatment for anxiety: Magic or myth? *Journal of Consulting and Clinical Psychology, 53,* 526–530.

LaBaw, W.L. (1975). Auto-hypnosis in haemophilia. *Haematologia, 9,* 103–110.

LaBerge, S. (1985). *Lucid dreaming.* Los Angeles: Tarcher.

Lamaze, F. & Vellay, P. (1956). *Psychologic analgesia in obstetrics.* New York: Pergamon.

Lamb, C.S. (1985). Hypnotically-induced deconditioning: Reconstruction of memories in the treatment of phobias. *American Journal of Clinical Hypnosis, 28,* 56–62.

Lankton, S. (1980). *Practical magic.* Cupertino, California, Meta Publications.

Lankton, S. & Lankton, C. (1983). *The answer within: A clinical framework of Ericksonian hypnotherapy.* New York: Bruner/Mazel.

Large, R.G. & James, F.R. (1988). Personalised evaluation of self–hypnosis as a treatment of chronic pain: A repertory grid analysis. *Pain, 35,* 155–169.

Lavigne, J.V., Schulein, M.J., & Hahn, Y.S. (1986). Psychological aspects of painful medical conditions in children. II. Personality factors, family characteristics and treatment. *Pain, 27,* 147–69.

LeBaron, S. & Zeltzer, L.K. (1984). Research on hypnosis in hemophilia—preliminary success and problems. *International Journal of Clinical and Experimental Hypnosis, 32,* 290–295.

Lenox, J.R. (1970). Effect of hypnotic analgesia on verbal report and cardiovascular responses to ischemic pain. *Journal of Abnormal Psychology, 75,* 199–206.

Leonie, S., Willer, J.C., & Michaux, D. (1987). Hypnotic suggestion of analgesia induces a profound depression of monosynaptic reflexes in man. *Pain,* Supplement 4, S192.

Levine, E.S. (1980). Indirect suggestions through personalized fairy tales for treatment of childhood insomnia. *American Journal of Clinical Hypnosis, 23,* 57–63.

Levine, M. (1960). Gagging—A problem in prosthodontica. *Journal of Canadian Dentistry, 26,* 70–75.

Lewinstein, L.N. (1978). Hypnosis as an anesthetic in pediatric opthalmology. *Anesthesiology, 49,* 144–145.

Lewinstein, L.N., Iwamoto, K., & Schwartz, H. (1981). Hypnosis in high risk opthalmic surgery. Op*thalmic Surgery, 12,* 39–41.

Lewis, J. (1961). Psychosomatic formulation in dentistry. *Journal of the American Dental Association, 63*, 626–629.

Lichtschein, L. (1898). Hypnotism in pregnancy and labour. *Medical News. 73*, 295–289.

Liébault, A. (1866). *Du sommeil et des états analogues, considérés surtout au point de vere de l'action du moral sur le physique*. Paris: Masson.

Loftus, E.F. & Loftus, G.R. (1980). On the permanence of stored information in the brain. *American Psychologist, 35*, 409–420.

London, P. & Cooper, L.M. (1969). Norms of hypnotic susceptibility in children. *Developmental Psychology, 1*, 113–124.

London, P. & Fuhrer, M. (1961). Hypnosis, motivation and performance. *Journal of Personality. 29*, 321–333.

Lozanov, G. (1978). *Suggestology and Outlines of Suggestopaedia*. London: Gordon Breach.

Lucas, D., Stratis, D.J., & Deniz, S. (1981). From the clinic: Hypnosis in conjunction with corrective therapy in a quadraplegic patient: A case report. *American Corrective Therapy Journal, 35*, 116–120.

Lucas, H. & Levy, M. (1984). The use of hypnosis in an unusual voice disorder—a combined clinical psychology and speech therapy approach. *Bulletin of the College of Speech Therapists, 383*, 1–2.

Ludwig, A. (1963). Hypnosis in fiction. *International Journal of Clinical and Experimental Hypnosis, 6*, 71–80.

Luthe, W. (1972). Autogenic therapy: Excerpts on applications to cardiovascular disorders and hypercholesteremia. In J. Stoyva, T.X. Barber, L. DiCara, J. Kamiya, N.E. Miller, & D. Shapiro (Eds.), *Biofeedback and Self–Control* (pp. 437–462). Chicago: Aldine-Atherton.

Luys, J. (1890a). Deux cas nouveaux d'accouchement sans douleur. *Revue Hypnologie Théorique et Pratique, 1*, 49–55.

Luys, J. (1890b). Accouchement en état de fascination: amnésie complète au reveil. *Revue d'Hypnologie Théorique et Pratique, 1*, 321–323.

Lynn, S.J. & Rhue, J.W. (1988). Fantasy proneness: Hypnosis, developmental antecedents and psychopathology. *American Psychologist, 43*, 35–44.

McConkey, K.M., Sheehan, P.W., & White, K.D. (1979). Comparison of the Creative Imagination Scale and the Harvard Group Scale of Hypnotic Susceptibility: Form A. *International Journal of Clinical and Experimental Hypnosis, 27*, 265–277.

McCue, P.A. (1987). Erickson's hypnosis and therapy: A critical view. *British Journal of Experimental and Clinical Hypnosis, 4*, 5–14.

McCue, P.A. (1988a). Milton H. Erickson: A critical perspective. In M. Heap (Ed.), *Hypnosis: Current clinical, experimental and forensic practices* (pp. 257–267). London: Croom Helm.

McCue, P.A. (1988b). Ericksonian hypnosis: A cautionary note. *The Psychologist, 1*, 261–262.

McDougall, W. (1908). *An introduction to social psychology*. London: Methuen.

Macfarlane, F.K. (1987). The use of hypnosis in speech therapy—a questionnaire study. *Trance: BSPHST Newsletter*, 7 November.

McGarry, J. (1987). Mesmerism vs hypnosis: A comparison of relaxation responses and evaluation of mental and psychophysiological outcomes. *Australian Journal of Clinical and Experimental Hypnosis, 8*, 7–36.

McGlashan, T.H., Evans, F.J., & Orne, M.T. (1969). The nature of hypnotic analgesia and the placebo response to experimental pain. *Psychosomatic Medicine, 31*, 227–246.

McGrady, A.V. (1984). Effects of psychological stress on male reproduction: A review. *Archives of Andrology, 13*, 1–7.

McKeegan, G.F. (1986). Hypnosis in the treatment of phobias. In F.A. De Piano & H.C. Salzberg (Eds.), *Clinical applications of hypnosis*. Norwood, New Jersey: Ablex Publishing Co.

Mackett, J. & Maden, W. (1989). Simple hypnotherapy for infertility. In D. Waxman, D. Pedersen, I. Wilkie, & P. Mellett (Eds.), *Hypnosis: The Fourth European Congress at Oxford* (pp. 201–205). London: Whurr Publishers.

MacMillan, P.M. (1988). The use of hypnosis and suggestopaedia in children with learning problems. In M. Heap (Ed.), *Hypnosis: Current clinical, experimental and forensic practices* (pp. 301–313). London: Croom Helm.

Maher-Loughnan, G.P. (1970). Hypnosis and autohypnosis for the treatment of asthma. *International Journal of Clinical and Experimental Hypnosis, 18,* 1–14.

Maher-Loughnan, G.P. (1984). Timing of clinical response to hypnotherapy. *Proceedings of the British Society of Medical and Dental Hypnosis, 5,* 1–16.

Maher-Loughnan, G.P. & Kinsley, D. (1968). Hypnosis for asthma—a controlled trial: A report to the Research Committee of the British Tuberculosis Association. *British Medical Journal, 4,* 71–76.

Maher-Loughnan, G.P., Macdonald, N., Mason, A.A., & Fry, L. (1962). Controlled trial of hypnosis in the symptomatic treatment of asthma. *British Medical Journal, 2,* 371–376.

Mairs, D.A.E. (1988). Hypnosis in sport. In M. Heap (Ed.), *Hypnosis: Current clinical, experimental and forensic practices* (pp. 340–348). London: Croom Helm.

Malmo, B., Boag, T.J., & Raginsky, B.B. (1954). Electromyographic study of hypnotic deafness. *Journal of Experimental and Clinical Hypnosis, 2,* 305–317.

Malyska, W. & Christenson, J. (1967). Autohypnosis and the prenatal class. *American Journal of Clinical Hypnosis, 9,* 188.

Mandy, A.J., Farcus, R., Scher, E., & Mandy, T.E. (1951). The natural childbirth illusion. *Southern Medical Journal, Birmingham (U.S.A.), 44,* 527–534.

Manganiello, A.J. (1986). Hypnotherapy in the rehabilitation of a stroke victim: A case study. *American Journal of Clinical Hypnosis, 29,* 64–68.

Mangioni, P.V. (1986). Hypnosis and behavioural self–management in the treatment of insomnia. *Australian Journal of Clinical and Experimental Hypnosis, 14,* 157–165.

Margolis, C.G. (1983). Hypnotic imagery with cancer patients. *American Journal of Clinical Hypnosis, 25,* 128–134.

Margolis, C.G. & DeClement, F.A. (1980). Hypnosis in the treatment of burns. *Burns, 6,* 253–254.

Margolis, C.G., Domangue, B.B., Ehleben, M.S., & Shrier, L. (1983). Hypnosis in the early treatment of burns: A pilot study. *American Journal of Clinical Hypnosis, 26,* 9–15.

Marks, I.M. (1974). *Fears and phobias.* London: Heinemann.

Marks, N., Karle, H., & Onisiphorou, C. (1985). A controlled trial of hypnotherapy in tinnitus arium. *Clinical Otolaryngology, 10,* 43–6.

Marmer, M.J. (1959). *Hypnosis in anesthesiology.* Springfield, Ill: C.C. Thomas.

Mason, A.A. (1952). A case of congenital ichthyosiform erythrodermia of Brocq treated by hypnosis. *British Medical Journal, 2,* 422–423.

Matheson, G. (1979). Modification of depressive symptoms through post-hypnotic suggestion. *American Journal of Clinical Hypnosis, 22,* 61–64.

Mattson, A. & Agle, D.P. (1979). Psychophysiological aspects of adolescence: Hemolytic disorders. *Adolescent Psychiatry, 7,* 269–280.

Meares, A. (1982/83). A form of intensive meditation associated with a regression of cancer. *American Journal of Clinical Hypnosis, 25,* 114–121.

Mellgren, A. (1966). Practical experiences with a modified hypnosis-delivery. *Psychotherapy and Psychosomatics, 14,* 425.

Melzack, R. (1973). *The puzzle of pain.* Harmondsworth: Penguin Books.

Melzack, R. (1975). The McGill Pain Questionnaire: Major properties and scoring methods. *Pain, 1,* 277–299.

Melzack, R. (1980). Psychological aspects of pain. In J.J. Bonica (Ed.), *Pain.* New York: Raven Press.

Melzack, R. (Ed.) (1983). *Pain measurement and assessment.* New York: Raven Press.

Melzack, R. (1985). Book review of *Hypnotherapy of pain in children with cancer*, J.R. Hilgard & S. Le Baron *Pain, 22,* 324.

Melzack, R. & Perry, C. (1975). Self regulation of pain: the use of alpha feedback and hypnotic training for the control of chronic pain. *Experimental Neurology, 46,* 452–469.

Melzack, R. & Torgerson, W.S. (1971). On the language of pain. *Anesthesiology, 34,* 50–59.

Melzack, R. & Wall, P. (1965). Pain mechanisms: A new theory. *Science, 150,* 971–979.

Melzack, R. & Wall, P. (1982). *The challenge of pain.* Harmondsworth: Penguin Books.

Mendelson, W.B., Gillin, C., & Wyatt, R.J. (1977). *Human sleep and its disorders.* New York: Plenum Press.

Mersky, H. (1987). Book review of B. Peter & T.C. Kraeker, *Hypnose and Kognition. Pain, 20,* 270.

Mersky, H. & Spear, E.G. (1967). *Pain: physiological and psychiatric aspects.* London: Baillière Tindall and Cassell.

Mesnet, E. (1888). De L'accouchement dans le somnambulisme provoqué. *Revue Hypnotisme, 1,* 33–42.

Meyer, R.G. & Tilker, H.S. (1969). The clinical use of direct hypnotic suggestion: A traditional technique in the light of current approaches. *International Journal of Clinical and Experimental Hypnosis, 17,* 81–88.

Milgram, S. (1963). Behavioral study of obedience. *Journal of Abnormal and Social Psychology, 67,* 371–378.

Milgram, S. (1974). *Obedience to authority.* London: Tavistock.

Mills, J.C. & Crowley, R.J. (1986). *Therapeutic metaphors for children and the child within.* New York: Bruner/Mazel.

Milne, G. (1985). Hypnorelaxation for essential hypertension. *Australian Journal of Clinical and Experimental Hypnosis, 13,* 113–116.

Mingay, D.J. (1988). Hypnosis and eye–witness testimony. In M. Heap (Ed.), *Hypnosis: Current clinical, experimental and forensic practices* (pp. 380–394). London: Croom Helm.

Mitchell, K.R. & White, R.G. (1977). Self management of severe predormital insomnia. *Journal of Behaviour Therapy and Experimental Psychiatry, 8,* 57–63.

Moghissi, K.S. & Wallach, E.E. (1983). Unexplained infertility. *Fertility and Sterility, 39,* 5.

Moon, T. & Moon, H. (1984). Hypnosis and childbirth: Self-report and comment. *British Journal of Experimental and Clinical Hypnosis, 1,* 49–52.

Moore, N. (1965). Behaviour therapy in bronchial asthma: A controlled study. *Journal of Psychosomatic Research, 9,* 257–276.

Morgan, A.H. (1973). The heritability of hypnotic susceptibility in twins. *Journal of Abnormal Psychology, 82,* 55–61.

Morgan, A.H. & Hilgard, E.R. (1973). Age differences in susceptibility to hypnosis. *International Journal of Clinical and Experimental Hypnosis, 21,* 78–87.

Morgan, A.H. & Hilgard, J.R. (1978a). Stanford Hypnotic Clinical Scale for Adults. *American Journal of Clinical Hypnosis, 21,* 134–147.

Morgan, A.H & Hilgard, J.R. (1978b). Stanford Hypnotic Scale for Children. *American Journal of Clinical Hypnosis, 21,* 148–168.

Morgan, G.E. (1940). How childhood fears towards dentistry can be controlled. *Journal of the American Dental Association, 27,* 766–768.

Morris, B.A.P. (1985). Successful treatment of multiple warts in a young girl using Simonton visualisation technique. *American Journal of Clinical Hypnosis, 27,* 237–240.

Morris, D.A., Nathan, R.G., Goebel, R.A., & Bluss, N.H. (1985). Hypnoanaesthesia in the morbidly obese. *Journal of the American Medical Association, 253,* 3292–3294.

Moss, A.A. (1963). Hypnosis for pain management in dentistry. *Journal of Dental Medicine, 18,* 110–112.

Motodo, K. (1971). A case report of the counter-conditioning treatment of an eczema patient by hypnosis. *Japanese Journal of Hypnosis, 15,* 46.

Myers, S.A. (1983). The Creative Imagination Scale: Group norms for children and adolescents. *International Journal of Clinical and Experimental Hypnosis, 31,* 28–36.

Myles, M.F. (1981). *Textbook for midwives.* London: Churchill Livingstone.

Nace, E.P., Orne, M.T., & Hammer, A.G. (1974). Posthypnotic amnesia as an active psychic process: The reversibility of amnesia. *Archives of General Psychiatry, 31,* 257–260.

Nash, M. (1987). What, if anything, is regressed about hypnotic age regression? A review of the empirical literature. *Psychological Bulletin, 102,* 42–52.

Nathan, R.G., Morris, D.A., Goebel, R.A., & Bluss, N.H. (1987). Preoperative and interoperative rehearsal in hypnoanesthesia for major surgery. *American Journal of Clinical Hypnosis, 29,* 238–241.

Neisser, U. (1967). *Cognitive psychology.* New York: Appleton Century Crofts.

Newman, M. (1971). The role of amnesia in dentistry: A case report. *American Journal of Clinical Hypnosis, 14,* 127–130.

Newton, B.W. (1982/83). The use of hypnosis in the treatment of cancer patients. *American Journal of Clinical Hypnosis, 25,* 104–113.

Newton, N. (1975). Trebly sensuous woman. *Psychology Today, 1,* 34–38.

Nicolaiev, A.P. (1959). "Conclusion" in Leningrad Congress, cited by L. Chertok, *Psychosomatic methods in painless childbirth: History, theory and practice* (trans. D. Leigh) London: Pergamon.

Nicolaou, P. (1988). Should professionals stick to their own lasts? One hypnodontist's point of view. *British Journal of Experimental and Clinical Hypnosis, 5,* 158–160.

Nixon, W.G.W. (1951). "Foreword" in H. Heardman *Physiotherapy in obstetrics and gynaecology.* Edinburgh: E. & Livingstone.

Oliver, B. (1977). Editorial. *Proceedings of the British Society of Medical and Dental Hypnosis, 3,* 2–3.

Olness, K. (1975). The use of self-hypnosis in the treatment of childhood nocturnal enuresis: A report on forty patients. *Clinical Pediatrics, 14,* 273–279.

Olness, K. (1981). Imagery (self-hypnosis) as an adjunct therapy in childhood cancer: Clinical experience with 25 patients. *American Journal of Pediatric Hematology/Oncology, 3,* 313–321.

Olness, K.N. & Conroy, M.M. (1985). A pilot study of voluntary control of transcutaneous PO_2 by children. *International Journal of Clinical and Experimental Hypnosis, 33,* 1–5.

Olness, K.N., Culbert, T., & Uden, D. (1989). Self-regulation of salivary immunoglobulin A by children. *Pediatrics, 83,* 66–71.

Olness, K., MacDonald, J., & Uden, D.L. (1987). Comparison of self-hypnosis and propranalol in the treatment of juvenile classic migraine. *Pediatrics, 79,* 593–597.

O'Moore, A.M., O'Moore, R.R., Harrison, R.F., Murphy, G., & Carruthers, M.E. (1983). Psychosomatic aspects of idiopathic infertility: Effects of treatment with autogenic training. *Journal of Psychosomatic Research, 27,* 145–151.

Orne, M.T. (1980a). On the construct of hypnosis: How its definition affects research and its clinical applications. In G.D. Burrows & L. Dennerstein (Eds.), *Handbook of hypnosis and psychosomatic medicine.* Amsterdam: Elsevier.

Orne, M.T. (1980b). Hypnotic control of pain. Toward a clarification of the different psychological processes involved. In J.J. Bonica (Ed.), *Pain,* New York: Raven Press.

Orne, M.T., Sheehan, P.W., & Evans, E.J. (1968). Occurrence of posthypnotic behaviour outside the experimental setting. *Journal of Abnormal and Social Psychology, 9,* 189–196.

Osgood, C.E., Suci, G.J., & Tannenbaum, P.H. (1957). *The measurement of meaning.* Urbana, Ill.: University of Illinois Press.

Oudet (1837). Séance du 24 janvier 1837. Cited by L. Chertok (1987). *Sense and nonsense in psychotherapy,* Oxford: Pergamon Press.

Oystragh, P. (1970). The use of hypnosis in general and obstetric practice. *Medical Journal of Australia, 2,* 731.

Pagano, R.R., Akots, N.J., & Wall, T.W. (1988). Hypnosis, cerebral laterality and relaxation. *International Journal of Clinical and Experimental Hypnosis, 36,* 350–358.

Pain (1984). Supplement 2.

Pajntar, M., Roskar, E., & Vodovnik, L. (1985). Some neuromuscular phenomena in hypnosis. In D. Waxman, P.C. Misra, M. Gibson, & M.A. Basker (Eds.), *Modern trends in hypnosis.* New York: Plenum Press.

Parsons, O.A. & Hart, R.P. (1984). Behavioral disorders associated with central nervous system dysfunction. In H.E. Adams & P.B. Sutker (Eds.), *Comprehensive handbook of psychopathology*. New York: Plenum Press.

Pascatto, R. & Mead, B. (1967). The use of post hypnotic suggestions in obstetrics. *American Journal of Clinical Hypnosis, 9,* 267.

Patel, C. (1973). Yoga and biofeedback in the management of hypertension. *Lancet, 2,* 1053–1055.

Patel, C. (1975). Twelve-month follow-up of yoga and biofeedback in the management of hypertension. *Lancet, 1,* 62–64.

Patterson, D.R., Ouestad, K.A., & Boltwood, M.D. (1987). Hypnotherapy as a treatment for pain in patients with burns: Research and clinical considerations. *Journal of Burn Care and Rehabilitation, 8,* 263–268.

Pattie, F.A. (1956). Mesmer's medical dissertation and its debt to Mead's "de imperia solis ac lunae". *Journal of the History of Medicine, 2,* 275.

Pearson, R.E. (1961). Response to suggestions given under general anesthesia. *American Journal of Clinical Hypnosis, 4,* 106–114.

Penfield, W. & Roberts, L. (1959). *Speech and brain mechanisms.* Princeton, N.J.: Princeton University Press.

Perchard, S.D. (1962). Hypnosis in pregnancy. *Obstetric and Gynecology Survey, 17,* 23.

Perls, F.S., Hefferline, R., & Goodman, P. (1973). *Gestalt therapy: Excitement and growth in the human personality.* Harmondsworth, Middlesex: Penguin Books.

Perry, C. (1978). The Abbé Faria: A neglected figure in the history of hypnosis. In F.H. Frankel & H.S. Zamansky (Eds.), *Hypnosis at its bicentennial.* New York: Plenum Press.

Perry, C. & Laurence, J.R. (1982). Book review of M. Reiser, *Handbook of investigative hypnosis. International Journal of Clinical and Experimental Hypnosis, 30,* 443–448.

Perry, C. & Laurence, J.R. (1983). The enhancement of memory by hypnosis in the legal investigative situation. *Canadian Psychology, 24,* 155–167.

Philips, H.C. (1988). *The psychological management of chronic pain.* New York: Springer.

Piccione, A., Contes, T.J., George, J.M., Rosenthal, D., & Kargmark, P. (1982). Nocturnal biofeedback for nocturnal bruxism. *Biofeedback and Self Regulation, 7,* 405–419.

Poe, E.A. (1871). Mesmeric revelation. In *The collected works of E.A. Poe, Vol. 1.* New York: W.J. Widdleton.

Pritzl, E. (1886). Un accouchement dans l'hypnose. *Revue de l'Hypnotisme Expérimentale et Thérapeutique, 1,* 157–158.

Pulos, L. (1980). Mesmerism revisited: The effectiveness of Esdaile's techniques in the production of deep hypnosis and total body hypnoanalgesia. *American Journal of Clinical Hypnosis, 22,* 206–211.

Rachman, S. (1968). The role of muscular relaxation in desensitization behaviour therapy. *Behaviour Research and Therapy, 6,* 159–166.

Rachman, S. & Hodgson, R. (1978). *Obsessions and compulsions.* Englewood Cliffs, N.J.: Prentice Hall.

Radin, H. (1972). Extractions using hypnosis for a patient with bacterial endocarditis. *British Journal of Clinical Hypnosis, 3,* 32–33.

Radtke, H.L. & Stam, H.J. (1987). Effects of hypnotic and placebo analgesia on magnitude scales for ischemic pain. *Pain,* Supplement 4, S424.

Read, G.D. (1933). *Natural childbirth.* London: Heinemann.

Read, G.D. (1942). *Revelation in childbirth.* London: Heinemann.

Read, G.D. (1953). *Childbirth without fear.* New York: Harper.

Redd, W.H., Andresen, G.V., & Minagawa, R.Y. (1982). Hypnotic control of anticipatory emesis in patients receiving chemotherapy. *Journal of Consulting and Clinical Psychology, 50,* 14–19.

Reiser, M. (1980). *Handbook of investigative hypnosis.* Los Angeles: LEHI.

Relinger, H. & Bortstein, P.H. (1979). Treatment of sleep onset insomnia by paradoxical instruction. *Behaviour Modification, 3,* 203–222.

Ritterman, M.K. (1983). *Using hypnosis in family therapy.* San Francisco: Jossey Bass.

Roberts, H., Wooten, L.T.D., McKane, K.M., & Hartnett, W.E. (1953). The value of antenatal preparation. *Journal of Obstetrics and Gynaecology of the British Empire, 60,* 404–408.

Robinson, G. (1977). Treatment of depression through hypnotic resensitization. *Dissertation Abstracts International, 38* (4–B), 1900.

Robyn, C., Delvoye, P., van Exter, C., Vekemans, M., Caufriez, A., de Nayer, P., Delogne-Desnoeck, J., & L'Hermite, M. (1977). Physiological and pharmacological factors influencing prolactin secretion and their relation to human reproduction. In P.C. Crosagnini & C. Robyn (Eds.), *Prolactin and human reproduction. Proceedings of the Seronon Symposia,* Vol. II. London: Academic Press.

Robyn, C., Delvoye, P., Vekemans, M., Caufriez, A., Delogne-Desnoeck, J., & L'Hermite, M. (1981). Anovulation and abnormal follicular maturation in hyperprolactinaemic women. In J.R.T. Coutts (Ed.), *Functional morphology of the human ovary.* Lancaster: MIT Press.

Rock, N., Shipley, T., & Campbell, C. (1969). Hypnosis with untrained nonvolunteer patients in labour. *International Journal of Clinical and Experimental Hypnosis, 17,* 25–6.

Roig-Garcia, S. (1961). The hypno-reflexogenous method: A new procedure in obstetrical psychoanalgesia. *Journal of Clinical Hypnosis, 6,* 15.

Rosen, H. (1960). Hypnosis: Deep sleep and danger. *Newsweek,* 23 May, 107A.

Rosenthal, R. (1963). On the social psychology of the psychological experiment: The experimenter's hypothesis as unintended determinant of experimental results. *American Scientist, 51,* 268–283.

Ross, C.A. (1984). Diagnosis of multiple personality during hypnosis: A case report. *International Journal of Clinical and Experimental Hypnosis, 32,* 222–235.

Ross, P.J. (1985). Ego-strengthening: A critical view. In M.Heap (Ed.), *Proceedings of the Second Annual Conference of the British Society of Experimental and Clinical Hypnosis* (pp. 74–76). BSECH publication.

Ross, P.J. (1988). The use of hypnosis with couples and families. In M. Heap (Ed.), *Hypnosis: Current clinical, experimental and forensic practices* (pp. 234–245). London: Croom Helm.

Rothschild, N. (1959). Practical gag reflex control. *Dental Survey, 35,* 1354–1355.

Rowley, D.T. (1986). *Hypnosis and hypnotherapy.* London: Croom Helm.

Rush, A.J., Beck, A.T., Kovac, M., & Hollon, S. (1977). Comparative efficacy of cognitive therapy and imipramine in the treatment of depressed outpatients. *Cognitive Therapy and Research, 1,* 17–37.

Sacerdote, P. (1982a). A non-statistical dissertation about hypnotizability scales and clinical goals: Comparison with individualised induction and deepening procedures. *International Journal of Clinical and Experimental Hypnosis, 33,* 354–376.

Sacerdote, P. (1982b). Further reflections on the hypnotizability scales: A comment. *International Journal of Clinical and Experimental Hypnosis, 33,* 393.

Sachs, B.C. (1987). Hypnosis and cancer patients. *Hypnos: Swedish Journal of Hypnosis in Psychotherapy and Psychosomatic Medicine, 14,* 46–51.

Sackheim, H.A. (1982). Lateral asymmetry in bodily response to hypnotic suggestion. *Biological Psychiatry, 17,* 437–447.

Sampimon, R.L.H. & Woodruff, M.F.A. (1946). Some observations concerning the use of hypnosis as a substitute for anesthesia. *Medical Journal of Australia, 1,* 393–395.

Sanders, R.S. & Reyher, J. (1969). Sensory deprivation and the enhancement of hypnotic susceptibility. *Journal of Abnormal Psychology, 74,* 735–781.

Sarbin, T.R. (1950). Contributions to role-taking theory: I. Hypnotic behavior. *Psychological Review, 57,* 255–270.

Sarbin, T.R. (1965). Hypnosis as a behavior modification technique. In L. Krasner & L.P. Ullmann (Eds.), *Research in behavior modification.* New York: Holt, Rinehart, Winston.

Sarbin, T.R. & Coe, W.C. (1972). *Hypnosis: A social psychological analysis of influence communication.* New York: Holt, Rinehart, & Winston.

Savage, R.D. & McGregor, A. (1970). Behavior therapy in prosthodontics. *Journal of Prosthetic Dentistry, 34,* 126–132.

Scagnelli, J. (1975). Therapy with eight schizophrenic and borderline patients: Summary of a therapy approach that employs a semi-symbiotic bond between patient and therapist. *Journal of Clinical Psychology, 31,* 519–525.

Scandrett, F.R. & Ervin, T.H. (1973). Occlusion and preventive dentistry. *Journal of the American Dental Association, 87,* 1231–1233.

Schafer, D.W. (1975). Hypnosis use on a burn unit. *International Journal of Clinical and Experimental Hypnosis, 23,* 1–14.

Schmidt, A.J.M. (1987). The behavioral management of pain. *Pain, 30,* 285–291.

Schneck, J.M. (1978). Henry James, George du Maurier and mesmerism. *International Journal of Clinical and Experimental Hypnosis, 26,* 76–80.

Schneiderman, M.J., Leu, R.H., & Glazeski, R.C. (1987). Use of hypnosis in spasmodic torticollis: A case report. *American Journal of Clinical Hypnosis, 29,* 260–263.

Schrenck-Notzing, A.F. von (1893). Eine Geburt in der Hypnose. *Zurschrift Hypnotismus, 1,* 49–52.

Scott, J.R. & Rose, N.B. (1976). Effects of psychoprophylaxis (Lamage preparation) on labour and delivery in primas. *New England Journal of Medicine, 294,* 1205–1207.

Sharpley, C. (1984). Predicate matching in NLP. A review of research on the preferred representational system. *Journal of Counselling Psychology, 31,* 238–248.

Sharpley, C. (1987). Research findings on neuro-linguistic programming: Non-supportive data or an untestable theory? *Journal of Counselling Psychology, 34,* 103–107.

Sharav, T. & Tal, M. (1987). Hypnotic anesthesia to electrical tooth-pulp stimulation: Sensation, reflex activity and placebo effect. *Pain,* Supplement 4, S271.

Shaw, L. & Ehrlich, A. (1987). Relaxation training as a treatment for chronic pain caused by ulcerative colitis. *Pain, 29,* 287–293.

Sheehan, P.W. & Perry, C.W. (1976). *Methodologies of hypnosis: A critical appraisal of contemporary paradigms of hypnosis.* Hillsdale, N.J.: Lawrence Erlbaum Associates Inc.

Shertzer, & Lookingbill, D.P. (1987). Effects of relaxation therapy and hypnotizability in chronic uticaria. *Archives of Dermatology, 123,* 913–916.

Shor, R.E. (1960). The frequency of naturally occurring "hypnotic like" experiences in the normal college population. *International Journal of Clinical and Experimental Hypnosis, 8,* 151–163.

Shor, R.E. (1972). The fundamental problem in hypnosis research as viewed from historic perspectives. In E. Fromm & R.E. Shor (Eds.), *Hypnosis: Research developments and perspectives.* Chicago: Aldine Atherton.

Shor, R.E. & Orne, E.C. (1962). *Harvard Group Scale of Hypnotic Susceptibility.* Palo Alto, California: Consulting Psychologists Press.

Shor, R.E., Orne, M.T., & O'Connell, D.N. (1962). Validation and cross-validation of a scale of self-reported personal experiences which predicts hypnotisability. *Journal of Psychology, 53,* 55–75.

Sigman, A. (1988). Hypnotic and biofeedback procedures for self-regulation of autonomic nervous system functions. In M. Heap (Ed.), *Hypnosis: Current clinical, experimental and forensic practices* (pp.126–138). London: Croom Helm.

Simonton, O.C., Matthews-Simonton, S., & Creighton, J.L. (1978). *Getting well again.* Los Angeles: Tarcher.

Sinclair-Gieben, A.H.C. & Chalmers, D. (1959). Evaluation of treatment of warts by hypnosis. *Lancet, 2,* 480–82.

Skynner, R. & Cleese, J. (1983). *Families and how to survive them.* London: Methuen.

Slater, E. (1965). Diagnosis of hysteria. *British Medical Journal, 1,* 1395–1399.

Smith, G.W.F. (1985). The treatment of dental phobia with a meditational and behavioral reorientation self-hypnosis. In D. Waxman, P. Misra, M. Gibson, & M.A. Basker (Eds.), *Modern trends in hypnosis.* New York: Plenum Press.

Snaith, R.P. (1983). The Hospital Anxiety and Distress Questionnaire. *Acta Psychiatrica Scandinavica, 67,* 361–370.

Snow, L. (1979). The relationship between "Rapid Induction" and placebo analgesia, hypnotic susceptibility and chronic pain intensity. *Dissertation Abstracts International, 40,* 937.

Spanos, N.P. (1986). Hypnosis and the modification of hypnotic susceptibility: A social psychological perspective. In P.L.N. Naish (Ed.), *What is hypnosis? Current theories and research.* Milton Keynes: Open University Press.

Spanos, N.P., de Moor, W., & Barber, T.X. (1973). Hypnosis and behavior therapy: Common denominators. *American Journal of Clinical Hypnosis, 16,* 45–64.

Spanos, N.P., Radke, H.L., Hodgkins, D.C., Stam, H.J., & Bertrand, L. (1983). The Carleton University Responsiveness to Suggestion Scale: Normative data and psychometric properties. *Psychological Reports, 53,* 523–535.

Sperry, R.W. (1968). Hemisphere deconnection and unity in conscious awareness. *American Psychologist, 23,* 723–733.

Spiegel, D. (1981). Vietnam grief work using hypnosis. *American Journal of Clinical Hypnosis, 24,* 33–40.

Spiegel, D. (1986). Dissociating damage. *American Journal of Clinical Hypnosis, 29,* 123–141.

Spiegel, D. & Chase, R.A. (1980). The treatment of contractures of the hand using self-hypnosis. *Journal of Hand Surgery, 5,* 428–432.

Spiegel, H. (1987). The answer is: Psychotherapy plus. *British Journal of Experimental and Clinical Hypnosis, 4,* 163–164.

Spiegel, H. & Spiegel, D. (1987). *Trance and treatment.* New York: Basic Books.

Spinhoven, P. (1987). Hypnosis and behaviour therapy: A review. *International Journal of Clinical and Experimental Hypnosis, 35,* 8–31.

Springer, S.P. & Deutsch, G. (1985). *Left brain, right brain* (2nd edn). New York: Freeman & Co.

Stampfl, T.G. & Lewis, D.J. (1967). Essentials of implosive therapy: A learning-based psychodynamic behavioral therapy. *Journal of Abnormal Psychology, 72,* 496–503.

Stampfl, T.G. & Lewis, D.J. (1968). Implosive therapy—A behavioural therapy? *Behaviour Research and Therapy, 6,* 31–36.

Standley, K., Soule, A.B., Copans, S.A., & Duchowny, M.S. (1974). Local-regional anesthesia during childbirth: Effect on newborn behaviors. *Science, 186,* 634–635.

Stanton, H.E. (1979a). Increasing internal control through hypnotic ego-enhancement. *Australian Journal of Clinical and Experimental Hypnosis, 7,* 219–223.

Stanton, H.E. (1979b). Short-term treatment of enuresis. *American Journal of Clinical Hypnosis, 22,* 103–107.

Stanton, H.E. (1988). Use of the "clenched fist" technique in the treatment of phobias. *British Journal of Experimental and Clinical Hypnosis, 5,* 125–129.

Stein, C. (1963). The clenched fist technique as a hypnotic procedure in clinical psychotherapy. *American Journal of Clinical Hypnosis, 6,* 113–119.

Stein, V.T. (1980). Hypnotherapy of involuntary movements in an 82-year-old male. *American Journal of Clinical Hypnosis, 23,* 128–131.

Stone, P. & Burrows, G.D. (1980). Hypnosis and obstetrics. In G.D. Burrows & L. Dennerstein (Eds.), *Handbook of hypnosis and psychosomatic medicine.* New York: Elsevier Press.

Storr, A. (1979). *The art of psychotherapy.* London: Secker and Warburg/Heinemann.

Straus, R.A. (1980). A naturalistic experiment investigating the effects of hypnotic induction upon Creative Imagination performance in a clinical setting. *International Journal of Clinical and Experimental Hypnosis, 28,* 218–224.

Stukát, K.G. (1958). *Suggestibility: A factorial and experimental analysis.* Stockholm: Almquist and Wiksell.

Surman, O.S., Gottlieb, S.K., Hackett, T.P., & Silverberg, E.L. (1973). *Archives of General Psychiatry, 28,* 439–441.

Surman, O.S. & Tolkoff-Rubin, N. (1984). Use of hypnosis in patients receiving hemodialysis for end stage renal disease. *General Hospital Psychiatry, 68,* 31–35.

Swirsky-Sacchetti, T. & Margolis, C.G. (1986). The effects of a comprehensive self-hypnosis training program on the use of Factor VIII in severe hemophilia. *International Journal of Clinical and Experimental Hypnosis, 34,* 71–83.

Syrjala, K.L., Cummings, C., Donaldson, G., & Chapman, C.R. (1987). Hypnosis for oral pain following chemotherapy and irradiation. *Pain,* Supplement 4, S171.

Tarde, G. (1907). *Les lois de l'imitation.* Paris: Alcan.

Tarnowski, K.J. & Smith, R.M. (1986). Clinical applications of hypnosis in the management of pain. In F.A. DePiano & H.C. Salzberg (Eds.), *Clinical applications of hypnosis.* Norwood, N.J.: Ablex.

Taub, E. & Stroebel, C.F. (1978). Biofeedback in the treatment of vasoconstrictive syndromes. *Biofeedback and Self-Regulation, 3,* 363–373.

Tellegen, A. & Atkinson, G. (1974). Openness to absorbency and self-altering experiences ("absorption"): A trait relating to hypnotic susceptibility. *Journal of Abnormal Psychology, 83,* 268–277.

Thompson, C.K., Hall, H.R., & Sison, C.E. (1986). Effects of hypnosis and imagery training on naming behaviour in aphasia. *Brain and Language, 28,* 141–143.

Thornton, E.M. (1976). *Hypnotism, hysteria and epilepsy: An historical synthesis.* London: Heinemann.

Tiba, J. (1986). The use of hypnosis, imagination and personality tests in the study of pregnancy and labour. *Hypnos: Swedish Journal of Hypnosis in Psychotherapy and Psychosomatic Medicine, 13,* 17–20.

Tilton, P. (1984). The hypnotic hero: A technique for hypnosis with children. *International Journal of Clinical and Experimental Hypnosis, 32,* 366–375.

Tinterow, M.M. (Ed.) (1970). *Foundations of hypnosis: From Mesmer to Freud.* Springfield, Illinois: Charles C. Thomas.

Todd, F.J. & Kelly, R.J. (1976). The use of hypnosis to facilitate conditioned relaxation responses: A report of three cases. In E. Dengrove (Ed.), *Hypnosis and behaviour therapy* (pp. 219–226). Springfield, Illinois: Charles C. Thomas.

Tom, K.S. (1960). Hypnosis in obstetrics. *Obstetrics and Gynecology, 16,* 222.

Topham, W. & Squire Ward, W. (1842). *Account of a case of successful amputation of the thigh during the mesmeric state without knowledge of the patient.* Paper read to the Royal Medical and Chirurgical Society of London, 22 November. London: Baillière.

Tosi, D.J. & Baisden, B.A. (1984). Cognitive-experiential therapy and hypnosis. In W.C. Wester & A.H. Smith (Eds.), *Clinical hypnosis: A multidisciplinary approach.* Philadelphia: Lippincott.

Towler, J. & Butler-Manuel, R. (1980). *Modern obstetrics for student midwives.* London: Lloyd–Luke Medical Books.

Venn, J. (1988). Misuse of hypnosis in sexual contexts: Two cases reports. *International Journal of Clinical and Experimental Hypnosis, 36,* 12–18.

Vingoe, F.J. (1981). Clinical hypnosis and behaviour therapy: A cognitive emphasis in the eighties? *Bulletin of the British Society of Experimental and Clinical Hypnosis, 4,* 6–10.

Vingoe, F.J. (1987). When is a placebo not a placebo? That is the question. *British Journal of Experimental and Clinical Hypnosis. 4,* 165–167.

Vingoe, F.J. & Kramer, E.F. (1966). Hypnotic susceptibility of hospitalized psvchotic patients: A pilot study. *International Journal of Clinical and Experimental Hypnosis, 4,* 47–54.

Voisin, A. (1896). Un accouchement dans l'état d'hypnotisme. *Revue hypnotisme, 6,* 360–361.

Wadden, T.A. & Anderton, C.H. (1982). The clinical use of hypnosis. *Psychological Bulletin, 91,* 215–243.

Wagstaff, G.F. (1981). *Hypnosis, compliance and belief.* Brighton: Harvester.

Wagstaff, G.F. (1987a). Is hypnotherapy a placebo? *British Journal of Experimental and Clinical Hypnosis, 4,* 135–139.

Wagstaff, G.F. (1987b). Hypnotic induction, hypnotherapy and the placebo effect. *British Journal of Experimental and Clinical Hypnosis, 4,* 168–170.

Wakeman, R.J. & Kaplan, J.A. (1978). An experimental study in hypnosis for painful burns. *American Journal of Clinical Hypnosis, 21,* 3–11.

Walker, L.G. (1979). Letter. *Proceedings of the British Society of Medical and Dental Hypnosis, 4,* 63.

Walker, L.G. (1984). Hypnotherapy for aversion to chemotherapy in patients with lymphoid tumours. In M. Heap (Ed.), *Proceedings of the First Annual Conference of the British Society of Experimental and Clinical Hypnosis* (pp. 86–91). BSECH publication.

Walker, L.G. (1988). Hypnosis in the treatment of irritable bowel syndrome. In M. Heap (Ed.), *Hypnosis: Current clinical, experimental and forensic practices* (pp. 167–177). London: Croom Helm.

Walker, L.G., Dawson, A.A., Pollet, S.M., Ratcliffe, M.A., & Hamilton, L. (1988). Hypnotherapy for chemotherapy side-effects. *British Journal of Experimental and Clinical Hypnosis, 5,* 79–82.

Wall, P. (1978). The gate control theory of pain mechanisms: A re-examination and a restatement. *Brain, 101,* 1–18.

Watkins, J.G. (1971). The affect bridge: A hypnoanalytic technique. *International Journal of Clinical and Experimental Hypnosis, 19,* 21–27.

Waxman, D. (1973). Behaviour therapy of psoriasis: A hypnoanalytic and counter-conditioning technique. *Postgraduate Medical Journal, 49,* 591–595.

Waxman, D. (1978a). Letter. *British Medical Journal*, 19 August.

Waxman, D. (1978b). Letter. *Proceedings of the British Society of Medical and Dental Hypnosis, 4,* 47–48.

Waxman, D. (1981). *Hypnosis: A guide for patients and practitioners.* London: George Allen & Unwin.

Weitzenhoffer, A.M. (1953). *Hypnotism: An objective study of suggestibility,* New York: Wiley.

Weitzenhoffer. A.M. (1972). Behavior therapeutic techniques and hypnotherapeutic methods. *American Journal of Clinical Hypnosis, 15,* 71–82.

Weitzenhoffer. A.M. (1985). In search of hypnosis. In D. Waxman, P.C. Misra, M. Gibson, & M.A. Basker (Eds.), *Modern trends in hypnosis.* New York: Plenum Press.

Weitzenhoffer, A.M. & Hilgard, E.R. (1959). *Stanford Hypnotic Susceptibility Scale: Forms A and B.* Palo Alto, California: Consulting Psychologists Press.

Werbel, E.W. (1965). *One surgeon's experience with hypnosis.* New York: Pagent Press.

Werner, W. (1959). Hypnosis from the viewpoint of obstetrics and clinical demonstration of the training of patients for delivery and hypnosis. *New York State Journal of Medicine, 4,* 1561.

Werner, W.E.F., Schauble, P.G., & Knudson, M.S. (1982). An argument for the revival of hypnosis in obstetrics. *American Journal of Clinical Hypnosis, 24,* 149–171.

Weyandt, J.A. (1972). Three case reports in dental hypnotherapy. *American Journal of Clinical Hypnosis, 15,* 49–55.

White, L.W., Tursky, B., & Schwartz, G.F. (Eds.)(1985). *Placebo: Theory, research and mechanisms.* New York and London: The Guilford Press.

Whorwell, P.J., Prior, A., & Colgan, S.M. (1987). Hypnotherapy in severe irritable bowel syndrome: Further experience. *Gut, 28,* 423–425.

Whorwell, P.J., Prior, A., & Faragher, E.B. (1984). Controlled trial of hypnotherapy in the treatment of severe refractory irritable bowel sydrome. *Lancet, 2,* 1232–1234.

Wickramasekera, S. (1973). Effects of electromyographic feedback on hypnotic susceptibility: More preliminary data. *Journal of Abnormal Psychology, 83,* 74–77.

Wilkinson, J.B. (1988a). Hyperventilation control techniques in combination with self-hypnosis for anxiety management. In M. Heap (Ed.), *Hypnosis: Current clinical, experimental and forensic practices* (pp. 115–125). London: Croom Helm.

Wilkinson, J.B. (1988b). Hypnosis in the treatment of asthma. In M. Heap (Ed.), *Hypnosis: Current clinical, experimental and forensic practices* (pp. 146–158). London: Croom Helm.

Williams, R.L. & Karacan, I. (1973). Clinical disorders of sleep. In G. Usdin (Ed.), *Sleep research and clinical practice.* London: Butterworths.

Winkelstein, L.B. (1958). Routine hypnosis for obstetrical delivery. *American Journal of Obstetrics and Gynecology, 76,* 153–159.

Wolberg, L.R. (1964). *Hypnoanalysis.* New York: Grune and Stratton.

Wolpe, J. (1958). *Psychotherapy by reciprocal inhibition.* Stanford, California: Stanford University Press.

Wolpe, J. & Rowan, V.C. (1988). Panic disorder: A product of classical conditioning. *Behaviour Research and Therapy, 26,* 441–450.

Womack, W.M., Smith, M.G., & Chen, A.C.N. (1988). Behavioral management of childhood headache: A pilot study and case report. *Pain, 32,* 279–283.

Wright, A.D. & Humphreys, A. (1984). The use of hypnosis to enhance covert sensitisation: Two case studies. *British Journal of Experimental and Clinical Hypnosis, 1,* 3–10.

Wright, S.M. (1980). An examination of the personality of dental patients who complain of retching with dentures. *British Dental Journal, 148,* 211–213.

Zeltzer, L., LeBaron, S., & Zeltzer, P.M. (1984). The effectiveness of behavioural interventions for reduction of nausea and vomiting in children and adolescents receiving chemotherapy. *Journal of Clinical Oncology, 2,* 683–690.

Zoist (1847-48). Report of the committee appointed by the government to observe and report on surgical operations by Dr J. Esdaile upon patients under the influence of alleged mesmeric agency. Printed by order by the Deputy Governor of Bengal, Calcutta, 1946. Quoted in *The Zoist, 5,* 51–52.

Zuspan, F. (1960). Hypnosis and the obstetrician-gynecologist. *Obstetrics and Gynecology, 16,* 740.

REFERENCE NOTES

1. Barber, J. (1976). *The efficacy of hypnotic analgesia for dental pain in individuals of both high and low hypnotic susceptibility.* Unpublished doctoral dissertation, University of Southern California.
2. Bowers, K.S. & van der Meulen, S. (1972). *A comparison of psychological and clinical techniques in the control of dental pain.* Paper delivered at the Society for Clinical and Experimental Hypnosis Convention. Boston (Fall).
3. Callow, G. (1988). *The use of story-telling in a case of childhood eczema.* Paper presented at the Fifth Annual Conference of the British Society of Experimental and Clinical Hypnosis, London.
4. Cladder, J.M. (1987). *A decision tree for anti-anxiety strategies.* Paper presented at the Fourth European Congress of Hypnosis in Psychotherapy and Psychosomatic Medicine, Oxford, U.K.
5. Coe, W.C (1974). *Personality correlates of hypnotic susceptibility: A validation study of Josephine Hilgard's hypotheses.* Paper presented to the Society for Clinical and Experimental Hypnosis, Montreal, 13 October.
6. Dane, J.R. (1988). *Radicular sympathetic dystrophies.* Paper presented at the Eleventh International Congress of Hypnosis and Psychosomatic Medicine, The Hague, Netherlands.
7. Elton, J., Burrows, G.D., & Stanley, G.V. (1978). *Hypnosis and chronic pain.* Paper presented at the Australian Society for Clinical and Experimental Hypnosis Conference, Muruchidore, Queensland, September.
8. Fellows, B.J. (1986). *The Creative Imagination Scale.* Paper presented at the Third Annual Conference of the British Society of Experimental and Clinical Hypnosis, University of Oxford, April.
9. Gillett, P.L. & Coe, W.C. (1983). *The effects of Rapid Induction Analgesia (RIA), hypnotic susceptibility and the severity of discomfort on reducing dental pain.* Paper presented at the Annual Meeting of the Western Psychological Association, San Francisco.
10. Greenleaf, M. & Fisher, S. (1988). *Preoperative training in self-hypnosis for patients undergoing coronary artery bypass surgery.* Paper presented at the Eleventh International Congress of Hypnosis and Psychosomatic Medicine, The Hague.
11. Hinton, R.A., Meadowcroft, J., Pike, D.C., & Wardle, P.G. (1988). *Hypnosis in infertility.* Paper presented at the International Congress of Hypnosis and Psychosomatic Medicine, The Hague, Netherlands.
12. Kirmayer, L.J. (1985). *Healing and the invention of metaphor: Erickson's implicit psychology.* Paper presented at the Tenth International Congress of Hypnosis and Psychosomatic Medicine, Toronto.
13. Kohen, D.P. (1985). *Relaxation/mental imagery (self-hypnosis) in asthma: Experience with 23 children.* Paper presented to the Tenth International Congress of Hypnosis and Psychosomatic Medicine, Toronto.
14. Orne, M.T. (1982). *Measurement and experimental control in hypnosis.* Paper presented at the Symposium of the Metropolitan Branch of the British Society of Experimental and Clinical Hypnosis, University College, London.
15. Spanos, N.P. (1987). *Comparison of hypnotic and non-hypnotic procedures in the remission of warts.* Paper presented at the Fourth European Congress of Hypnosis in Psychotherapy and Psychosomatic Medicine, Oxford, U.K.
16. van Strein, J.J.A. & Weele, K. (1987). *The role of hypnosis in the treatment of patients with verified hernia nuclei pulposi.* Paper presented at the Fourth European Congress of Hypnosis in Psychotherapy and Psychosomatic Medicine, Oxford, U.K.
17. Van Gorp, W. & Meyer, R.G. (1983). *Efficiency of Rapid Induction Analgesia and standard hypnosis in pain.* Paper presented to the Annual Meeting of the American Psychological Association, Anaheim, California, U.S.A.

Author Index

Subject Index